Close Calls on High Walls

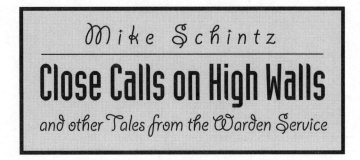

Mike Schintz

Close Calls on High Walls

and other Tales from the Warden Service

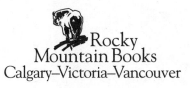

Rocky
Mountain Books
Calgary–Victoria–Vancouver

Rocky Mountain Books
#108 – 17665 66A Avenue
Surrey, BC V3S2A7
www.rmbooks.com

Library and Archives Canada Cataloguing in Publication
Schintz, Michael J.
    Close calls on high walls: and other tales from the warden service / Mike Schintz.

ISBN 13: 978-1-894765-55-8   ISBN 10: 1-894765-55-9

1. Schintz, Michael J. 2. Park rangers—Canada—Biography.
3. National parks and reserves—Canada. I. Title.

SB481.6.S33A3 2005   333.78'3'092   C2005-901217-X

Edited by Sheila Macklin
Book design by Frances Hunter
Cover design by Frances Hunter
Front cover photo of Bill Vroom by Bruno Engler
All illustrations by author

Printed in Canada

Rocky Mountain Books acknowledges the financial support for its publishing program from the Government of Canada through the Book Publishing Industry Development Program (BPIDP).

*This book is dedicated to the men and women
of Parks Canada's Warden Service.*

Acknowledgments

My first big thank you goes rightly to Rocky Mountain Books. For a little known author, finding a publisher can be a discouraging business. When David Finch approached me on behalf of the company, that worry was resolved. Thank you, David! I am also very grateful to my friend and editor, Sheila Macklin. If this books reads well, much credit goes to her. To know Sheila is a pleasure and, to work with her, a privilege.

Next, my sincere thanks to friends and former colleagues with Parks Canada—Gail Harrison, Giselle Dubé and Kurt Seel, for their help with word processing, editing and for constructive comments. A special thanks goes to my daughter-in-law, Julie, for the final typing, fine tuning and the putting together of it all. Many thanks go to Peter Fuhrmann for all the years of friendship and support, and for his assistance with technical details of search and rescue. And to Faris Evans, who survived three days entombed in the ice of Crowfoot Glacier, thank you for sharing that remarkable experience with us in "Last Seen Point."

The biggest thanks of all goes to Glennys, who braved the grizzly bears to be my partner and who has been a great help throughout the preparation of this book.

Photo credits go to the Bruno Engler Family for the wonderful cover photo of Bill Vroom, a brave and resourceful rescue warden, for whom the title of this book would have special meaning.

Contents

Introduction

PART ONE

*Getting started in the Warden Service;
backcountry districts in the mountains;
highway work; training, travel and survival.*

PART TWO

*Jasper and frontcountry; law enforcement
in the Hippie era.*

PART THREE

*Strange, remarkable and sometimes
haunting stories of search and rescue.*

Part Four

Moving east; Pukaskwa and tales from the haunted North Shore of Lake Superior; aerial adventure.

Part Five

On the move again; stories from Newfoundland and the Atlantic Region.

Part Six

Back to the west; the Wardens go to Expo '86; exploring the Queen Charlottes; my last job for Parks buying horses for the Ya-Ha-Tinda.

Introduction

On a warm summer day early in the last century, a man trod softly along a faint, meandering game trail in a remote mountain valley. He wore heavy, knee-high boots, and wide-hipped breeks of dark, greenish-brown material. Above that was a faded cotton shirt, sweat-stained where the straps of his pack crossed his shoulders. Pinned to the front of his shirt was a small, shield-shaped, silver badge. On his head was a heavy felt hat, flat-brimmed with a peaked crown, somewhat like that worn by the Royal Canadian Mounted Police (RCMP). The man carried a long, heavy rifle slung over his left shoulder, and in his right hand he balanced an axe. He moved slowly and deliberately, his eyes always searching the path ahead. He moved like a man with many miles behind him and many more to go.

Over and around him was a forest of dark green spruce, the heavy branches casting deep shadows over the trail. Rising high above the spruces were the towering cathedrals of the Rocky Mountains. On the limestone cliffs, tumbling waterfalls gleamed in the afternoon sun, the spray forming small rainbows against the grey rock. On a narrow ledge spotted with bright yellow moss, a small band of mountain goats picked their way precariously across the mountainside.

Down in the valley where the man walked there were frequent signs of wild animals. Damp places on the trail revealed the tracks of deer and moose, and claw marks of the grizzly bear. He had the company of a pair of Canada jays—gliding through the shadows on silent wings. The traveller felt a sense of kinship with these denizens of the wild; he had been at home with them for most of his life. Added to that sense of kinship was a newly acquired feeling of custodianship for the badge on his chest bore the words "Dominion Parks, Fire & Game Guardian." He and a handful of others were the first generation of what would later be known as park wardens.

The man had not seen a human being for over a week, and would not see his own kind for many days to come. A long valley stretched behind him, and over each pass was another. The game trail wandered on, at times nearly invisible. Frequently, confronted by a tangled mass of deadfall, the traveller would try two or three possibilities before finding the best route. Once satisfied, he would select a prominent tree on the right hand side of the trail. There with a swing of his axe he would slice an upright sliver of bark off the trunk and complete the blaze with a short horizontal cut at the base of the strip.

Slowly and methodically, with the sure pace of the mountaineer, the guardian moved on into the deepening shadows. Soon even the small sounds of his passing were gone. Behind him the dark spruce closed in again, the tops gently sighing in the breeze.

In the years to come, more park wardens would travel this and other trails. Visitors would arrive on foot and horseback, wearing the trails deeper. In some of the main valleys the paths would in time become highways.

Travel with some of these park wardens in the stories that follow. Walk sunny trails with them and, on other days, snowshoe through lonely, frozen woods where the only sounds are the moaning of the north wind and the far away howl of the wolf. At the end of a day's journey throw down your pack on the steps of some cold and silent cabin, while the Canada jays come to greet you and the crafty old pack rat watches warily from his perch underneath the eaves. On evenings when the animals sense a change in the weather, the great grizzly may come, so the cabin walls had better be stout and the door securely latched!

If you care to travel on, you could tie into a climbing rope and help to rescue someone who has had a close call on a high wall of a limestone castle. Or, on one of those trails which have now become busy highways, a park warden may ask for your help to save the life of someone hurt in a collision. Strange characters lurk along this trail you are about to start, with events which will make you laugh and a few which may make you weep. Not all days with a park warden are fun, but few are dull.

After awhile, the story takes you to Pukaskwa National Park, a wild and beautiful park on the North Shore of Lake Superior where you can still find some of the old fur trappers' trails, and sense the spirits of the Ojibway lurking in the shadows of the forest. Here, travel the lake with the first park patrolmen—your canoe nearly swamped by towering seas. Explore the back country in winter when all the land is white like the sky so there is no landscape pattern to guide you. In these conditions, if you don't fall off a granite cliff, you can wander forever or until you freeze. Not for nothing is this known as the haunted shore. Dark deeds are done on the big lake on black and stormy nights; Superior never gives up her dead, those who disappear overboard become the stuff of legends.

Again we move on still going east, from the lonely balds of the Canadian Shield to the fogbound shores of the North Atlantic. We visit the wonderful hardwood forest of "Kedgie" (Kejimkujik, Nova Scotia) National Park and drive the beautiful Cabot Trail in Cape Breton, linking the Scots village of Ingonish to the French-Canadian hamlet of Cheticamp. And then late one night we find ourselves wandering the wet, cobbled streets of eighteenth century Louisbourg. It is very quiet. The mist almost hides the lights of an occasional lantern in a window or over a door. Somewhere a shutter creaks in the chill, sea wind. Then an eerie, terrified scream of a woman rips the darkness; a bottle shatters on the cobblestones and we hear the drunken oath of a sailor. We can imagine that it's 1758 and one of General Wolfe's men is celebrating the last and final conquest of the fortress.

Come, let us begin our journey. The mountains beckon from behind their mantle of clouds. They wait for us beyond the rain curtain—misty, moody and mysterious. Ahead are the great valleys; sombre spruce and sighing pines; quiet trails and secret places; beaver ponds at dusk; the call of the loon at dawn. Higher up are the alpine meadows in their autumn colours—golden larch against the blue September shadows. On a scree slope above timberline a grizzly bear up-ends stones in search of supper. And finally, we reach the great icefields, where the snow snakes weave and wander before the endless winds—snow that tells tales that crevasses make secret.

So pick up your pack and take the alpenstock in hand. Who knows? In one of those quiet valleys we may even find those candle-flame blazes where that old guardian wandered so many years ago.

Part One

Getting started in the Warden Service;
backcountry districts in the mountains;
highway work; training, travel
and survival.

Picking Up the Trail

I had been awake in the cold, dark cabin for some time, huddled on the borderline of discomfort in the blankets. Chief among my waking impressions was the silence of that first morning on the trail. There was no muted hum of traffic, no cutting in of the furnace, no voices, none of the comforting indications of easily obtainable warmth, transportation and assistance to which most people in this country awake each day. Nothing moved; the silence was absolute. I was on my own.

Finally, at 6:05 am, I mustered the courage for the first move of the day. Scrambling up in socks and long underwear, I first lit the candle, then threw kindling in the stove, and thirdly lit the lamp. The hiss of the Coleman and the crackle of the wood made me feel better, although now I was conscious of a sharp pain in each groin from yesterday's snowshoeing. I also had a couple of blisters on my heels that would be raw before this second day was over.

During breakfast, I had been temporarily diverted, from my earlier reluctance to meet the day, by reading a few pages of my pocket novel. Too soon I was charged with a vague anxiety, a need to get moving. Today meant going over the pass. Six more gruelling miles to the summit, then the great barrier fields of snow, open to the wind, and finally down again into friendlier country.

When the dishes were put away, the bedding folded and stored, water pail and kettle emptied, I prepared three fuzz sticks with which to light the stove on my return trip. To make one of these sticks I selected a piece of straight-grained kindling. Then, with a sharp knife I peeled back a number of shavings around the stick, without actually cutting them off. When touched with a match, these shavings would ignite immediately. Satisfied that all was in order, I locked the door and closed the shutters. It was now just short of 8:00 am. I strapped on the snowshoes, heaved up the pack, and turned my face to the trail. As I trudged along, my thoughts turned to how it all began.

Small things, seemingly inconsequential at the time, can sometimes influence our careers, even the course of our lives. I remember my father telling us once that the fact of his having attended agricultural college during his youth in Holland was instrumental in allowing us to immigrate to Canada in 1939. This was just before the outbreak of war in Europe and a most fortunate move for us. Growing up by the Highwood River in southern Alberta and taking school by correspondence, I had almost no exposure to towns or cities, except with Banff. Banff was a mecca for artists and my dad was an artist. My first visit there was when I accompanied him to visit Carl Rungius at his studio on Banff Avenue. I fell in love with the mountains, and have drawn spiritual sustenance from them all my life. When it came time to choose a town where I could attend high school, I asked for Banff and got my wish. Good luck again.

After a couple of bad experiences at finding board and lodging, one with a family who found me too independent and another who were a bit rough even for me, I ended up with Charlie and Monty Watts on Otter Street. It was an arrangement made in heaven. Mr. and Mrs. Watts were sensible, solid people, with a son of my age who became my friend and running-mate. Charlie was the head gardener at the Cascade Gardens, and he gave me enough part-time work to augment the money from home and get me through school. When I graduated in the spring of 1952, it was only a short walk to the Chief Warden's Office of Banff National Park. Two weeks later, I was in the fire lookout tower on Mt. Sarback, Saskatchewan Crossing District.

By the age of nineteen, I was an assistant park warden for the Saskatchewan Crossing District. I spent much of the summer with my horses and a small crew of men, clearing a trail up the Alexandra River. Those who followed this trail in later years concluded that it must have been cleared after a heavy snowfall, because all the stumps were at least a foot high. Later, I was mortified when it was pointed out that the cutting should have been done at ground level.

I had my first encounter with a grizzly bear on a windy morning in November. It was still the practice in some parks, even as late as the 1950s, for backcountry wardens to take an animal for winter meat, on the understanding that only elk could be taken. That fall the Saskatchewan Crossing park wardens had already stockpiled two animals and the quarters were hanging in a root cellar halfway between the house and the barn.

The district warden had gone to Banff for the weekend, leaving me in charge. Shortly before lunch I went for a piece of meat, only to find the heavy timber door torn off its hinges and a hindquarter of elk missing. Fresh tracks led into the woods east of the barn. In retrospect, my next action made no sense whatever, but it must be remembered that I was a teenager, raised in the foothills. Although no stranger to the outdoors, I knew little about grizzlies. My education was almost over before it began.

Accompanied by my boss' little dog, Tuffy, a Heinz 57 terrier-type, I started to follow the bear's trail into the timber to see which way it went. In fact, the grizzly hadn't gone very far at all. Just within the edge of the timber was a round, clear opening about 50 yards across. The bear had taken the hind-quarter of the elk to the far side, where he ate for awhile, then covered the remains with leaves and brush. When the dog and I came into the clearing, he was curled up on top of the pile, having a snooze.

The grizzly, a beautiful silvertip, caught our scent the same instant that we noticed him. His reaction was spontaneous, and deadly. Without a second's hesitation, the bear jumped to his feet and came after us at full charge. I did what most people would do, I simply turned and ran for the house as fast as my legs would carry me. However, a person's speed is no match for an animal that can travel at 35 miles an hour. I glanced hurriedly over my right shoulder and saw the big silver hump of the grizzly two or three yards behind me and gaining fast.

It is very likely that my young park warden's career would have been ended almost before it began, had it not been for the dog. Various scars attested that the little mongrel had been badly knocked about by bears before, but he remained utterly fearless. As all three of us ran pell-mell toward the house, the dog continued to go in circles around the grizzly, jumping at its nose and nipping at its heels. It was only this remarkable act of skill and courage which enabled the dog and me to gain the back porch a scant few feet ahead of our pursuer. Seconds later, Tuffy and I were lying on the kitchen floor gasping for breath while the big bear, having stopped at the porch, ambled back to his cache. On the many lonely trails that still waited, the shadow of that silvertip would be forever at my elbow.

Before going up to the fire-lookout tower, I had received a brief introduction to telephone line work. As an assistant park warden, this became one of my main duties. Since the early days, the park wardens had been responsible for building and maintaining a system of forestry telephone lines in the mountain parks. Prior to the advent of two-way radios, the telephone network was designed to link all district cabins to the administration building in each park. For the park wardens and their families, the telephone provided a link with the outside world in case of sickness or accident. For the chief park wardens, it was a means of keeping tabs on the movements of men, some of whom, if left to their own devices, would not come to town or even report in for months at a time.

The line itself was a heavy-gauge wire, suspended from trees by porcelain insulators (split knobs), at a height of 16 feet. Where possible, the lines were constructed along the side of existing trails, both to eliminate the need for having to cut a new right-of-way, and also to facilitate maintenance of the line. Where a divergence was necessary, a narrow, three to four-foot-wide right-of-way was constructed. Trees intended to serve as telephone poles had to be sturdy enough to support a man's weight and be large enough in diameter to provide good contact for the climbing spurs. If too large in diameter there was a problem in getting the safety belt around it. Straight, clean-limbed trees were preferable. Where open country had to be traversed, poles were cut as close to the line as possible, peeled, and skidded to the site. Most park wardens in the outlying districts had in their string, one all-purpose horse that had been trained to work in single harness, as well as for riding and packing. These horses were especially valuable on the districts, as they were also used to skid firewood to the cabins.

In muskeg, the line would be suspended from three light-weight poles wired together to form a tripod. The split knobs were an oval, or sometimes hexagon-shaped insulator, built in two halves. These halves could be placed around the phone line, and bound together by a piece of light, flexible tie wire. After a couple of twists, the remaining ends of the tie wire were used to hang the insulator from a large staple on a tree or telephone pole.

While the wire ran freely through these insulators, it was necessary every mile or so, to have a solid tie. This consisted of a heavy glass insulator that screwed onto a wooden bracket that was then secured to the tree or pole by two big spikes. The phone line was firmly anchored to this insulator, again with a length of tie wire, but used in a different manner. In the case of a break in the line, usually caused by falling trees, these anchor points prevented the line from recoiling endlessly through the running insulators, making rejoining and splicing of the telephone wire a hell of a job. Solid ties were also used on either side of a river crossing or where the line crossed a highway.

Although considered primitive by today's standards, the single line worked extremely well, sometimes against all the laws of reason. For example, in crossing the Sunwapta Pass summit, the old line between Lake Louise and Jasper was actually looped around tree stumps in places. Once on Snow Creek summit, a park warden reported the line was tangled up in the antlers of a live moose and still working!

The park warden's telephone equipment included climbing spurs, a climber's belt and a splicing tool—a Nicropress. This was somewhat like a powerful set of pliers which was used to crimp the two ends of a hollow tube or sleeve, around the two ends of the wire. For conductivity, these tubes had to be of the same material as the line.

Probably the most indispensable tools of all were the specially designed telephone pliers—somewhat similar to the fencing pliers still in use by farmers and ranchers, and an axe. Finally, there was a pulley device, each end of which clamped onto the opposite ends of the broken telephone wire to bring them together. Once one included some spare insulators, staples and tie wire, this equipment constituted a considerable weight. It was particularly burdensome for a park warden on foot patrol, already carrying his food, spare clothes and rifle.

However, makeshift solutions were possible. My boss taught me an ingenious trick. He showed me how to take a piece of multiple strand rope, such as a halter shank off one of the horses' halters, and by temporarily spreading the weave, wrap the rope around the telephone line in such a way that the line became embedded in the core of the rope. Once wrapped in this manner for a foot or two and then allowed to tighten, this rope will slide down the wire in one direction, but when pulled the other way, clenched itself tightly on the line. It was an easy step from there, using two pieces of rope, to devise a simple pulley, which could be used instead of the much heavier mechanical one. Of course, this was in the days of grass ropes, before polypropylene products were invented. Not only does a synthetic halter rope burn the skin off your hands, when a pack horse pulls back, but you can't use it for the wire trick either.

Another item, which proved to be extremely useful when working phone lines, was a canvas bucket, usually one that had been condemned from the fire stores. Tied to the end of a light rope, the bucket could be lowered by the man up the pole to his helper on the ground, in order to haul up more insulators or whatever might be needed.

Working the phone lines entailed a number of hazards. A rather common accident was to over-climb a pole. It is common practice when climbing a telephone pole to have the head bowed to ensure that the climbing spurs are firmly embedded in the pole at each step. Normally, one instinctively looks up when approaching the line height, but if the line had not yet been hung, the warden, charging up the pole could be at the top and suddenly reach out and get an armful of empty air. One day this happened to my boss, Neil Woledge. Like a cat, he did a back flip and landed squarely on his feet at the foot of the pole!

☆　☆　☆

Working line on a stormy day in the summer also provided some thrills. Lightning, although seldom dangerous when working on the line, often travelled down the wire giving the park warden a hearty shock, if he was in contact with the wire. Anyone attempting to use a phone sent a pretty good tingle down the line when they cranked the generator in the telephone box to produce a ring. Frozen trees in the winter could be downright dangerous as well, in that the spurs tended to slip and snow-laden, leaning trees were difficult to climb; it didn't matter how hard one tried to stay on the upper side, the law of gravity usually prevailed.

The forestry telephone consisted of a rectangular wooden box, approximately 10 inches wide by 24 inches long by 8 inches deep, normally mounted vertically on a wall of a park warden's cabin or house. From the front centre of the box projected a mouthpiece, or speaking tube, while a receiver hung on a hook on the left side of the phone box. At the top front of the box were two bells and on the right hand side a crank, which turned the generator inside.

When making a telephone call, one removed the receiver from its cradle and used the generator crank to send out a specific signal. Special arrangements of long and short rings were used on forestry lines before today's dial system. Thus, to raise the Jasper switchboard one might use one long ring, about four revolutions of the crank handle, and to call the Maligne Lake Station, three short rings, about one crank of the handle each. When speaking, the voice was powered by three cylindrical batteries arranged inside the phone box.

In the case of very long telephone lines, such as from Banff to Jasper, it was necessary to relay messages through small switchboards at key park warden stations, such as Lake Louise and Saskatchewan River Crossing. It fell to the park wardens' wives to act as switchboard operators. If once in awhile one of these ladies developed a reputation as a bit of an eavesdropper, one could hardly blame her as the gleaning of a choice bit of news was the only compensation any of them received for this 24 hours a day, seven days a week job!

Working the lines could be very hard work, particularly when alone or when unexpected damage was encountered on a day's patrol. Picture please, a hot summer day, about two in the afternoon. I have been hard at work since 4:30 that morning when I set out before breakfast to find my horses. Now I am moving along with my pack string in heavy spruce forest when I come upon a typical blow-down, a place where a violent storm has cut a swath through the timber. Half a dozen spruce trees, some nearly two feet in diameter, lie across the trail and telephone line, blocking access. Several insulators are down; the line has snapped and recoiled for a quarter of a mile. The next cabin is still six miles away. Slowly I dismount, tie up my horses, unpack my tools and begin the wearying work.

On another bitter-cold day, this time in mid-winter, I am on patrol along a pine-covered ridge. Conditions are terrible. I've had to stop to rest with the last stopping place still visible on my back trail. Just ahead, a loose telephone insulator can be seen; the line hanging no more than 18 inches from the ground and the staple, from which the wire was originally hung, is 15 feet up a flimsy-looking leaner. I am sorely tempted to ignore it and press on. I have no tools with me, except for a small pair of pliers. However, my pride gets in the way. There is no shame greater than allowing a moose or elk to get hung up and killed in your telephone line wire. Too tired even to swear, I take off my pack and snowshoes.

Standing facing the tree, I raise the line behind me and hook the tie wire onto the back of my belt. The weight of the line adds to my extreme feeling of inertia. Then, summoning every available ounce of energy, I scramble up the tree using my arms and knees. Two-thirds of the way up, my body swings suddenly to the underside of the tree and I almost fall. Finally reaching my objective, I cling with one arm to the tree and, with the other, I reach behind my back and unhook the tie wire that's attached to the insulator. Wrestling it over my head, I finally manage to drop the tie wire into the staple and make the regulation tie before dropping into the snow—exhausted. There is an hour of daylight left and four long miles to go.

Work on the warden districts was cyclical in nature, changing with the seasons. Summers were for telephone line and trail maintenance, coupled with extensive horse patrols into the backcountry. In the fall, before oil or propane furnaces were installed in park warden stations, about two weeks had to be spent hauling in and sawing up firewood that was stacked in the basement of the main house. After that was done, and with the snows beginning to pile up on the passes north and south, the warden of the Saskatchewan District and I settled in for the winter.

Much of our time was spent on a vigorous program of patrols. Using wooden skis with bear-trap bindings, we travelled all of the main valleys regularly and often forayed into remote and rugged areas high above timberline. Here I received the first instruction in route selection and wilderness skiing, always with a wary eye for avalanche terrain. My boss was a bluff and hearty man, quick to temper, but surprisingly patient when it came to teaching his young helper—together we passed a very pleasant winter.

The toughest trip we made that year was shortly before Christmas. On a good cool day for travelling, we drained the pump, closed the house, then headed into town for the holidays. One of the interesting features of the trail in those days was the tea pail, strategically hidden in the bush about halfway between cabins. These tea pails were usually the four-pound honey tins that were around at that time. In the tin would be a scrap of paper or stub of candle for quick fire starts, some tea, sugar and matches. We reached our first tea pail around noon, travelling well, and by about three were at the cabin on Lower Waterfowl Lake.

That night the weather changed, it began to rain and in the morning it was a different story altogether. We set off in three feet of wet snow and literally trenched our way toward the Bow Summit. The older warden was bull-headed on occasion, and very strong. It was he who got us through that day. Although in good condition, I was tiring by midday and by the afternoon my world was becoming a nightmare. I finally gave up any pretence of breaking trail and settled down simply to try to stay with my boss as he led our way to the summit. We finally reached the Bow Summit Station in late afternoon. I staggered into the house on wooden legs and sank weakly into a chair. As our host made tea, exhaustion made the room swim before my eyes.

In February 1954, I entered a competition for park warden positions in Banff and Jasper National Parks. I was called for an interview in early March, and told to report to the third floor boardroom of the administration building in Banff. This park office is easily the most impressive of any in Canada, built like a castle and set in the beautiful Cascade Gardens overlooking the Bow River. Many wonderful and prestigious careers in the National Parks Service have either had their beginning or end in this building. For me it was a beginning.

I was already familiar with the outside of the "Ivory Tower," as it was referred to by most park staff. My part-time work in the gardens as a labourer had allowed me the use of the basement washrooms but I had never had reason to venture into the hallowed halls above. The only glimpse that I had been allowed of the boardroom was from the outside, when washing windows.

Now, as a young assistant warden, I found myself actually sitting at a long conference table, across from two chief park wardens and a personnel officer. I felt very much in awe of my surroundings and of them. Here were two of the highest-ranking park wardens in Canada—big, rugged men, loaded with responsibility and oozing authority. Both were carefully barbered, and their forest green uniforms were tailored to a "T." Each man wore on his arm the three gold stars of rank and on the right lower sleeve the yellow chevrons denoting service. Every chevron meant five years and these gentlemen each had a row of them halfway up to the elbow.

A large picture of King George hung on a dark panelled wall, and one of the Queen on another. The moth-eaten head of a large buffalo bull brooded from its place over the doorway. The personnel officer explained the rules of competition, and the interview got underway. When they turned me loose half an hour later, I had no idea how I had made out. The questioning had been gentle, the attitude of the chief park wardens almost fatherly. The personnel type walked me to the door and informed me I would get a letter in about 10 days. I went back to the Saskatchewan River Crossing Station and forgot all about it.

Two weeks later, I did get a letter and was excited beyond words to learn that I had qualified for a backcountry district in Jasper National Park. I was instructed to report to the chief park warden of Jasper on April first. Before leaving the Crossing, I made one more trip to Banff: to give the glad tidings to the great people who had rented me a little suite during high school, to say good bye to all my friends at the greenhouse and finally, to the chief park warden who had given me a start. As we shook hands, I looked at the sign that hung on the wall behind the chief's desk. The sign read, "If you lose your horses, don't call this office. They are not here!"

Jasper National Park is an area of over 4000 square miles. Most of it is wilderness—mountains and icefields, wild rivers and forests, and beautiful valleys. The Brazeau River District, to which I was assigned, comprises over 500 square miles, and lies in the southeast quarter of the park. Although it can be approached by vehicle from the east, through provincial forest reserve, there is no access from the park side except by foot or horseback. This way, one may go in over Nigel Pass to the south, or by way of Poboktan Pass from the west, or over Cairn Pass at the north end of the district.

The main Brazeau Valley is one of the friendliest stretches of country in the entire park. Herds of bighorn sheep and mountain goat graze on the mountainsides, while some of the oldest populations of elk in the Rockies feed on the meadows beside the river. There are moose and deer, black and grizzly bears, wolves and wolverines, and a host of smaller, shyer animals not so easily seen. It is a valley that seems to get more than its share of sunshine. Wandering through that pleasant country, the traveller feels at home and at peace. When I went there, I had seven patrol cabins scattered throughout the district, the headquarters being about two and a half miles below Brazeau Lake. The forestry telephone line came from the highway at Poboktan Creek, over the pass and ended at the main cabin.

The snowshoe trip is my first winter patrol on the Brazeau. The cabin where you join me is Waterfalls Cabin, on the way to Poboktan Pass. It is not a particularly cold day, but cold enough to discourage resting. Nor is there much hope of sunshine to brighten the mid-hours. When it finally gets light enough to gauge the conditions, the sky is grey and without movement and dusk is only eight hours away. On my first five-minute stop to take stock of the weather, I am aware again of the silence. I stand still in order to detect even the slightest sound; all I hear is the minute rustle of my parka caused by the beating of my own heart.

I move on. I am in the old burn now, breaking trail in 10 inches of new snow. I am beginning to feel more confident; the muscles beginning to lose their stiffness and the pace settling down. Last night's cabin is far behind; ahead lies the open high-country.

Just before 10:00 am, I judge that things are going well enough that I can afford the time for a short diversionary trip. The valley up which I travelled has become quite narrow and the banks on each side steeper. On the opposite side from the trail, a very small log shelter stands half-buried in the snow, on the side of a tributary to the creek which I am following. Before crossing over to check the place out, I debate leaving my pack on the trail, but decide that rather than crossing back, I will travel the far bank for awhile in hopes of better going.

As soon as I leave the trail, I realize that heavy as the travelling has been, it is considerably worse off the track. The light crust under the recent snow is insufficient to carry my weight and I am now ploughing through a good foot and a half to two feet. I am sweating when I reached the cabin.

I clear away the four feet of snow which barricades the tiny door and squeeze inside. It is a very poor place indeed. Built of small unpeeled balsam logs, with a dirt floor and one very small window, it is dark and cramped. But the worst feature is the mildew and the smell of mice. The inside surfaces of the logs are mouldy, as is the mattress on the pole bunk. Little pockets of mouse droppings lie in every depression. The small air-tight heater, a few very dubious cans of food, and left-over nails are in various stages of rust. The place gives me claustrophobia. It will be a very frosty Friday before I spend a night in this spot.

The cold, fresh air actually feels good as I step outside and latch the creaky little door. It is now 11:00 am. I had travelled five miles, plus a side trip. When I regain the trail, there will be eight miles to go. There is now a very pale, late morning winter sun. It shines upon the right-hand side of the gully, the side on which I stand. It makes that part of the landscape considerably more inviting than the cold, shadowy, left-hand side. Deciding to stay on that side for awhile, I head once more toward the pass, following a narrow strip of ground flanked on the downside by a steep slope and on the upper by dwarf balsam fir and spruce.

During the next few minutes a small defect in my equipment is going to be the critical factor in a calamity which has been building for some time. It has to do with my snowshoe harnesses. The leather piece which encases the toe of my boot is not fastened firmly enough to the webbing of the snowshoe. The lacing has stretched, allowing the foot considerable leeway to swivel sideways, as well as the necessary up and down movement. The result is a lack of control over the snowshoe, irritating on the trail and a severe hindrance in deep snow.

Travelling too close to the rim of the gully, I have been skittering along a bit of hard pack, when my left foot sinks unexpectedly into soft snow, throwing me off balance. At the same time, my pack, 40 pounds or so, swings sideways, tipping me completely over and knocking me head first down the slope. Away I go, upside down and out of control, accompanied by my own personal avalanche. After about 30 feet of this, I hit a rather nasty stretch. The snow is thinned here by wind action, so various sharp and unforgiving rock protrusions impact painfully on my person. The fact that I have lost a mitt and am trying to brake speed with my bare hand does not help matters. It is my passage over the rocks that shocks me into realizing that this is indeed becoming a serious business. With a spurt of strength impelled by pain, I regain an upright position. A moment later I find myself standing at the bottom of the gully, buried to the knees in snow and debris. My pack hangs over one shoulder.

I clear the snow from my clothing, pack and mitt and generally set myself to rights and feel the urge to hurry on. I re-tie my snowshoes—awkward bloody things, but do not feel that I can afford to work on the slipping problem. Time was wasting, I must push off. Climbing up to the old trail I pause once to look back at the scene. There is a spot at the top where I had gotten entangled and lost my balance. It was quite obvious from here that it had been a poor choice of route. Why did I go that way? And there is the track of my ignominious descent, rock scraped bare and all—an embarrassing testimony to my ineptitude and lack of experience. I hope snow and wind will cover up the story before some other, wiser park warden comes this way.

Lift and push. Lift the snowshoe and push it ahead. Each time I lift, the ankles complain; each time I push and swing the snowshoe forward, the groin complains. Each time I set a foot down, the blisters hurt. 18 inches forward to the step and six miles to go. That is 6 times 5,280 which equals 31,680 feet, divided by 1½ which equals 21,120 steps. Twenty-one thousand, one hundred and twenty steps will get me to the cabin! It seemed an impossible task. Lift and push. This is a great adventure?

I stop at noon in the shelter of a small gully—pale sunshine with an illusion of warmth. All of the trees of any stature are far behind me; up ahead are a few small ridges with clumps of balsam fir barely visible in five to six feet of snow. Beyond that, the rolling fields lead to the pass. White upon white, grey upon white, white upon grey, no real points of reference—just shadows upon shadows. I stomp out a little patch of snow and ease off my pack. First a sip of warm tea, then a SPAM sandwich, half frozen. Finally, I savour a small piece of Christmas cake and the last of my cup of tea. Then I sit for a few minutes while the digestive process turn the food into new energy, new strength and new hope. Let's see, 12:45 now—a little better than four miles to go, about three hours of daylight left—should be okay, but there's no time to spare.

I travel well for the first hour or so after refuelling. By slightly after two o'clock I am on the summit and able to look down the southeast aspect of the watershed. To my left, or northeast, the snow reaches up in gentle undulations to a high ridge which culminates at the southeast end in bare rock, and a steep face dropping into a slightly smaller valley which runs counter to the one I am on. At the head of that short valley is an open basin, good caribou country in the summer, backed by a huge massif which forms a barrier to the west. Lower down, below the basin, I can just make out the tops of the spruce trees which fill the bottom end of the valley. It seems such a long way off, like a site at the end of the universe. Continuing the circle, my gaze takes in a series of peaks that rise to the west, directly across from me. And below these peaks, as on my side, are vast empty slopes of unbroken snow. The scale of the landscape makes me feel small, an insignificant speck in this enormous bowl of snow and silence.

Glancing once more to the slope above, I search for a sign, any sign, to indicate that some other creature lives and moves in this empty wilderness. There is, in fact, a track about 200 yards higher and parallel to my own. It belongs to a wolverine, a tireless super-traveller of the high country. The animal, typically, is not in sight, but its trail leads up the slope and appears to be going to the very top of the ridge. Unlike most other beings, including man, the wolverine seems to scorn even the stern protection of the timbered valley, electing instead to travel in solitary grandeur where lesser creatures would fear to tread. Slowly I move on.

I now encounter a new problem, or rather, an old one re-occurs. Unlike the deep, soft snow on the north side of the pass, I am now travelling on a sun and wind-glazed crust. A crust that supports me on one step, only to break on the next. Furthermore, because the centre of the basin here forms a steep-walled gully, I am forced to travel on the sidehill. This means that the ill-fitting snowshoes are constantly either sliding out from under me or else breaking through. It is torturous going, and after awhile I have to rest again. "Mother said there would be days like this," I told myself, "but she never said how damn many!"

By this time I am very tired and extremely thirsty. The term air hunger, learned in first-aid practice, occurs to me and I think, "I'm hungry for a drink." Hunger seems to better describe the urgency of my need, rather than the word thirst. The Thermos still contains a mouthful of tea but I feel it would be wise to conserve that precious commodity until later. I begin to watch for water as I go along.

After awhile, working my way across a narrow gully, I discern the muted gurgle of a tiny stream beneath the snow. The problem is how to reach it. The gully is narrow and steep, the angle of descent exaggerated by the fact that five feet of snow on each bank tapers down to only a few inches over the surface of the unseen water. To climb down into the declivity on my clumsy snowshoes would be awkward, and would likely result in actually stepping into the water with one or both feet before I was done. Previous experience while travelling a frozen but partially flooded river had taught me the folly of allowing one's snowshoes to get wet on a cold day.

On future trips, remembering today's travails, I would be travelling with a long ski pole complete with a large basket, a disc near the tip of the ski pole to stop it from sinking into the snow. This would help immeasurably in keeping my balance on the trail. In my pack would be a small plastic cup which, in a situation like this, I could wire to the end of the pole and lower it neatly into the stream from a comfortable standing position. Today, however, I am not so well equipped. Finally removing both pack and snowshoes, I stretch out carefully on the snow, head down, and proceed to worm my way toward the enticing gurgle.

By the time I am actually within reach of the water I am very nearly upside down. It is a sense of extreme vulnerability which causes me to pause and glance back over each shoulder. People who travel the trail alone develop an aversion to placing themselves in a position or situation from which they cannot react effectively to an unforeseen threat. I begin to explore the strength of the snow layer covering the streamlet.

One second later, the weight of my body disrupts the stability of the snowpack, on which I rest, and it collapses with a slight hissing sound. I am forced to support myself on my outstretched arms and hands which promptly go through the light crust and into the water below. At least I can finally drink, and seldom has anything tasted as good as that ice-cold mountain-spring water. I drink again, and then fight my way back to a standing position. The water is a lifesaver, but I am dismayed by my loss of energy and the sudden pull of tiredness. My right mitt is soaked; I wring the water from the liner and pull it back on, regain my snowshoes, shoulder the pack, and carry on into a greying afternoon.

It is just short of four in the afternoon when I reach the lower rim of the basin and prepare to descend into the short valley, which lies at a right angle before me. Just ahead is a tricky bit of steep, open sidehill before the first fringe of timber. I have barely started across this stretch when my right foot slews wildly to one side, upsetting my balance and dumping me heavily on my back. When looking for the cause of this latest disaster, I find that one of the leather laces, which holds the footplate of my harness to the snowshoe, has broken—a logical outcome of many hours of wear. Not a big deal either, but there is no escaping a repair job now.

Digging into my pack I find some scraps of leather which I carry for occasions like this, and single out one which will do nicely if trimmed in half. I am somewhat surprised at the difficulty with which I extricate the pocket knife from my trouser pocket. My fingers, although not noticeably cold, seem numb and clumsy, probably due to the frozen mitts. I finally get the blade open and look for a firm surface on which to place the leather for cutting. There is no firm surface. All around is snow—no rock or tree stump to be seen.

Finally I devise a rather unsatisfactory system whereby I stand upon one end of the leather and with my left hand stretch it as taut as possible. I then take the knife and press the point of the blade through the leather, in order to start the cut. I apply pressure, then more pressure, until in one sickening motion the bright steel goes through—as if through Kleenex, and bites into my left index finger until it hits bone.

The shock makes me yell. I seize the injured finger in my other hand and clasp both hands between my knees. And there I crouch in the snow, biting my lip while a cold, sick sweat breaks out on my forehead. After a moment, I carefully part my knees and raise the unfortunate member for inspection. It is bleeding profusely—dark red. I reach into my pack once again with my free hand and rummage for my shaving kit, in which I find a gauze bandage.

No ointment to moisten the gauze, it will be a bitch to get off when the blood dries. "Hell with it. No time to mess around." Wrap the gauze snug, not too tight, mustn't stop the circulation altogether. Splitting the end of the gauze in order to make a wrap and tie is tricky—do it with my teeth. As I finish, the blood is already coming through. "It will have to do," I think, "I must get to that cabin."

I try to get the injured hand into the mitt. The shock is leaving the finger now and it hurts like the devil. Putting the mitt on is agony. Then I remember the snowshoe still needs fixing. Another thought, "I'm in trouble." Then, "No, I'm not in trouble, no big deal." And then I continued, "Well, if I'm not in trouble, I'm awful darned close to it."

I look around. Darkness is approaching. Immediately in front of me, the open slope curves down towards the timber, snow-laden spruces, silent and stately. Somewhere in the midst of those trees is the cabin, perhaps a mile away in a straight line. But though I strain my eyes I can not pick it out in the gloom—I can only estimate its whereabouts. To my right, at the head of the valley, the massif rises dark against the evening sky. And behind are the great peaks—impassive, stoic, timeless and unforgiving, that had looked down upon me as I toiled all afternoon making my way through the basin.

Being a man of reason, I wonder at my plight. The day had not in any way been remarkable. The distance to be covered was not unusual, the temperature was cold but I had not been caught in a blizzard or a surprise thaw, both of which can put a man in trouble. Why am I in difficulty? Why do I feel so wiped?

Bits and pieces of wilderness first aid training come back to me. Trauma. Shock. Any accident, any unforeseen event that interrupts— sometimes in a violent manner, the normal planned activities of mind and body, produces shock. To the mind these incidents mean surprise, insecurity, loss of control over one's movement, fear and anxiety. Accidents, even small ones, cause physical reactions: adrenaline flow, heart rate up, strenuous unplanned activity to extricate oneself from a dilemma, subjugation of the threat, the effort of regaining control.

In many of man's legends and superstitions, bad luck is believed to occur in threes and, indeed, such frequently appears to be the case. Roy Mason, British Columbia Coastal Range pilot, survivor of many hair-raising landings on lakes and glaciers in the high country, dwells on the three factor in his fascinating book, *Ice Runway*.

Had I been asked, I would have admitted to shock when I cut myself, though in actual fact, I had been the victim of shock three times that day. Precious time and energy had been squandered in ways unforeseen.

"I must be careful now, I'm extremely tired; the night will be long and dangerously cold for one not equipped to bivouac... essential to find the cabin without further incident."

While I complete the emergency repair job, my eyes scan the remaining snow slope, picking out the exact route I will have to take. Then I locate and memorize the spot where I will enter the timber. And finally, because by then I can expect to be completely in darkness, I estimate the direction and distance to the cabin.

I start off slowly, each step taken with utmost care. The cabin is a goal that will require my greatest effort. Somehow, I made it.

A Bride in the Backcountry

When I started off for the Brazeau District in mid-June of 1955, I was astride a four-year old grey gelding, and leading three pack horses. The first of these was a strong, deep-chested bay mare, with a kind heart and a nervous disposition. The other two were black, twin geldings and their presence made the mare even jumpier than usual. The twins were half-broke, green-timber wild ones and they specialized in violent and unpredictable behaviour. They were already well on the way to becoming a regular pair of outlaws.

If the blacks were bad news and the mare a bit of a liability, the grey, called Silver, was already a valuable companion. The gelding had barely seen a saddle when assigned to me early in May and I spent most of the month finishing the horse. Each day that passed, I found out a little more about the animal's temperament and personality and the more I learned, the better I liked him. Silver was a serious-minded, intelligent horse, with a large measure of common sense and a sincere desire to do things properly. By the time we hit the trail, we were already working well together.

There was, however, a problem with the name. In the past month I had grown thoroughly sick of being hailed as the Lone Ranger with his horse Silver. I had no intention of putting up with it all summer. Early in our relationship, the gelding escaped from the corral at Poboktan Creek and gracefully eluded capture for several days. This gave me cause to change his name to Slippery. Slippery soon became Slip which, over time, became Old Slip.

In the years to come, Slip and I would literally travel thousands of miles together. Together we would face wild rivers, deadfall and swamp.

Together we would coax, bully and provide leadership for balky, nervous, recalcitrant, confused and suspicious pack horses. Together we carefully circumnavigated the unpredictable grizzly and fought our way through rain and mud. Our friendship and understanding eventually grew to a degree seldom found even between members of the same species. It was a remarkable bonding of man and horse.

In appearance and accoutrements, my saddle horse and I were more or less typical of backcountry park wardens in the mountain national parks of Canada in the 1950s. A photograph taken in the Brazeau Valley shows me wearing the Park Warden Stetson with a pronounced curl to the front corners of the brim—cowboy-style. The hat badge is clean and polished. I wear a faded, light-green Parks-issue shirt with narrow dark-green tie and an Eisenhower-jacket of the same colour with black and gold shoulder flashes. Below my broad leather belt, the park warden image gives way to blue jeans, because they were simply more comfortable for riding than the issued uniform slacks. As for footgear, while some park wardens wore riding boots, I still favoured a heavy work boot with a built-up heel, in those days made by Dayton. The boot laced well above the ankle and, when equipped with toe and heel plates, was well suited to rough, rocky terrain. On those days when the jingled-out horses were hard to find, my boots were much better for hiking than were cowboy boots. They were also better for fording creeks and rivers, although the weight became a bit troublesome once the water level rose above a person's nose!

The saddle on the grey gelding was a standard Stock Association model, the only distinguishing mark being a ram's head branded into the leather at the back of the cantle. This was the National Parks Service horse brand, and it appeared also on the gelding's left shoulder. Draped over the saddle skirts behind the cantle were a pair of saddle bags. On most days one contained a SPAM sandwich or else two left-over hotcakes wrapped in wax paper, and an orange. The other side sometimes held a mickey of rye, fortification against mosquito bites, grizzly bites and frostbite.

On the right side of the gelding, an ancient Lee-Enfield .303 carbine hung in a scabbard, the lower part of which passed under the stirrup leather. The butt of the rifle rode high on the horse's withers just ahead of the saddle tree, ready to my right hand. Many of the park wardens had been issued new .270 calibre rifles but I'd had poor results with mine and went back to the trusty old carbine with the filed-down bolt that made it fit easily into the scabbard.

An old-fashioned grass lariat was also tied to the right side of the tree and hung on the outside of the rifle. Usually tied to the left side of the saddle horn was a pair of stout leather gloves and, hanging in a scabbard under my left leg, was a trail axe. I was quite proud of my axe. I had it made in the blacksmith shop in Jasper by taking a full-sized axe blade of particularly good steel and cutting away nearly two-thirds of the width of the head of the axe, while still maintaining the full width of the blade. Always well sharpened, it was a very effective tool or weapon, very light and easily swung with one hand.

Tied behind the cantle, in a compact roll no more than 16 inches long, was the traditional yellow slicker. This method of rolling and tying the slicker was a hallmark of the park wardens of Jasper National Park at the time, as was the very neat, tied-off-at-the-top method of throwing the diamond hitch. The whole aspect of a good park warden trail outfit was one of neatness and utilitarianism—nothing flapping, nothing dragging, no loose ends.

Finally, draped across the front of my saddle, were my broad, leather chaps, smooth side out to shed the rain. Chaps are heavy and cumbersome when mounting, dismounting or walking along the trail. By hanging one half of them on each side of the saddle horn, I could quickly wrap them around my legs in case of a storm, and could just as quickly free myself and jump off my horse if trouble erupted in the pack string. The chaps also had deep, very useful pockets. As I often travelled in very wild terrain where trails were nearly indistinguishable, I was a firm believer in topographic maps. The left pocket of my chaps always contained a "topo" map of Jasper-South, neatly folded into a plastic cover, protection against rain. Such a smooth traveller was the gelding that many a day I simply spread the map over the front of the saddle and studied it at leisure as we ambled down some quiet trail.

My horses and I reached the summit of Poboktan Pass around 10:00 am, on the morning of the second day. Although the trees were in leaf and the grass already well started in the main Athabasca Valley, conditions on the pass resembled very early spring. Snow drifts as deep as six feet lay across the trail in many places, and had to be skirted around. Every rivulet and gully was filled with run-off. After struggling through the drifts and slipping and sliding down the steep trail into Jonas Creek, conditions began to improve. Once below Brazeau Lake, little patches of green grass began to appear and, as I rode into the pasture at the district headquarters in the late afternoon, the setting was almost idyllic. Here, the new grass was already half-a-foot high, and several early wildflowers added their colours to the scene. Up on the shoulder of Chocolate Mountain, a band of bighorn sheep grazed peacefully and the Brazeau River seemed actually to welcome me. I felt instantly at home.

My sense of well-being lasted about 10 seconds. Once safely down off the pass, I turned the three packhorses loose to see if they would follow without having to be led. This worked very nicely and, in fact, for the last four or five miles they had been trailing along as good as gold. Whether it was the sight of all the green grass or the idea that they had reached their destination, the two pea-brained blacks decided to celebrate by bucking off their packs.

They startled me halfway out of my wits when they came roaring by, one on each side, creating an avalanche of flying tarps, tin cans and a hail-storm of macaroni. The jittery bay mare, her nerves on edge after a hard day, came totally unglued by the explosion. With eyes as big as saucers, she galloped past the cabin and plunged headlong into the river, where she soon found herself in swimming water and promptly vanished around the next bend. Meanwhile, the two blacks, rid of their packs but still trailing latigos and lash ropes, turned around and fled back up the trail toward Brazeau Lake.

The whole debacle hadn't taken more than five minutes. My grey horse and I stood in the pasture amid splintered packboxes and scattered groceries, and wondered how a beautiful day could go to hell so rapidly. However, there was no time to waste. I decided that the mare was my first priority. If she wasn't drowned, she was probably on the other side of the river by now, which meant she was out of the park and heading into the provincial forest reserve, a premise which was soon verified by fresh tracks on the far bank.

Up to this point I had not swum a river with Slip so I sat and studied the Brazeau River for a long minute, trying to find the best place to cross. That we were going to have to swim in any case was obvious. The trick

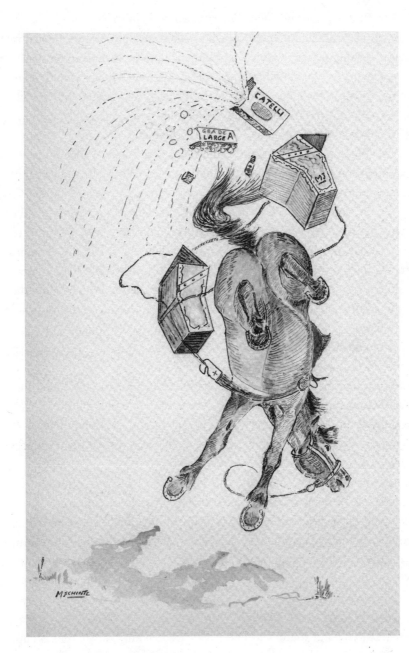

A Hailstorm of Macaroni

was to choose a spot where the current would help to carry us to the far side, to ensure that we would not be sucked into any deadly rapids, to pick a landing where the horse would be able to get a footing on the far side. Having run quickly through these calculations, I spoke a word of encouragement to the grey, patted him on the neck, and steered him quickly and surely into the torrent. To my relief, Slip responded nobly, going in with hardly any hesitation and swimming high and strongly. In a matter of a couple of minutes we were hauling ourselves out on a friendly gravel bar, and soon found the mare, trembling and unhappy, all tangled up in a patch of brush.

By the time I got back to my own side of the river and unpacked the mare, the shadows were lengthening and I would have been very glad to call it a day, but this day was far from over. There was still the dynamic duo to track down and bring back. Hauling myself wearily onto a soggy saddle, I headed Slippery back up the trail. At the log bridge below the outlet of Brazeau Lake, the tracks turned right, up the side of the lake and, for a minute, I was afraid I might not find them in the timber.

I shouldn't have worried. The two runaways left a trail of destruction equal to that of a small tornado. When I caught up with them a few minutes later, they were standing, side by side, in a mass of deadfall, thoroughly entangled in their lash ropes. The smaller one gave a little whicker of relief at the sight of Slippery and I began the task of getting them free. Having done so, I tied the two rascals together and trotted them smartly back to the cabin.

By the time I got there the sun had set on what was probably the longest day of the year and certainly that as far as I was concerned. After stripping all the gear and stacking it neatly on the porch, I gave everyone, good guys and bad guys alike, a helping of oats. Then I opened the cabin, hauled a pail of water and made sure there was enough firewood for supper and breakfast. As I completed these chores, my thoughts turned with mounting anticipation to a tall, cold drink. With great foresight I had decided to carry some Gordon's Gin in a saddle pocket, where it had remained safe and sound through all the excitement. Now I took a cup, shook the mouse droppings out, poured a large dollop of gin and topped it off with river water. Taking my drink to the front porch, I sat on a block of firewood and relaxed for the first time in 18 hours.

After a second Brazeau Martini, I put hobbles on the horses and a bell each on Slippery and on the neck of the steadier of the two blacks, and turned them loose. I knew that the mare had been on the district previously and, as hoped, she soon led the little group to the east corner of the meadow. Here the trail down the valley led through a small band of spruce, after which came a series of beautiful little pastures much loved by all the generations of horses to visit the Brazeau. In a few minutes the bells faded away.

Now I turned to the last chore of the day. Taking an empty pannier from the equipment shed, I walked slowly around the pasture, in the soft June dusk, picking up what I could of my widely scattered groceries. From a nearby pine tree, two whiskey jacks watched my every move, noting where items like spilled bread and cracker crumbs might be left in the grass.

On the way back to the cabin I was surprised to hear a very quiet tinkle of a bell, and even more surprised to see Slippery's grey head sticking out from behind the tack shed. Having seen the rest of his colleagues well down the trail through the woods, the canny animal had ducked back to scrounge a second feed of oats, knowing his only hope of getting it was to appear alone. It was a scene which would be repeated many times. Over the second oats and the third gin, my horse and I commiserated with each other. After awhile the grey went to look for his friends, and I went into the cabin to make a very late supper. I decided the next day would be a take-it-easy day.

By the end of the month, I had finished my first patrol of the district, stopping over two days at Isaac Creek and again at Cairn Pass. These layovers were used to tidy up and repair the cabins, and make short trips into side valleys, noting game trails and feeding areas. The horses behaved well. The Brazeau is friendly country with plenty of feed and, by morning, the ponies were seldom more than half a mile from the cabin. Towards the far end of the district, however, the topography changes somewhat and so does the local weather. Where the Southesk River comes brawling down from the west to join the Brazeau, the timber is thicker, and the temperatures more extreme. Thunderstorms are common in the summer and it was here, on my second patrol, that I ran into a severe one.

On a day near the middle of July, my horses and I were following a winding trail beneath heavy timber. Close by on the right, the Southesk River ran swiftly on its way toward the foothills. The air was warm and very still beneath the spruce and pine. Sounds were muted in the mid-day hush; I was quiet, slightly uneasy at the prospect of an oncoming storm. Another traveller, a few bends up the trail, would have been unaware of the pack train until one of the horses snorted, or a hoof thumped against an exposed root on the trail. Above the timber to the west, thunderheads piled high above the pass, the edges of cumulus shining against the summer sky. All the while, the sky below the clouds blackened and heavy shadows moved across the alpine meadows.

I turned in the saddle, with right hand resting on the cantle, and eyed the line of diamond hitches strung along behind. Full tarps were on all the loads, corners neatly tucked in, ropes snug, boxes riding nice and even on each side. Things were shipshape as far as I could tell. I had learned to pack in Banff National Park, where, at that time, they taught you to take the tail-end of the lash rope back down the rear of the left hand box and tie off with a double hitch underneath, up by the front cinch. This way there were no loops anywhere on top to snag on branches or deadfall along the trail.

When wardens in Jasper National Park saw me do this, I was haughtily informed that trails in that park were maintained to a level which precluded any possibility of catching packs on snags and branches. Besides, it was pointed out, Jasper Park Wardens did not favour the head-and-tail method of trailing pack horses, which admittedly is hard on the horses. Instead, they tied the halter shank of the second horse to the loop on top of the pack on the first horse. The knot used was one which could be untied with a swift pull by a rider alongside. There were advantages to this method in terms of well-being of the horses and expediency in case of emergency.

The air is oppressive now, so very hot and still that only violence can break the tension. The sun is gone. The towering cumuli roll across the pass and boil down into the valley—distant thunder rumbles—menacing.

As the storm gets closer, I face a nice little problem. It has to do with the yellow slicker neatly rolled and tied on the back of my saddle. The grey was proving to be an exceptionally intelligent horse. However, he was still young, and clearly tense at the prospect of an oncoming storm. Unfurling the slicker while in the saddle could have disastrous results. On the other hand, if I dismounted and put the thing on, the horse might not let me back up.

A sudden change in the air, heralding the imminence of the storm, makes up my mind and my right hand reaches back for the saddle strings, while my left moves up to the horse's neck for a reassuring pat. Seeing that I was already firmly in the saddle, it was better to have it out from there than give it up and try to fight my way back. I now address my horse: "It's OK, Old Timer. It's just me putting this old slicker on. A little spooky, but nothing to get excited about. Easy now! Don't start that, you son of a bitch! There, there, that's a good horse."

The last button is hardly fastened and the skirts of the slicker smoothed into place, when a jagged streak of lightning splits the black sky and snakes to earth nearly on top of us. In the next second, the first drop of rain hits the brim of my Stetson. Barely has the first drop knocked the dust out of my hat, when the next dozen fall like bullets, and the storm is on us. In minutes the hot stillness is gone, replaced by a rush of wind that bends the spruces over and pounds us with a drenching, driving downpour. In another five minutes my Stetson is leaking and I tip its brim forward, sending a deluge of water onto the saddle horn. Horses' manes are dripping, my gloves are soaked through.

Just as things are getting thoroughly miserable, the rain stops and a breath of warm, flower-scented air drifts by. Then, in the manner of mountain storms, the hail comes. Now the wind is truly cold and the horses show signs of extreme discomfort, shaking their heads and ducking under the stinging fusillade of ice. Hailstones collect in the folds of slicker and tarpaulin, and pile up along the edges of the trail. Coming to the first ford on the river, our little group emerges from the timber to see the water, wild at any time, erupting in fountains where the hailstones strike. In we plunge, too wet and numb to care about the cold.

But as we emerge on the farther bank, with clang of hooves on slippery stones and seek the trail once more in the stirrup-high brush, the sun comes out and lights the dancing river and turns the slicker a brilliant yellow that contrasts vividly with the retreating dark clouds. By common consent, the pack train stops. I dismount and check my saddle cinch and those of the pack horses, for cinches can become too tight when wet. Black Pete blows his nose, the mare braces her legs and gives herself such a shake that everything in her boxes rattles, another takes the opportunity to relieve himself, with a big sigh. And I speak kindly to my horse and the bond between us grows.

Most of the time that I was in the backcountry, I was supremely happy as my personality is inclined more than a little to that of a lone wolf. Strangely enough, the lack of companionship, female companionship, bothered me acutely on my trips to Jasper for supplies. Most evenings on the town found me gazing morosely into the bottom of a beer glass, wishing very much for a nice girl to keep me company.

For some time I dated the young lady who clerked in the chief park warden's office. Although she was good company, I came to suspect that she was more interested in my new Jeep than she was in me. It was about this time that I discovered the partner I was searching for. Her name was Glennys and she worked in the front of the bakeshop in Jasper. She had soft brown curls, a sunny personality and was rather a short girl, which made us well matched. We got along from the very beginning, and our friendship soon progressed to a more intimate relationship. By Christmas, there was a growing understanding that we might be going to start our lives together.

So it was that in April, when Glennys disclosed that she was in the family way, there was no hesitation on either side as to getting married. When I got the news, I had been spending springtime on the district, as it was common practise to be either out of, or in, town during the break up, due to the poor travelling in the valleys. Through most of April I had been doing my spring thing, which was getting up very early in the morning to travel the high country. There, my skis gliding effortlessly over the frozen snow, I tracked the movement of caribou and wolverine and found the wintering places of the ptarmigan. By afternoon, my day's patrol over, I would be back at one of the cabins, basking in the warm April sun. And always I watched in the spring snow for the first sign of grizzly bear.

The news of Glennys' pregnancy ended my carefree days. We agreed that my presence in town was required in order to make clear my intentions to her parents and to plan the wedding in the near future. The route by which I chose to come out led over Nigel Pass, this being considerably shorter than over Poboktan. The first half of the trail went well enough, the snow being nearly gone on my side of the pass, but when I struggled to the summit shortly before noon, a discouraging sight lay before me. The entire six miles from the top of the pass to the highway was deeply covered in three to four feet of snow. Ten minutes convinced me that it would be nearly impossible to get through. This side of the summit had been exposed to the sun all morning and there was literally no bottom to the snow. With or without snowshoes, I sank to my hips at each step. After half an hour, I was soaking wet and exhausted.

Strangely enough, it did not for an instant occur to me to turn back. I could have returned to the main cabin and waited for a cold snap in the weather or waited until the snow melted further. A week or so would have made no difference and could have been easily explained. In my state of mind, however, waiting was not an option. I was eager and anxious to see my bride-to-be and could only look ahead. Sitting on my pack, nursing a thermos cup of tea, I noticed the creek.

Nigel Creek was running freely. Although some ice bridges remained, there were frequent lengths of open water. Furthermore, it flowed in the direction I wished to go. Making up my mind, I put away my Thermos, tied my snowshoes to the pack, and waded into the icy water. It was fortunate that the weather was warm, because I was soon thoroughly wet. The creek dropped steeply in a number of places, forming a series of small waterfalls and pools. It was hardly any time at all before I had lost my footing and slid into a deep pool on my back. From there on I made no attempt to stay dry but determined to make time instead. Wading, swimming and sliding, I arrived at the highway waterlogged but exhilarated and by evening I was recounting my experiences to Glennys and her folks. Her father mused that a man must have wolverine blood in his veins to be able to travel that way, and "Wolverine" became my family nickname.

We were married in a simple ceremony. For no good reason other than that it rhymed with Jasper, we chose Casper, Wyoming, for a honeymoon destination. We were away for 10 days, which was the maximum time the Park Warden Service allowed for honeymoons. It was a marvellous time, as hopefully most honeymoons are, but ours was especially notable for the wonderful weather and the equally sunny disposition of the people we encountered along the way. At nearly every stopping place we were treated to little specialties and freebies by restaurant keepers and motel managers. It made us feel very fortunate and very special.

By the time we returned, the high country was passable for horses. We set to at once getting our assigned pack string shod and gathering supplies. On a day late in June, with me in the lead, Glennys took her place at the rear of the outfit and headed for her new home. She was 19 that year, and nothing in her previous experience had prepared her for life in the backcountry. The long ride in nearly killed her but, from the moment she climbed off her horse at Headquarters Cabin, she tackled her new role with courage and determination.

Horsemanship and backcountry cooking were immediate challenges. On moving days I would go out to find the horses at dawn, leaving Glennys to make breakfast. Doing the dishes and cleaning up the cabin were her duties, while I saddled the horses and did outside chores. Then, with everything ready to go, we packed the horses together. Because I so often travelled alone, I favoured the one-man diamond hitch but, with my wife pulling slack on the off side, the operation could be speeded up. The whole procedure of hanging the packboxes on the pack saddle, adjusting the top pack, covering the load with a tarpaulin, and tying the diamond was reversed upon arriving. Again, we worked quickly and efficiently with one on each side.

Cooking on a variety of wood stoves was also a learning experience. Only two cabins in our district had stoves with ovens. At the others, all of the cooking had to be done on top of the wood heater, or in a curious drum-shaped oven built into the chimney. The chimney ovens required careful regulation of heat in order to be effective but, if properly handled, could be used to bake bread or biscuits, or even pies. After some rocky experiments, Glennys became as good with the cooking as she was with the horses.

On frequent occasions during the summer she was required to prepare meals, under primitive circumstances with rudimentary materials, for other park wardens and trail riders as well. One of these occasions provided her with a new backcountry recipe and, of even greater value, a more relaxed and confident approach to backcountry cooking. It was on a fall boundary patrol that five or six park wardens arrived together at Isaac Creek one evening. While they were caring for their horses and setting up camp, Glennys was in her cabin wondering what on earth to feed that crew. None of the ingredients at hand appeared likely to make a meal for half a dozen hungry men. It was her good fortune that there was a wonderful trail hand in the group.

A blacksmith by trade, Gene Merrill was highly skilled in all aspects of backcountry travel, including cooking. Furthermore, he was one of those rare individuals who takes the time to observe how everyone else is coping and step in quietly to lend a hand where necessary. His thoughtful meandering soon brought him to the lamp-lit cabin where the young woman was in growing panic. "Well," he said cheerfully after realizing her problem, "I tell you what we'll do; we'll give 'em Hishy-Hashy-Hell-Fired-Stew!" And with this, he showed her how to combine in a large frying pan bologna, canned SPAM, onions and diced potatoes, plus cans of mixed vegetables, to make a tasty and satisfying supper. Many were the compliments around the table that night, as my bride sat flushed with her success and the wise, old hand smiled to see her pleasure.

Although days on the trail were long and often demanding, Glennys enjoyed these days very much. She had great confidence in my ability and the horses were also comforting and companionable presences. Where the real courage was required were those occasions that found her alone for days at a time in one of the cabins. As usual, the source of her anxiety was the grizzly bear.

It used to be that many backcountry cabins in the mountain parks had what might almost have been considered a resident sow grizzly. These females produced a new litter every two years, and while they couldn't possibly have been the same bears, some of them seemed to have been around forever. When I was in camp with my horses, these old girls tended to take their babies and fade into the timber. As soon as the outfit took off down the trail, they came ambling back out and sometimes almost camped on the doorstep until I returned. For a warden's wife, this was company she would have preferred to do without.

Although these stay-at-home times were infrequent during the first summer, they became a regular occurrence in the next year after the baby had arrived. Long, hard days in the saddle were simply not practical with a little child, and more and more often, Glennys had to stay at the main cabin while I was on patrol. It was as a result of these lonely vigils that a strange phenomenon occurred. Although Glennys might be nervous during my absences, immediately on my return the anxiety would be gone and everything would be fine. The baby, however, would remain unsettled and jumpy, crying at unexpected noises for as long as 24 hours after I came back. We finally realized that it was Glennys' nervousness, transmitted to the child during the time they were alone, that caused this unsettled behaviour. It was a troubling thought, with no immediate solution.

It was decided early that Glennys should learn to handle a rifle. In the beginning, she practiced with a .22 calibre, and eventually graduated to the old Army .303 carbine. As it happened, we had an assistant on the district that summer. This man was a World War II veteran who prided himself on his shooting ability. The highlight of my young wife's training came the evening that she outscored the war veteran in a shoot-out behind the main cabin. After that, the old carbine hung on the cabin wall when she was home alone. Ironically, she regarded it with almost as much apprehension as she did the occasional grizzly that came along, for even though she had learned to shoot, the noise and recoil frightened her terribly.

When we rode into the district for our second summer together, we had with us a blond baby boy. This child, less than a year old, rode on the saddle in front of his mother. A wide sash was tied around the two of them so that he could not fall off, leaving her hands free to handle the reins and, if necessary, lead a pack horse. As usual there were still huge snowfields covering the pass and the early summer sun was warm and bright. We did not realize that the baby was acquiring a terrible sunburn until we were nearly to the cabin. By that time the poor little fellow was bright red and beginning to complain. He continued to complain for the next two days.

After getting over the sunburn the baby did fine, although he invariably caught a "bug" on our infrequent trips to town. Slippery was now an indispensable member of the family, and was on his best behaviour when carrying mother and baby. I wrote a letter to my father on a dreamy summer afternoon, while my wife and son napped in the cabin and the ponies drowsed in the meadow. In the letter I wrote, "I have never been so happy and content."

The following year found us in another backcountry district, still lonely and rugged, but somewhat closer to civilization according to the pattern used for moves and promotions. This time the main cabin was only eight miles from the nearest road, instead of 28. There was also a precious mountain lake in front of the cabin, full of wonderful trout, and a resident bull moose known to generations of park wardens as "Uncle Joe."

When I took the Rocky River District over from the previous park warden, we went through an exercise known as hand-over/take-over. To do this we rode through the district together with both horse outfits. At each cabin the outgoing park warden pointed out the main items of interest, such as the ponies' favourite feeding areas, good river crossings and local trails. Then the cabin inventory was carefully checked, and the previous incumbent emptied the cupboards of his possessions to make way for the new man.

It was at noon on the second day of our ride-through that we approached a dark, somewhat sinister looking little cabin, standing quietly beneath big spruce trees. Its name was Grizzly Shelter. Here I learned that I had been promoted into the most notorious bear district in the entire park. Approaching the cabin with some curiosity, I noted the outer walls heavily scarred with claw marks. The windows were protected by heavy rails, permanently nailed across; the hinges and latch on the heavy door were extra thick. But the most curious sight to behold were the eight-inch deep indentations at regular intervals in the earth around the cabin.

"What are those holes?" I asked.

The other park warden gave a tight smile. "That is where the grizzlies walk," he said.

However, the strangest sight of all still awaited me, for when we unlocked the scarred and battered door and stepped cautiously inside, I saw that the forestry telephone was mounted on the east wall, at floor level! While we fired up the stove and made tea, I was told the story that led to this odd positioning of the telephone.

In 1937, the Rocky River District in Jasper National Park was in the care of a park warden by the name of Ed McDonald. One day as Ed approached the shelter with his horses, he surprised a grizzly near the cabin. In the confusion which ensued, Ed was thrown from his horse, and landed on the ground with a broken pelvis. The horses left, and it seems, so did the bear. Now normally, a person with this injury is completely immobile, but Ed had to get to the telephone or die. In three days he managed to drag himself into the cabin and, by piling boxes and furniture against the wall, was able, on the third day, to reach high enough to crank the phone. It took two more days for his fellow park wardens to get in to him on horseback and then they had to sling a stretcher between two pack horses. That is how Ed went out with his broken pelvis. It would take a brave man to travel that particular trail, in that manner, in good health!

Ed spent over a year in a hospital in Edmonton getting over that episode and when he returned to Jasper, they sent him right back to the Rocky River District, the park administration having kindly kept it open for him, as was the custom in those days—after all, it was his home. Those last three days must have burned their way into his mind during the long months in the hospital. On his first trip back into the district, he took the telephone off the wall and mounted it on the floor. It had remained there ever since, in memory of Ed.

When we rode away some time later, I was unusually thoughtful. I sensed that the big bears would be very much a part of our lives as long as we were on that district. In fact, it was to be much longer than that, for dreams about grizzlies were to haunt me for years afterward.

I was to hear one more bear story when we did the hand-over/take-over at the main cabin. It was probably a good thing that it at least had a humorous touch. We were having a late cup of coffee one evening after checking on the horses, when the other warden looked out of the window at the gathering dusk. "I guess one young park warden had a hell of a scare here one time," he said. "This young guy, I can't remember his name, but it doesn't matter for the sake of the story, was sitting here one night in November. He hadn't been in the Service very long and he still wasn't too comfortable out in the boonies. Then too, this little valley isn't one of the most cheerful places I have ever seen, being kind of shut in, and with all them big spruce hangin' over you.

"Anyway, this young park warden is sitting here at the table one night, maybe readin' a book, or doing up his diary, when some movement outside the window makes him look up. Well, I guess he's pretty near startled out of his wits to see this big old grizzly lookin' at him through the glass. Now as you know this cabin has shutters and not railings nailed permanently across the windows like some cabins. The bear is so close that the warden is sure it's coming right in and, without waiting any longer, he grabs his rifle off the wall and fires point blank.

"When the smoke clears, the bear is gone but the young fellow is too nervous to go out in the dark to investigate. After awhile he takes the rifle to bed and tries to get some sleep, but I bet he leaves the lamp on all night. In the morning, when daylight finally arrives, he tiptoes outside and around the corner, and there's Mr. Bear lying stone dead alongside the cabin. Well, the beast is too heavy for him to move and, it being November, he's already turned his horses in. So, he's kind'a puzzled as to what to do next. After awhile he goes in and phones the park warden up at Maligne Lake."

In Jasper National Park, under the old district system, the park warden at Maligne Lake was generally senior to the man on the Rocky River for which Jacques Lake was the main cabin. It was policy in those days for park wardens on more senior districts to keep an eye on, and help and advise, young park wardens on backcountry districts adjacent to their own.

The story continued. "Well, the warden at Maligne Lake at that time was a long and lanky man, with a very deep and growly voice, for which he was well known. Now, after serious consideration to the bear problem, he spoke as follows: 'Well, son,' he said slowly in his growly voice, 'I guess you'd better dig a hole and bury 'im.'

"This hole digging turns out to be quite a job. Digging at Jacques Lake is no fun at the best of times, the ground being made up mostly of boulders, and on top of that, the first six inches is frozen as well. Although the warden struggles bravely all day, the hole is still a little short of complete when darkness falls.

"Next morning when he goes out to finish the job, he is astounded to find that some of the bear's cousins have been around in the night, and dragged the remains clean over to the other side of the clearing. Maybe they didn't care for the original burial site. Anyway, this poses a new problem and the young feller decides to phone the warden at Maligne Lake again. Maybe he is hoping, in the back of his mind, that the other fellow will come over and lend a hand. If so, he was in for a disappointment.

"After explaining the latest problem, he ended with a rather plaintive 'What the heck should I do now?' To which the man at Maligne replied in his deepest, growliest voice, 'Well, son,' he said, 'I guess you'd better dig another hole.'"

Old Baldy

When my little family and I moved to our second district, on the Rocky River, we had in our pack string a delightful old pinto called Baldy. He was a steady and faithful animal, always careful with his pack, but he had a number of eccentricities. One was a passion for bread and hotcakes. He would literally follow us into the cabin for a pancake. In fact, his love of bread was probably the reason the National Parks Service was able to purchase him for a ridiculously low price. Shortly before the arrival of the prospective buyer, Baldy had consumed most of a case of bread that was sitting on the station platform. Both he and his owner were somewhat unpopular as a result.

The horse's penchant for strange edibles also caused us some anxious moments. During World War II a group of British commandos, destined for winter infiltration into German-occupied Norway, were sent to Canada for training. They ended up in Jasper National Park, where they were instructed in skiing and mountaineering at the Columbia Icefields and in some of the other valleys. One of these other valleys lay in what was now our district. The Lovett Scouts, as the commandos were known, apparently experimented with dried foods in their search for easy-to-carry, non-perishable groceries, for when they departed they left behind several large, one-gallon tins of dried carrots.

Neither I, nor any of my successors developed a great liking for dried carrots, with the result that the cans ended up rusting away at the rear of the main cabin. Here the local sow grizzly found them one day and tore the lids off, hoping for something she and her cubs could eat. Not finding dried carrots to her liking either, she up-ended the cans before ambling away. Not long after this, Baldy discovered the mess and apparently decided that dried carrots were the next best thing to sliced bread, because he cleaned up every shred. When his feast was discovered, we were afraid to let the old packhorse near water, in case he swelled up and burst. For the next two or three days, we kept anxious eyes on him but, apart from a few thunderous explosions, he seemed perfectly happy.

Unfortunately, the lovable old weirdo was accident prone as well as eccentric. Some of his misadventures were hilarious, like the time he went for a roll after work and ended up on his back with a hind leg on each side of a pine tree. There he lay, completely hobbled, until I extricated him. Other incidents were more serious. I was alone at the time and was riding through an area of big, over-mature timber at the side of Jacques Lake. There were numerous sections of corduroy spanning wet places on the trail, and one of these sections over a small ravine had begun to sag on the downhill side. This caused the deck to slope and, to make matters worse, the logs were wet from recent rain. It was an accident waiting to happen and a horse was coming that couldn't pass up an accident.

Old Baldy was halfway across the corduroy when his legs shot out from under him, and the next thing he knew he was flat on his back in the gully—all four legs in the air. I was off my horse at once, grounding the reins, leaving Slippery to hold the head of the line. Baldy was in quite a predicament, the weight of his packs held him squarely on his back; he could neither roll over nor climb up. Quickly I loosened the cinches and removed all encumbrances but, just about the time Old Baldy had a chance to get up, he quit fighting. Like an old horse down on the ice, he seemed to have come to the conclusion he was finished and all the spunk went out of him.

It was not a pretty picture. The packhorse was lying there with his eyes rolled back in his head and no amount of tugging and pushing was to any avail. The other horses were gazing down at him with eyes as big as saucers and Slippery rolled his pink nostril and gave that low, snoring sound that horses make when they sense trouble. I stood with my hands on my hips—thinking. There are various ways that a horse can be helped out of a difficult situation but the animal has to have some motivation to help itself. I thought, "Well this horse needs help in the worst way and that's just the way he's going to get it!" Then I dropped into the gully with a knee on either side of Baldy's upturned head, and firmly clapped a hand over each nostril, cutting off the air. In desperation the horse began to struggle and finally in one great, convulsive effort he launched himself up and onto his feet. Speaking softly now and steadying him, I helped old fellow back onto the trail where he stood, shaky and subdued, soon to be re-saddled and packed.

Old Baldy survived this and various other minor mishaps in the time we were on the Rocky River but the old horse was so lovable and so good with his pack that we kept him on the outfit and tried to protect him from himself. As a result, he was still with us when we moved to our first highway district, 45 miles south of the town of Jasper.

Finally the old horse met with his last accident on a wild wet, thundery night at the Waterfalls Cabin. I was staying overnight with just the two horses, Old Baldy and Slippery. When the storm struck, late at night, the grey did what he usually did on bad nights, he came to the cabin and stood with his head under the porch roof. The old packhorse had other ideas however; he wanted to go back down the trail to the home corral. When I woke up to the clumping of hoofs and the clanging of the bell, I went out to find Baldy trying to haze the grey away from the cabin. He seemed in quite a panic. I decided I had better tie the pair of them up for the night, just to be sure. For some reason I had only one halter with me and I decided to use this for the saddle horse. For Baldy I fashioned a makeshift headstall with my lariat. After securing both animals I tried to go back to sleep.

Aroused by another commotion a short time later, I went out again. This time I was startled to find the packhorse on his back. Furthermore, the knot under the horse's jaw had slipped and the rope was pulled very tight. The old fellow appeared to be strangling. Having rushed to the cabin for a knife, I knelt and cut away the rope but it was too late. Old Baldy had either broken his neck when he threw himself backwards or else had strangled in the makeshift halter. Kneeling by the horse, in wind and rain, I was sick with anguish, the knife forgotten in my hand. Meanwhile, the grey stood quietly by, self-possessed as always, although watching, with deep concern, the passing of a friend.

While my little family and I were still back on the Rocky River there were some happy days. For the first time since our marriage we were able to

Old Baldy

have my parents and Glennys' mother in for a visit, bringing them the last eight miles on horseback. Glennys' mom particularly enjoyed the lake and the fishing for trout. We would take her out in the old rowboat in the evening and she would troll happily for an hour or two; the only sounds were the creak of the oarlocks and the splash when a fish was brought in. Then, as shadows deepened in the little valley, I would go to check on my horses, after which everyone gathered in the cabin for hot chocolate or coffee, and a late snack. Those were the good times!

Meanwhile, the district lived up to its reputation for grizzly bears. Any day that I went up the trail, except in the dead of winter, I could count on finding fresh tracks within five minutes of any cabin. It worried me more in the spring and fall when I was on foot. The tracks coming towards me weren't too bad, for they indicated a bear already past; it was the ones travelling up the trail in front of me that were the problem, especially when the huge claw marks were so fresh they were practically smoking in the mud.

As for Glennys, she saw her first grizzlies at Jacques Lake. She and baby Ted were alone at the cabin; I had been upcountry with the horses, and was expected home that day. Glen decided to freshen up in preparation for my arrival. At Jacques Lake this meant stripping off at the wash stand for a sponge bath while Ted was in his crib. Hearing what could best be described as a snort from just outside the cabin, she looked up at the mirror in time to see the reflection of a grizzly mama and two cubs at the window on the north side of the cabin. Naturally her first fright was that the bears might break in and get her but what really panicked her was the thought that some other warden might come along before me and find her naked corpse. She rushed to get dressed!

We were fortunate to have with us at Jacques Lake a wonderful black Labrador. Jock had been a town bum in Jasper and had ultimately ended up in the pound—unloved and unwanted. We rescued him and gave him a home in the bush, which he appreciated and he was to show his gratitude in remarkable fashion. The incident occurred at a time when Glennys was alone at the cabin with the baby, as she was much of the time. It was early evening and she had given the little boy his bath and put him to bed, when she decided to fetch a pail of water from the spring. Preparing to step off the porch she was confronted by Jock, who refused to allow her to set foot on the ground. Without showing his teeth or threatening any harm, he nonetheless made plain that he would not let her leave the cabin.

Thoroughly mystified by the dog's behaviour, Glennys waited a few minutes before trying again, only to be met with the same determined resistance. Moments later a large grizzly bear walked into the yard. As brave as he was resolute, Jock now gave chase to the bear and did not give up until he had it a safe distance away. Then he came back for his mistress, invited her off the porch and happily escorted her across the meadow to the well. It was an extraordinary display of courage, forethought and planning for the protection of someone that he obviously considered in his care. After this, I felt much better about leaving my little family alone, knowing the Lab was with them.

"Uncle Jo," the moose, was often to be seen, either in the meadow or feeding in the lake. On a quick trip to the spring for water one day, my young wife was startled to look up and find herself in close proximity to the big fellow. He was just as surprised and for a moment they stood and stared at each other; she with bucket in hand, he with a drippy underwater morsel hanging from his mouth. Then she spoke his name and he actually seemed to relax. The worst thing Joe ever did was to pull the clothesline down with his antlers.

When the willow bushes in the pasture turned from gold to russet, it was obvious that winter would soon come to the little valley and my wife and I had to make a decision. The question was whether she should go to town for the winter, as she had done the year before, or try to stick it out with the baby on the district. Eight miles of snowshoeing over a very low pass did not seem nearly so intimidating as 28 miles over a very high pass. It was decided that she would try a winter in the bush.

Now it became necessary to devise some kind of sleigh that would navigate the trail and could be handled on snowshoes. For a time we had carried the baby around in a papoose bag but he was getting bigger now and objected to the close confinement when strapped into the bag. So, I began by going into the woods around the main cabin and selecting two young spruce trees growing out from the bank of the creek. These trees were about four inches in diameter at the base, and curved upward in an identical manner in order to reach for the sunlight. From these I fashioned the runners of the sled. Then I found two more identical rails, each with a slight curve at one end, and fastened them to the front of the runners in such a way that they swept back and up to hip height at the rear of the sleigh. Vertical struts supported these handles. Finally, a box about the size of an apple box was fastened between these handles, about nine inches above the runners.

When it was finished, we had a sturdy little sled that could be pulled by one person on snowshoes in front, and steered and pushed by the other member of the team at the back. All in all, it worked very well, although we soon discovered that all the paraphernalia needed to keep the baby clean and warm and fed, far outweighed the boy himself. We also remembered the unfortunate incident with sunburn of the previous year and watched our son anxiously for signs of frostbite. Using the sleigh, we were able to go into town for Christmas and made one or two other trips as well. The eight miles usually took about six hours, all of it hard work for two small people.

After the Christmas break, we went back to patrol the district, leaving the baby with his grandmother. We had never made a long winter patrol together and were looking forward to the freedom of travelling without the sleigh. I was happy to have company and Glennys was pleased to be making a trip instead of waiting alone at the main cabin. Even so, it was not all pure joy. The trail up the main valley was rougher and steeper than she was used to and the days of travel much longer. On the afternoon of the second day, she slipped sideways on a snowshoe and twisted an ankle, making the remaining miles slow and painful.

Just before dark, we arrived at that gloomy, claw-marked little cabin under the spruces, with the deep footprints of bears around the outside walls. Primitive as it was, it seemed a wonderful haven once the lamp was lit and supper on the stove. After the dishes were done and our supplies stored out of reach of the mice, we sat at the little table and played 300 Rummy. It was something we had started doing on evenings together on the Brazeau. There were no prizes, but the catch was that the loser had to get up first and start the stove in the morning, a daunting task in the dark, ice-cold cabin in the winter. I won more often than I lost and, in later years, Glennys would claim jokingly that I used to cheat.

After the long, hard day, the supper and the warmth of the cabin made us drowsy and we tucked into the blankets early. It was well that we did because, shortly after midnight, we were awakened by the mice. The little rascals at this cabin were a noisy energetic crew and it was impossible to sleep while they were clumping around rearranging things.

As we lay speculating on these goings on, I asked my wife, "Ever wonder why the bears try so hard to get into these shacks?" She replied that she assumed it was in an attempt to get at whatever food was cached inside.

"Well, partly that, yes, but in many cases it's because of the mice. You see, when they built these places, the park warden or trail crew cut and skidded the logs in early summer. Then they would peel and rack them, and leave them to cure. Or it might be in the fall, in which case they would go back the next summer and build the cabin. For insulation, they would gather up the dried bark and shavings, and put them under the pole floor. This layer of insulation under the floor would turn out to be a perfect haven for countless generations of mice over the years. I'm sure that's the reason the bears try so hard to get into the place."

The next morning we discovered that at least part of the racket was being made while portions of the felt insoles from our boots were being smuggled down below the pole floor. That day was a long one and very difficult for Glennys with her sprained ankle. We would not even have attempted it but for the fact that Grizzly Shelter was such a dark, depressing place, whereas the next cabin was actually the nicest one on the district. It was an exhausted and footsore young woman who stumbled into that place long after the daylight was gone.

She sank onto the bed while I got the two stoves lit and went for water. After awhile, with a warm drink inside her, she had revived enough to hobble around and help with supper and, by bedtime, she had reason to believe she might survive. With a few days stopover to mend the ankle, the rest of the trip was completed in good style. It was another accomplishment for my backcountry bride.

Close Calls On High Walls

We had only been on the Rocky River for a year when we were moved to the Sunwapta River District south of Jasper. At the time we welcomed what was seen as a promotion, providing as it did easy road access and a reasonably good house. In retrospect we would come to realize that the idyllic days in the Service and, indeed in our marriage, came to an end the day we left the backcountry. Something in our lives began to change and seldom again would we share each other and enjoy life together as we had done in the outlying districts. For me, my first day on the new station was an indicator of things to come.

It was on an afternoon in mid-April, that a Parks' truck moved our few belongings down the South Highway. While unloading was in progress, I decided to make my first patrol to the Columbia Icefields. Arriving at the Icefields Chalet in the late afternoon, I had barely turned off the motor when I was approached by a group of excited people. I learned that a skier had been caught in a small avalanche in the high gully between Mt. Athabasca and Mt. Andromeda. The man's thigh had been broken.

I looked anxiously at the mountains. They seemed huge and forbidding. I had no knowledge of the area in question and could not see the site of the accident. My stomach gave a nervous twinge. I could see that in order to get the victim to safety, the skier would somehow have to be transported over a series of ice-covered rock ledges lying below the high gully. My skis were in the truck; other than that I had no other special equipment of any kind. Although I had had some rudimentary training, I had never organized or led a rescue. The people stood around, looking at me expectantly.

It was fortunate for everyone that an extremely capable man was already on the scene, and had in fact made arrangements for a rescue party to come from the town of Jasper. Fred Schleiss had been hired by the Park Warden Service to monitor the mountaineering activities in the area of the Columbia Icefields. He registered parties out for climbing or overnight trips, checked on overdue parties, and when necessary went to their rescue. Although less than medium in height, he was an accomplished mountaineer and a tremendous athlete. On this occasion he had already reached the victim, immobilized the leg and was proceeding toward the lip of the gully with the rescue sled. He reached the upper edge of the rock bands at nearly the same time as the back-up party from Jasper with me in tow. In the next hour I observed first hand as a top-notch search and rescue leader directed the safe transportation of a seriously injured person over difficult and dangerous terrain. The experience left me humble and subdued.

I returned to the Icefields early the next morning to find Fred cleaning up the rescue gear and storing it away. At least eight new parties had already signed out that morning. Some of them could be seen strung out along the tongue of the Athabasca Glacier; other tiny figures were scaling the headwall. After the gear was stored we sat down to make out the accident report.

Just as the stopover at Grizzly Shelter had led me to apprehend the nature of life in that backcountry district, so the next few hours provided an insight into one of the more daunting aspects of the Sunwapta area. After finishing the report about the previous day's rescue, the young mountaineer took me for a trip on the glacier, pointing out the routes up Mounts Athabasca, Andromeda and Snow Dome. I was shown the mill holes where meltwaters tunnelled down into the bowels of the glacier; I peered nervously into crevasses that could swallow a freight car. Then, roped together, we climbed the headwall and Fred pointed out Mount Columbia to the west, one of the most popular climbs in the area.

It was late in the afternoon when we returned to the lower portion of the glacier. Fred, although a fine mountaineer, was also an impatient man. By four o'clock he was obviously anxious to be done with the day's work and get gussied-up for his second favourite sport—courting the pretty waitress at the Icefields Chalet. As a result, I found myself loosely held on the end of the rope, while my guide loped down the tongue of the glacier. Rather than going around the various crevasses that crossed our path, Fred, who knew them all by heart, simply leapt across, towing me behind. I swiftly learned that one's legs can indeed stretch incredible distances when the owner is looking down into a dark green crack 60 feet deep!

The run was exhilarating, but the day left me with a growing recognition of the serious implications and responsibilities of this new district. For the time being I could rely on Fred but, I realized that as the district warden, I must work hard to improve my mountaineering skills. The ever-watchful chief warden was evidently of the same opinion, because from this point on my training was noticeably stepped up.

The climbing and rescue schools, at which I now became a regular participant, involved wardens from all the mountain national parks. The aim of the program was to produce a first rate Search and Rescue Service, able to operate in any of the terrain frequented by mountain climbers. On the face of it, it was a formidable task.

The wardens of the 1950s were a mixed bag of individuals, bringing with them a variety of skills and abilities. Many were cowboys and horsemen from the east slope of the Rockies—capable, versatile men who could ride a bronc, put up a teepee or bake a loaf of bread on a tin stove. Some were World War II veterans—quiet, careful men with watchful eyes and a gift for stepping in and providing leadership when it was needed. A few were just kids like myself, fresh out of school, with the outdoor skills needed to survive in the bush. Our gear and clothing were primitive. We came to those early schools with our jeans tucked into wool socks, and green forage caps and rubber boots, and the same parka we used in our previous lives.

All were highly independent characters, some to the point where they preferred to break their own trail through two feet of heavy snow rather than travel with a partner. Even though their mountaineering skills were minimal, they had two qualities in common: resourcefulness, and a willingness to learn. The challenge was to make them work together as a team, while teaching them the skills needed for mountain search and rescue.

The man chosen by the National Parks Service to perform this miracle was Walter Perren, a diminutive Swiss guide with a gentle voice, a twinkling eye, and a will of iron. With the aid of a small group of senior park wardens, he would devise and implement a training program, which eventually produced a world-class rescue organization. From the very beginning, proficiency in travel and survival in mountainous terrain under all weather conditions were the foundations upon which the training was based. In school after school, it was pounded into us that we could not help a park visitor out of difficulty if we could not first help ourselves.

Because it was essential, first of all, to get everyone in good physical condition, the early schools were basically route marches. The park wardens would start off in the valley bottoms, wading through muskeg, perhaps fording a river. Then we would be led up steep, deadfall-choked mountainsides until we reached the timberline. In blistering heat we would struggle ever higher, following our wiry little guide across slopes that would make us sweat and claw and scramble. And when we believed we had reached our destination for the day, it was only to learn that another pass still lay ahead. Finally, the instructor camped us above the snow line at night, wet and exhausted, without a fire. Next day, the whole procedure was repeated.

At the same time the park wardens were being introduced to the art of route selection. We learned to plot our course in order to reach the destination as safely and easily as possible. Usually this meant avoiding scree slopes, where one step ahead often meant two backwards, and the steep rock faces with extreme exposure. Instead we followed ridge tops and when higher-up looked for ledges, where as the instructor said, "It goes." And always it was drummed into us to beware of loose rock, and to watch out for those below. It was advice well taken, because at this time we still climbed without protection on our heads, other than worn-out cowboy hats or little forestry caps. While the park wardens suffered and toiled, and silently cursed their seemingly indefatigable leader, three things began to happen. First, we began to copy the deceptive pace of the mountaineer— one step at a time, always ahead, never back, minute after minute, hour after hour, day after day, never hurrying, never stopping. Only by keeping on the move could we ever reach the seemingly impossible goals set for us. Only by pacing ourselves could we survive the gruelling marches. And only by getting a doctor's certificate could we avoid training. One could leave the Service, and some did, but if one wanted to be a park warden, one trained!

We also learned to take care of our clothing and gear. It was critical that clothing be kept as dry as possible, equipment carefully stored and inspected before use. The importance of this was driven home to us early in our training by a freak occurrence that could have had serious consequences. It happened during a regional climbing and rescue school in the Flint's Park area of Banff.

The techniques being taught involved the use of climbing ropes, and at the end of the day a 200-foot rope was passed around a tree at the top of a rock face. The wardens used it to rappel out of the area but, intending to return the next day, left it in place. Walking along the foot of the cliff the following morning, one fellow, in a playful mood, seized the ends of the rope, took a couple of running steps up the rock and threw his weight backwards onto the line. He was astonished, a moment later, to find himself lying in a heap on the pathway, while 200 feet of rope collapsed upon him. When they examined it, they saw that a pack rat had chewed nearly through the rope where it passed around the tree.

It brought home to us that you couldn't be too careful. When you thought you had all the bases covered, it was the rolling stone underfoot that did you in; the joker who pulled the chair out from under you, after God had invited you to sit down! And out of it all, the most important lesson we learned was to be vigilant in watching out for each other, because the mountains never forgave. Men who had been fiercely independent all their lives, if not outright loners, learned to work together as a team.

The team spirit was a necessary development for a group of men involved in hard, difficult, and often dangerous work. It was also a thing carefully nurtured by the instructors. They knew that when it came to technical climbing, not everyone would be able to function at the same level. When certain park wardens arrived at the painful realization that they simply could not function in exposed, high-angle situations, it was crucial that they still continue to think of themselves as part of the team.

So while they continued to push every man to the limit of his physical endurance, Walter Perren and the chief wardens were carefully evaluating each person's ability to function under stress. The training, under controlled conditions, was designed to expose all members to every aspect of climbing and skiing. Then, when it was obvious who were destined to become leaders and who were not, those who were not found themselves with useful support roles, indispensable to the team effort. The result was that each park warden felt a sense of responsibility for his fellows. During the next 30 years, not one of these men, or those that followed, were lost either during a rescue or in training. A remarkable record!

I did not enjoy technical terrain but I worked hard to do what was asked of me. On potentially dangerous ground, I followed instructions to the letter and, on rare occasions when I knew that I was very apt to fall, I placed my faith in my companions. One factor that concerned me on the training schools was my size. At five-feet-eight and only 137 pounds it was obvious that I could not carry a colleague who weighed 180 pounds, or even 160, so I and other small park wardens often acted as the victims to be rescued by our bigger companions. But I was haunted by the spectre of a real accident and someday having to rescue an injured climber who outweighed me.

Another concern was the matter of belaying, for in this the instructors gave no preference to big or small. They apparently believed that a small man, if in a proper belay position, could stop the fall of a much heavier person. They devised a brutal but effective method to test this theory. During belay practice, a piton anchor would be established on a tiny ledge above a high cliff. Here, each candidate in turn would be carefully placed by the instructor and anchored to the wall. The student would then be told to assume an effective belay position, while a 200-pound log was tied to the other end of a 100-foot-long climbing rope. When the candidate shouted, "On belay," the log would be tossed off the cliff, while the rest of the class watched with interest. If the belayer withstood the shock without tightening his connection to the cliff, he was deemed to have passed the test. However, if he was jerked into a position of dependency on the anchor, his technique was obviously faulty and the test would be repeated.

Meanwhile, I still loved the mountains, although the love was becoming tempered with a healthy respect. It was still delightful to hike up a cool, limestone canyon on a hot summer day. And how wonderful it felt after an exhausting climb, to lower one's face into a pool of ice-cold, alpine spring water! At the same time, how treacherous was a loose pebble underfoot on one of those limestone walls, how dangerous the water when it turned to ice on a high ledge!

Although the Search and Rescue record of the Park Warden Service has been an enviable one, let it not be supposed that all was smooth sailing. There were glitches and close calls. That these incidents did not turn into tragedies must be attributed at least in part to teamwork, quick thinking and an instinct for survival. If the mountains don't forgive, surely once in awhile they did turn a blind eye. Some of the following vignettes have become part of park warden folklore. Others are less well known. They are sketched here to impart the flavour of the work and the times.

Two park wardens are ascending a rock face, known as the Black Wall, south of the Columbia Icefields. They work their way cautiously up a narrow chimney, treacherous with loose rock. A thousand feet below, the North Fork of the North Saskatchewan River is a mere silver thread. The leader of the rope is a long, rangy, hard-bitten mountain man. The one below him smaller, and younger. Neither one is happy to be there.

The big man stops and looked down. "You know, little buddy," he says softly, "You want to take a good long look at me."

"Now why would I want to do that?"

"Because," the first one replies, and the corners of his mouth pull down as he smiles, "You ain't never going to see me in this place again!"

On another day, the class has been assigned to climb Mount Athabasca. After several hours of skirting crevasses, we arrive at the upper end of a steep slope just below the final ascent. The slope consists of frozen snow, polished to an icy surface by sun and wind. Here, with our ice axes held in a certain position, we are told to launch ourselves down the slope, as in a fall. When it comes to my turn, I am surprised at the speed with which I begin to slide. Within seconds I am hurtling downwards on my back, bumped and bruised by protuberances of rock and ice. It was essential to hang onto the ice axe. Carefully, remembering my instructions, I roll over on my left side. Then, with one hand on the handle of the axe and the other clenched around its head, I apply its point to the icy surface. When it begins to bite, I roll the weight of my body on top of the ice axe causing it to cut even deeper into the ice and snow. The effect is rapid and reassuring. Within a few more seconds I come to a complete stop. Getting carefully to my feet, I set my crampons into the slope and work my way to the top.

Half an hour later, three other park wardens are roped-up in the last few yards of the ascent of Mount Athabasca. They are on a knife-edged snowridge with lots of empty space on both sides. The warden in the middle position, overcome by fear of heights collapses on the ridge, hanging on with an arm and a leg on each side. Suddenly a small hand taps him on the shoulder. Peering cautiously upward, he encounters a pair of twinkling blue eyes. "Stand up," says the instructor, "You won't bump your head."

As I led my rope cautiously towards the peak, I went over the procedure I should use if one of us should lose his balance and go over the edge. The "rule book" called for the next man on the rope to throw himself over the opposite side of the knife-edged ridge, as a counter balance. With sudden unease, I realized that I was not sure how both men were supposed to regain the ridge after that. I assumed it would be up to the third man to assist the first two, provided he was still on top. It worried me that I did not have the procedure in my head. All of a sudden the whole situation seemed much more precarious than before.

On the winter schools, the instructors took their motley crew into the high country on skis. Now the art of route selection gained additional significance, for wherever possible, it was necessary to avoid travelling beneath cornices or across deadly avalanche paths. When they did have to cross such places, it was usually done near the upper end of a slope, where the slide path was at its narrowest. Here, the skis were taken off and carried and, the men crossed one at a time, each trailing a length of bright-red avalanche cord. Meanwhile, the rest of the crew carefully watched the terrain above, avalanche probes and shovels at the ready. Survival meant reducing all the hazards to the smallest possible calculated risk, and then, as always, looking out for each other. Sometimes, little miracles also played a part.

One day in the late 1950s, the Tucker Sno-Cat towed half a dozen skiers up the south face of Brewster Rock, at the Sunshine Ski Area in Banff National Park, on a Warden Winter School. We were dressed in heavy, rough winter clothing; modern, lightweight mountain gear was either not yet invented or was not available to us at the time. Some did have the new fibreglass Head Standard ski, and the Ramy-Securis combined downhill and touring harness. I was in charge of this particular group. A good downhill skier in high school, my time at the Saskatchewan Crossing Warden Station had also given me some cross-country and mountaineering skills. Although still quite young, I had been marked as a potential instructor for park wardens.

Now, this was my first class. There were no ski lifts in that part of the Sunshine Ski Area in those days; in fact, there was no development of any kind on Brewster Rock. The south face of the Rock is the skiable part. The north side is a sheer drop of 2000 to 3000 feet. Soon after the Sno-Cat left us at the top, the weather closed in and a whiteout developed. The group, most of whom were older than I, were what might be called novice to intermediate skiers. Snow conditions on the south slope were unadulterated crud—two or three feet of snow with sun and wind crusts. The surface was just hard enough to allow the skis to run like crazy but, as soon as we attempted to brake or turn, we broke through the crusts. It was the type of condition that a big powerful skier could handle with panache by going straight down the fall line and throwing chunks of hard-pack right and left. No one in this group could ski like that, not even me for I was just too light in weight.

I decided to take them down in long, easy traverses with a good, strong stem-Christie at each turn. Those who wanted to could even do a little kick-turn in the fog and his companions would pretend not to notice. Days like this were for getting through in one piece, not for glamour. And getting through in one piece is what we very nearly didn't.

Although a reasonably competent traveller, nothing in my brief experience had caused me to be aware of the fact that persons in this hemisphere who become disoriented will, in almost every instance, bear subconsciously to the right. As a result of this unawareness, I was not leading my little group straight down the mountain but, instead each traverse to the right was in fact longer than the return trip to the left. Meanwhile, my crew followed dutifully, glad of having a track to follow and concentrating on staying upright.

After some dozen or so traverses, and while moving to the right, I felt my skis hesitate, as if I had run over something. Puzzled, I stopped to investigate and found that I had skied over a small piece of shale. Even more surprising, the snow at this point was only a few inches deep. As all of the south face was heavily covered with snow, I was obviously not where I had believed myself to be. Taking off my skis, I stood them up crosswise over my tracks as a warning to the others, and walked cautiously ahead into the murk. In less than a dozen steps I appeared to reach the end of land. Peering over the edge, I found myself looking down the north face of Brewster Rock. There was nothing but air between my nose and the scree slopes far below. But for a tiny piece of stone, it would have been the greatest disaster in all the history of the Warden Service.

Later that winter, in a different area of the same park, the class was being trained in searching avalanches for victims. Three straw-filled dummies had been placed on an avalanche path and a snow slide released on top of them. When the wardens arrived on site shortly after, it was observed that only the left side of the basin had released. On the remaining half, the snow pack hung, ominous and threatening. Three skiers proceeded onto the slide. I was posted as lookout on a small ridge across from the slide. From that position of safety, I could clearly see the entire basin and could shout a warning to those doing the hasty search.

For the first few minutes the men on the slide were very tense, conscious of the danger hanging over them, but as the time went by they grew engrossed in their work. I swung my arms to keep warm, watched and waited. Meanwhile, the follow-up party had been organized and were proceeding to the scene, dragging the long, heavy iron probes and carrying shovels. The sun hit the rim of the basin and began moving slowly to the right. At 10:20 am, I, who was also serving as chronicler, noted the arrival of the follow-up party. These men paused to take in the situation, glanced up into the bowl and prepared to cross over to the toe of the avalanche. The temperature was moderating rapidly. Two minutes later, the right hand side of the bowl released.

I had taken my eyes off the slope for a minute to talk to one of the new arrivals. The fracture line up in the basin was already widening noticeably when I saw it and gave a warning shout. New fracture lines appeared now, as masses of snow began to converge. I shouted again and was astounded to see the three searchers on the slide still going about their business. They could not hear! By this time the second avalanche was well under way, on a course that would intersect the first one. I was frantic, jumping up and down, and yelling, and several members of the second party were shouting as well.

Suddenly the three looked up. There was no time, under the circumstances, to climb out of danger. They did the only thing left to them; pointing their skis straight down, went into a crouch and skied the run of their lives. The rest of us watched spellbound. All three made it to safety.

One of them lived to be a future Director General of the Canadian Parks Service.

Later that day, as the temperature cooled rapidly, my companions and I stood shoulder-to-shoulder on the probe line. The hasty search had found one dummy body; two others were presumed still in the slide. "Probe left; probe right; step ahead," the probe master called. On the hasty search, performed on skis by the first wardens to reach the slide, they took into consideration the last seen point, or the point where the tracks of the skiers were seen to enter the slide path. Below that point they looked for the places where a body might hang up: rock outcroppings, ledges, depressions, trees.

"Probe left; probe right; step ahead. What's this?" The probe didn't go into the slide so far this time. Give it a twist and withdraw carefully. A small blue thread clings to the end of the rod. Shovel! One more to go, freezing fingers, toes turning to ice in the old leather boots, but you can't leave the line. "Probe left; probe right; step ahead." This is a serious business. The instructors watch like hawks. Today is practice; tomorrow may be real. If you haven't found the victim, it's because you haven't looked where he is! Beneath the cold blue snow, a life is slipping away while you look in the wrong place. "Probe left; probe right; step ahead." The shadows lengthen.

Because mountain climbing was, for most park wardens, a pretty serious business, it was fortunate that some individuals among us were always able to provide a bit of humour. A group of us are setting up a traverse on a rock face somewhere on the Colin Range in Jasper National Park. It is a crummy limestone slab and all the hand holds slope outwards. As if this isn't bad enough, every ledge is covered with loose debris that rolls under the climbing boot and could fire a man off into space before he knew what was happening. Safe climbing requires that the leaders clear the ledges as they pick out the route, but in the days before the Warden Service adopted hard hats for climbing, even this constitutes a hazard for those below.

After scrambling around on this hill for a few hours, everyone is getting cranky and shaky in the knees. One fellow, negotiating a particularly unfriendly piece of rock, pauses to look up at his rope mates. "Don't you fellers let me drop now," he says. "You let me drop and I'll come back to haunt you!" Everyone has a good laugh at this.

In common with most of my fellow wardens, I developed an enormous respect for the instructors who guided and watched over us during those arduous training courses. The first of these remarkable men to join the National Parks Service was the Swiss guide already alluded to, Walter Perren. Hired in the late 1950s at the rank and pay of an Assistant Chief Park Warden in Banff National Park, he was the head instructor responsible for the design and implementation of the search and rescue program in the mountain parks at that time. When Walter died of cancer, his work was taken over by Peter Fuhrmann at Banff, and Willie Pfisterer in Jasper National Park. It was Peter who introduced to Canada the helicopter-sling method for evacuating injured climbers. This technique, already in use in some European countries, largely replaced the rope and cable system and is still being used today. These three alpiners, ably assisted by various guides and a number of senior wardens over the years, made a lasting contribution to visitor safety in our mountain national parks.

Willie, the Jasper alpine specialist, was a big, powerful man. All, however, remember him fondly for the soundness and safety of his teachings and for his sense of humour. It was he who, after years of alleged research, astounded the alpine community with his announcement that only 50 per cent of all mountain climbing was uphill! This was also the man who liked to tell his struggling students that if you need a helping hand, you will find it on the end of your arm. Nonetheless, he looked after the park wardens as he would his own children. Because of his concern for the safety of his charges, the following tale should be taken with a grain of salt, but it is still worth telling.

When Willie first began to work for Parks, he was operating a little shop for mountaineering equipment in Jasper. During that time it seems he received an order of bootlaces from the Old Country. He was particularly proud of these. For some reason, they did not sell very well and he decided to do some promotional advertising.

So on the next climbing school, which took place on that godforsaken Weeping Wall south of the Columbia Icefields, the wardens found themselves doing a double rappel late one afternoon. They would be helped into position and started off on the first rope length by one of the instructors, the spot for the changeover to the second rope being hidden by an overhang. Arriving tense and breathless, at this point they found themselves on a little platform not much larger than a dinner plate. Here, Will awaited them, and in a very brisk and business-like manner transferred the shaky warden over to the second rope. In the act of backing off into space, the warden's line of vision would inevitably come on a level with the anchor and here they just about went bonkers to see the belay carabiner apparently tied to the anchor piton with a red bootlace. The immediate impulse was to mutiny, but with their arses already hanging out in space, the boys were in a poor position to argue. Besides, the instructor wasn't having any of it. With a rapid sales pitch on the virtues of the mighty bootlace, he launched them on their way. Then, just as the unhappy warden began his wide-legged kick jumps down the wall, he got this advice from the ledge above, "Oh, by the way. No bouncing too hard. Okay?"

When my compatriots and I were first introduced to mountain rescue techniques, we were taught to handle ropes. This usually meant that all members of the team had to climb and play a role in reaching and lowering a victim. Although the fledgling climbers often felt severely challenged in rigging traverses and lowering devices, the rope systems were in fact limited in scope. Using the standard climbing ropes, the greatest distance that could be managed on any particular set-up was 200 feet. At that point a safe area had to be found, ropes retrieved, new anchors established and a whole new raising or lowering apparatus put in place. It wasn't long, however, before the wardens arrived at a climbing school to find some scary, new equipment waiting for them. Sensing that a new phase in their training was about to commence, everyone watched carefully.

What we saw were drums of slender steel cable, much longer than the ropes, and capable of being linked while an operation was in progress. Along with the cable was a braking drum, a multi-grooved wooden disk around which the cable was fed, either up or down the mountain. Along with the usual array of carabiners and other assorted paraphernalia was also a curious little device called a frog which, when tied to anchor, could be clamped onto the cable to stop its progress. Weighted down with all this gear, we trudged slowly up to the infamous Weeping Wall for the first lesson. Even without the weight, it is doubtful if any speed records would have been broken.

The system we practiced that day entailed setting up the brake drum and spools of cable at the foot of the cliff. The drum was anchored to a tree. Then, a good climber took the end of the cable up to the top of the cliff by the easiest route and built an anchor above the position of the injured party. This anchor consisted of three or four pitons driven into the rock. A pulley was then anchored to the pitons, the cable run through the pulley, and the rescuer and mine-rescue basket attached to the end of the cable. When all was in readiness, the wardens at the bottom would feed cable up the line, and the rescuer would be lowered to the level of the injured party to begin the evacuation.

One unfortunate aspect of this system, which plagued the instructors for some time, was the fact that the weight of the steel cable would cause it to sag, or belly, on its way up the cliff. It seemed there was nothing that could be done to get rid of that slack. The result was that when the weight of the rescuer and the basket, containing the victim, first hit the end of the cable, there would be a sickening drop of six to ten feet before tension was taken up. Naturally, this put an unwanted strain on the upper anchor, not to mention the already overtaxed sphincter muscles of the rescue warden and the victim.

The cable system, coming as it did between ropes and helicopter-sling rescue which was to arrive later, brought a change in roles for some of us. To begin with, many of us found it hard to get used to the increased sense of exposure. The end of a 300 to 400-foot length of very thin cable seemed a much lonelier place than the end of a 100-foot climbing rope. Furthermore, there was now a requirement to have two or three people responsible for setting up the anchor and braking drum, while only one went down on the cable. Although everyone was encouraged to take part in all aspects of the operation, the wardens were beginning to separate into future specialists and support personnel.

It was now that the teamwork and sense of comradeship developed on the ropes really paid off. For while the more timid park wardens readily admitted that they had no stomach for 1000-foot drops, they strained every nerve and muscle to ensure the safety of those who did. Everyone did his best at what he could manage. Everyone at one time held the life of another in his hands, and never had anyone let another down. The real heroes, of course, without which the Service could never have managed, were those who were scared spitless, but still able to perform in a professional way doing whatever had to be done. As usual when experimenting with new techniques, there were glitches and close calls.

On another school, the following year, a small group of wardens was again gathered around the cable brake drum at the base of the Weeping Wall. A rescue practice was in progress. The slender steel cable stretched, like a silver thread on the menacing black rock, for 200 to 300 feet above them. At the top of the wall the cable was lost to sight for those below. Above the wall was a steep scree slope, dotted with the occasional shrubby little spruce tree. Near the bottom of the scree, just above the cliff edge, the rescue warden was securing his companion in the mine basket that was still being used at the time.

Possibly 50 or 60 feet above these two, Walter and I were searching for some means of establishing an anchor for the pulley through which the cable had to pass on its way from the braking drum below, and back down to the rescue basket. There was nothing that would hold a piton, nor were there any large, solid rocks to be had. Walter finally chose a wiry little spruce, about twice the height of a man. He passed the cable over the pulley with a locking carabiner, and secured the whole to the base of the tree with a number of sling ropes. Both of us then threw our combined weight against the anchor. It appeared solid. Walter took the end of the cable down to the basket, leaving me to ensure that the pulley did not twist or foul in any way.

Down below, a last-minute check of the lower anchor was in progress, ensuring all vital pieces were properly in place. The warden on the brake checked for the tenth time to see that he had the required number of turns on the drum. His eyes and hands would not leave the drum until the rescued and the rescuer were safely down. On the upper edge of the cliff all was in readiness, and the rescue warden was stepping carefully backwards over the edge. His eyes were locked on those of the instructor who, at times like these, literally willed his man to take that most difficult of all steps. The warden in the basket was thoroughly strapped in and could not have climbed out at this point if he had wanted to. His life was totally in the hands of his comrades. Now the last step was taken and instantly the weight of both men was transferred to the cable. As the slack was taken up, they dropped a good six feet.

In spite of himself, the man in the basket gave a cry of surprise and apprehension and an expletive pierced the air. Walter was carefully watching the progress of the cable over the rim of the cliff; I was several yards below the little spruce tree, removing a sharp-edged stone from under the cable. As the cable tightened, I glanced up at the tree and nearly fainted. Walter, who tended to whistle tunelessly at times of stress, heard me call his name and looked up. The whistle stopped abruptly, leaving his mouth formed in a soundless little "o." The tree was moving—sliding gently down the slope, surrounded by a little island of scree!

Walter flew up the hill and now for the second time that day, we two rather small men threw our combined weight against the tree. This time we were trying to hold it in place. Heels dug into the shale, shoulders braced against the tree, we prayed silently while the cable rolled through the pulley. And then it was over. The men below radioed to say the victim and rescuer had arrived safely. We lay weakly on the scree; another perilous incident in our interesting careers was miraculously over.

One more scare awaited us on the way home from the cable rescue school. When we were getting ready to leave for this school, the superintendent graciously allowed us to use his official car for the trip, to avoid the need for two or three half-ton trucks. The chief park warden put me in charge of the vehicle. Now, a mile or two north of the Icefields Chalet, I was approaching the sharp right-hand curve on the cliff above Dead Horse Canyon. On my side of the road was a shallow ditch and a rock wall; on the other, a sheer drop into the canyon. I was halfway around the turn when I came face to face with an oncoming car. It was a tourist, scared to death of the drop-off on his side, hogging the wrong lane. I drove the superintendent's car into the rock wall.

When we finally got back to Jasper, I had to inform the chief park warden that we had wrecked the superintendent's car. The only thing I had to be thankful for was that I had witnesses to vouch for my actions.

In the not too distant future, one of the alpine specialists would visit Europe and return with the germ of an idea for a new alpine-rescue technique which would revolutionize the Search and Rescue (SAR) in the Parks Service. Once the system was perfected, one highly trained warden, working closely with a specially trained SAR pilot, would perform rescue evacuations in one or two hours which in earlier times might have taken six men up to two days.

It began as a spring day in 1971, when two neighbours in Harvie

Heights (Canmore, AB) hung over a garden fence studying a mountain rescue magazine. This in itself was not surprising as both were avid mountaineers, but what held Peter Fuhrmann and Bruno Engler's attention was an article which Bruno had discovered in *Bergwacht*.

It dealt with heli-rescue, a new concept currently being explored in Europe for the evacuation of alpine casualties. The way the system was described, a rescuer would hang below the machine harnessed to a long line. In this fashion he would be airlifted to the site of an injured climber and lowered to the ground, where he would release himself from the sling. After providing first aid, the warden would place the injured party in a mine-rescue basket, hook himself to the frame and radio the pilot to return. Once reconnected to the sling, both rescuer and victim would be airlifted to the nearest hospital.

It didn't take Peter long to make up his mind. In June, travelling on his own time, he flew to Munich to visit the rescue chief for the Bavarian Red Cross of Germany. Ludwig Gramminger had a number of search and rescue innovations to his credit, including the cable-rescue system described earlier, and had already designed a special stretcher to be used beneath the helicopter. When Peter returned to Canada, he was armed with enough equipment and information about the new system that he was able to convince Jim Davies, the Banff Warden Service SAR pilot, to give it a try.

Very carefully at first, Peter and Jim began to experiment. They went to Banff Airfield with Jim's helicopter, an Allouette II, to which a long line had been securely attached. Here Peter, communicating with the pilot by means of a two-way radio, hooked himself to the line and was airlifted first 10 feet, then 100 feet, and finally flown in a huge circle over the airfield. Growing increasingly optimistic they next tried a lift off Cascade Mountain, and when that proved successful, the wardens, who were keenly watching, agreed that here was a system that could work. Soon everyone wanted to fly!

My introduction to the procedure occurred on a summer day in 1971, when Peter drove north to introduce heli-slinging to Willie and the Jasper wardens. Using the local airfield as a base and Mount Colin as the rescue site, we took turns playing the role of victim and rescuer. From a personal point of view, I was relieved to find the only moments of concern occurred during take off and landing. This was due in part to the fact that the Bell-G2 was somewhat underpowered for the task of lifting two men. Therefore, instead of a clean, vertical lift, the pilot had to put the nose down and move forward while lifting. The same was true when coming down, making for a moment when the victim and rescuer were dragged along the ground and vulnerable to danger. When Parks eventually went to the use of Jet Rangers, this problem was eliminated.

It was while returning to Banff later on that day that Peter had the opportunity to put his new system into actual practice. He passed the Columbia Icefields and motored down into the steep valley where the North Fork of the North Saskatchewan River has its beginning. Emerging from the shadows of the notorious Weeping Wall and the equally infamous Black Slab, he was approaching the confluence of the North Fork and the Alexandra Rivers. It was at this point, with evening not far away, that he began to pick up radio transmissions indicating that rescue efforts were underway for a fourteen-year-old boy on Sunset Pass.

As he approached the Graveyard Flats, so named because at sunset the bleached trunks of countless trees washed down by the two rivers dot the gravel flats like the bones of ancient dinosaurs, he observed a cluster of warden vehicles at the base of the trail leading up to the summit. Here he learned that the boy was lying near the entrance to a ravine above Pinto Lake, in the cradle of the pass. The youngster had apparently fallen several hundred feet, suffering a badly broken leg and losing a number of fingers on one hand. He was presently unconscious, and entering hypothermia. The rescue plan was to airlift him out in a helicopter, this time using a Bell-G2 obtained from the Peter Lougheed Park. A number of wardens were at the scene, caring for the boy and attempting to prepare a landing pad for the machine. Concern was being expressed as to whether or not the pad could be completed in time for a daylight evacuation.

Peter's mind was churning, weighing the facts, assessing the possibilities. He believed the boy's condition to be very serious; failure to get him to a hospital quickly could be fatal. It was questionable if the landing would be possible before dark. On the other hand, the helicopter was there and Peter had all the equipment necessary for a sling rescue right in his station wagon. Furthermore, the method had been successfully tested twice under mountain conditions, the most recent occasion having been that very day. He decided to talk to the pilot. That individual had never heard of sling rescue but he did have some long-lining experience. When Peter explained the technique, the pilot agreed to give it a try.

Here were two men who had never worked together before, setting out to perform a potentially dangerous mission for the first time in the history of search and rescue in Canada. That they were able to do it successfully says a great deal for the professionalism of both men, and particularly to the coordinating skills and cool nerve of the alpine specialist. Even so, the position of the victim and the limited power of the G2 caused some precarious moments. The boy was lying in some trees near the base of the canyon, opposite a rock wall. Old snow still lingered in the bottom of the chasm. When the pilot lowered the rescuer onto the site, he nosed the machine into the canyon, deposited Peter on the snow in front of the incredulous wardens, then executed a 180° turn to circle over the lake until he would be recalled.

Returning to pick up the loaded stretcher, the pilot again came in nose first but was unable to lift off with the combined weight of patient and rescuer. After an extremely tense moment during which the G2 struggled valiantly above the canyon, Peter radioed for slack and hastily released the cable. On his next attempt, the pilot came down the ravine from above. Now the declination of the ground worked in their favour. Hooking on as the machine swooped overhead, the specialist and his patient were plucked from the ground before the astonished eyes of the wardens and whisked into the air high above Pinto Lake.

With his two charges dangling 60 feet below, the pilot now executed a number of broad circles over the lake, gaining altitude until he was able to slide over the ridge on the west side. Now preparing to descend to the gravel flats, Peter was pre-occupied with the details of landing. The prospect of being dragged over tree trunks and boulders, while trying to support the stretcher and undo the sling all at the same time, was a daunting one. Looking at the little group of wardens standing on the road below, their eyes glued to the aerial acrobats, the specialist had an idea.

Thumbing his two-way radio, he instructed the wardens to walk out to a relatively clear spot on the flats. Here he had them form up in two lines about four feet apart, in the path of the approaching helicopter. As he neared the ground the pilot slung the basket, with Peter attached, between the waiting men. Seizing the basket from either side and supporting it, they moved forward with the machine, giving Peter an opportunity to release the sling. Seconds later a very relieved pilot was once more safely aloft and patient and rescuer were on the ground. The first heli-sling rescue on Canadian soil was successfully completed.

As it turned out, it would also fall to Peter to perform the second Parks Canada rescue of an injured climber by the heli-sling method. In 1971, a Canadian Forces climber, working his way up the east face of Mount Edith in Banff National Park, was almost killed when a rock crashed down on his head. Bleeding badly, he clung for his life to a narrow ledge.

Fuhrmann and other members of the rescue crew were airlifted to the site. They provided what medical aid they could, strapped him to a stretcher, hitched him and Fuhrmann to the chopper cable and prepared to take off. "But the helicopter didn't have enough power—these were 1971 machines—to lift up the load," Fuhrmann recalled.

"After some hurried consultation with the pilot, the rescue team went ahead with a daring plan. On the count of three, they threw the stretcher over the edge and I jumped." Fuhrmann and the injured climber plummeted toward the valley three kilometres below. The helicopter began its own rapid descent, picking up forward speed as it dropped. Within a few seconds the speed was great enough to provide the power needed to carry the humans dangling below. Fuhrmann said, "A few minutes later we were on the lawn of the Mineral Springs Hospital, in Banff." A ground rescue would have taken two days, but the helicopter cut it down to 45 minutes.

Although the procedure was now officially launched and would save many lives in the years to come, there was one issue which would continue to be a serious concern for a considerable time. This was the seemingly irreconcilable fact that Department of Transport (DOT) regulations did not permit the transport of any load beneath a helicopter which could not be released from the cargo hook by the pilot. The wardens on the other hand, and with some justification, were disinclined to commit their lives to any kind of contraption which could be released by the pilot. It was a considerable time before a solution was worked out with DOT. In the meantime, the sling was safeguarded by a strong strap which actually passed through the body of the helicopter, making release, whether by accident or intention, impossible. And the park wardens were supposed to carry a large knife with which to cut themselves free if, by getting entangled in something on the ground, they were endangering the machine. As with a lot of warden operations, the system worked because of a great deal of faith on both sides. When I returned to the West in 1980, I was surprised and alarmed to find this situation on-going, and it became a priority to get DOT sanction as soon as possible.

Meanwhile the wardens and alpine specialists continued to innovate and improve the systems wherever possible. One such improvement was the adoption of a specially designed conveyance called a Jenny Bag, which allowed a patient to be securely zipped in during flight, as opposed to the old mine-rescue basket, from the confines of which at least one person attempted to escape en route to the hospital!

There was a never-ending requirement to keep on improving, as mountain climbers continued to push their limits. Now that the easier routes were becoming passé, it was the fashion to tackle the north and east faces of mountains and, when that got too easy, it was northeast faces in the winter. In the 1970s, in order to meet these rising challenges, the alpine specialists would gather up their best SAR wardens and organize a series of expedition climbs in the Yukon. Those days were still ahead.

The Highway

When we went into the second year on the Sunwapta District, I was 28 and Glennys 24. By this time we had two sons, and the problem of schooling for our children was the next thing that had to be faced.

Although the move to the highway was supposedly a promotion, I did not enjoy it. The station was 45 miles from Jasper, which meant an hour or more before help in the form of police or an ambulance could be expected to arrive. Many times I would have to cope single-handedly with multiple injury accidents, acting as medic, traffic control and policeman, all in one.

Far from the idyllic existence which many perceive to be a warden's lot, highway work can be difficult and dangerous. Working alone, the warden is often first responder at the scene of an accident where he or she must protect the site and fill the roles of first-aider and police officer until help arrives.

Training and equipment were rudimentary in the early days—a standard first-aid course, taught by St. John Ambulance and basic first-aid kits, often made up by the wardens themselves. Casualties were transported in mine-rescue baskets, often in the back of pick-up trucks. In 1960, which is roughly when the following incident took place, some warden trucks were equipped with a single revolving red light, often referred to as a party hat, mounted on top of the cab. At about the same time, VHF (very high frequency) radio systems were being installed in a number of national parks, a great improvement over the old forestry phone lines.

In addition to the human tragedy that a warden frequently encounters, the continuing destruction of game on our park highways is particularly distressing to those who spend their lives protecting the wildlife.

Events happen quickly on a mountain road. I am patrolling north toward Jasper on the Icefields Parkway on a bright, sunny July day. There are happy tourists and happy bears all over the place, all breaking park regulations and having a great time. Approaching the Big Bend about 20 miles south of the town, the mighty Athabasca River rolling along majestically on my left, all is peaceful and serene. A moment later, around the bend, I am in the middle of a warden's nightmare.

The first thing I see is the cow elk, obviously injured, her hindquarters down on the highway—then the overturned car in the right-hand ditch, doors flung wide. I see a man, blood running from his neck and face, staggering around on the road, and two small children lying near the car as if thrown there by a careless hand that also flung a cooler and its contents. And finally, I see the woman, lying in the grass on the far side of the embankment and even at a distance, I get a bad feeling. There's something about the way she lies—so still.

Later, when I am able to piece together the story, I learn that the injured man was the woman's husband and father of the two children. He had been driving, perhaps not as carefully as he should have, when a calf elk ran across the highway. Alerted by his wife's cry of alarm, he looked up to see the mother, her hooves skittering on the pavement, attempting to follow. In spite of his last-minute attempt to avoid the animal, she caromed onto the hood, smacking into the windshield and obliterating his vision. With the wheel pulled hard over, the vehicle went into a sideways skid, hit an obstruction at the edge of the road and rolled over.

I arrive moments later. Turning on my recently installed hazard light and thumbing the mike button on the VHF radio, I place an urgent call for police and ambulance. It will be at least half an hour before they arrive; meanwhile I must do what I can to ensure there is no further injury or loss of life. Even before I can position my truck to protect the injured elk, two other vehicles, both travelling too fast, arrive on the scene. The occupants of the first car, going south, are gawking around looking for the Columbia Icefields, still 40 miles away. They nearly run over the man, who is still wandering around distractedly on the road. The driver finally gets his vehicle stopped some way past the accident scene, and after hesitating, backs up and parks half in the driving lane, half on the shoulder of the road. The people in the second car are also looking for the Icefields, having unknowingly passed them some time ago. They become aware just in time to avoid hitting the back of my truck, swerve left to avoid it and sideswipe the parked car. Before lurching to a halt in the middle of the road, they manage to hit the cow elk again as the poor animal is trying to drag herself off the pavement. So much for protecting the scene.

I have to do something about the guy before he gets himself killed. In the small crowd beginning to gather are two big ladies and to them falls the job of sitting him firmly down in the grass at the side of the road and making sure he stays there. A young husband and wife stay with the kids and comfort them. One has a broken arm, but other than that damage appears to be superficial. Both are making a lot of noise, which is usually a good sign.

Off to one side, the mother still lies, unattended and quiet—so still and quiet. She is a handsome, dark-haired lady, probably in her late 30s; sprawled on her back, black skirt and white blouse in disarray, shoes missing. An obscene blue fly brazenly explores the corner of a half-closed eye. Few outward signs of damage, but pale and clammy skin, with a faint sheen of perspiration. I have difficulty finding the weak, rapid pulse, and breathing is shallow and intermittent. I wonder if she might actually have been under the car at some point; I suspect severe internal damage. I kneel beside her, monitoring pulse and respiration. I'm still there when the ambulance arrives, but by this time the half-lidded eyes have a faraway look, as if she sees already a strange and distant realm. I fear greatly for her.

Meanwhile, the Royal Canadian Mounted Police are on the scene, getting the traffic sorted out and taking the first of many statements. As for me, I have one more sad duty to perform before I can go home. With a heavy heart I take the rifle from behind the seat of my truck and walk back to the cow elk. Sensing my approach, she twists toward me, and with a supreme effort rises up on her front legs to confront me. Her battered hindquarters were already sticking to the blood that was congealing on the pavement. A handsome lady, strong legs in dark stocking—a young mother, mortally damaged, chin held high, eyes brave and challenging, even in the face of death. Praying for forgiveness, I look directly into those eyes and pull the trigger.

The sudden shot startles everybody. People stare at me in shocked silence and the Mounties' hands drop to their holsters. And somewhere in the shelter of the timber a terrified calf elk becomes an orphan.

"The National Parks of Canada are hereby dedicated to the people of Canada for their benefit, education and enjoyment," I think bitterly as I pull the carcass off the road, "and the national parks shall be maintained and made use of as to leave them unimpaired for the enjoyment of future generations."

Such a fine animal, I think sadly as I turn away. Such a nice family and what a wonderful day. I am as close to tears as a warden is allowed to get.

Sunwapta was an extremely busy area, particularly in the summer months. Incidents ranged all the way from various types of mountaineering accidents, to forest fires, drownings, missing persons and bear attacks. The year before we arrived, a little girl had been mauled by a black bear at Sunwapta Falls. Two youngsters were drowned there during my tenure and a future suicide still waited in the wings.

Invariably, when I felt that the day's work was done, I would find myself back in the green truck heading off to another problem. Even on the days when nothing happened, I, like most district wardens at the time, was never free of responsibility. I was often tired and irritable. It all seemed so stupid, people endlessly getting into trouble—lighting fires, feeding bears, crashing cars, maiming wildlife—it went on and on!

It did not seem to matter how many improvements were made to the highway, the accidents continued. Although the road was rebuilt for the third time in its history while we were on the Sunwapta District, I could discern no abatement of collisions and mishaps. Indeed, wider, straighter roads seemed simply to encourage people to drive faster and with less care. On a rainy summer morning I rounded the rockcut just south of the Sunwapta Teahouse to find one of the construction camp trucks on its side in the right hand ditch, both male occupants thrown out and lying crumpled on the muddy ground.

Kneeling by the driver first, I smelled the sick-sweet odour of injury and fright, rising like steam in the pouring rain. In spite of shock and pain, however, the victim had correctly assessed his own damage as a broken pelvis. He was shivering violently, but was otherwise calm and self-possessed. Already curled up on his side in the fetal position, he asked only to be left untouched until help arrived. Peering at the Teahouse through sheets of rain, wishing someone would come forth, I took a grey blanket from my homemade first-aid kit and tucked it carefully around the patient. Unfortunately, there was nothing waterproof to lay over that. I made a mental note to add a piece of plastic to the assorted first-aid items stored behind the seat of the old green pick-up. Later I would bring the subject up with my colleagues, all of whom were forever looking for new and better ways to care for injured visitors far from the nearest hospital.

Then I moved quickly to the second casualty. This person, a hefty young man of about twenty, was in the act of trying to get back on his feet, but when I spoke to him there was no response. In fact, it was as if the person were sleep walking and unaware of his surroundings. As it turned out, he had received a blow to the head and was suffering from amnesia and concussion.

In any case, he presented me with a serious problem. It was obvious that the patient was badly hurt and could come to further harm if left to his own devices. Yet, in order to diagnose his injuries and care for him, it would be necessary to sit the man down and keep him still. With a strong young labourer, weighing a good 50 pounds more than I, this was easier said than done. I held my patient as firmly as I could, alternately holding him back when in his bewilderment he would have charged madly off, then supporting him when a fall might have been fatal. Meanwhile, the other victim gazed helplessly from the ditch, which was now running water, and the rain came down harder than ever.

Eventually, a number of motorists stopped to offer assistance. Three vehicles from the north and two from the south drove up within minutes of each other and parked on the roadsides. One visitor was dispatched to the Teahouse with a message calling for an ambulance and the police, and two hefty ladies were called upon to help subdue and comfort the big young man with the head injury.

With things now more or less in hand, I began to breathe easier, but my respite was short-lived. A doctor, chancing upon the scene, stopped his car in the only clear lane left to see if he could be of any assistance. At the same instant a car full of teenagers, travelling north after an all-night party at Lake Louise, came cruising happily around the rockcut, almost collided with the doctor's vehicle and ended up damaging the park truck. The resulting injuries were not serious, but the complications and implications, insofar as handling the whole scene, were considerable.

It was mid-afternoon when I drove wearily back to the station. I was dispirited and somewhat apprehensive over the damage to my truck. Although not serious, it would have to be mentioned as part of the incident report. Going to the big wooden telephone in the hallway, I cranked the handle and asked the switchboard operator in Jasper to connect me to the chief warden's office. The chief listened carefully as I relayed the details of my activities, including the involvement of the Park vehicle. Although noncommittal, I noted that my boss's voice deepened perceptively during our conversation, a sure sign of concern.

Promptly at eight the next morning the phone rang again. I put down my coffee cup and went to answer it, thinking that the ring sounded like trouble. What else is new, I wondered? It was the chief again, still wearing his serious voice, to let me know that an official from the administration building would be coming out that morning to go over the accident and prepare a report for the Department. After hanging up, I poured another cup and sat down and thought about the previous day's events once more. When I first came upon the overturned truck and the two injured men, I had parked my patrol vehicle as far over on the right hand shoulder as I dared, without actually going into the ditch, which was all mud and running water.

My truck, an old Willys Jeep, carried no emergency lights of any sort and in the confusion of the moment, I could not remember if I had left a signal on. At any rate, no blinker lights were operating when I returned to my vehicle after seeing it struck. Sitting there mulling the whole thing over, it seemed that my actions had been reasonable until I remembered that I had neglected to place a reflector light, which the truck did carry, on the road behind the vehicle. After first stopping, my immediate priority had been to help the injured; after that it simply slipped my mind. Not that it would have made much difference, I told myself; the kids probably wouldn't have seen it and, at any rate by the time they came around the corner, the whole road was blocked anyway and the bodies were in the ditch. Well, it was too late now to worry. I went out and began cleaning the corral, waiting for my visitor.

At 9:30 am, I saw the superintendent's black sedan pull into the driveway and, at first, thought the "Old Man" himself had come to see me. When the lone occupant stepped out however, it turned out to be the town sanitary engineer, whose duties at the time included investigating accidents involving Parks vehicles. No one could figure out why. The engineer was a tall, thin, lawyerly individual in his early thirties, serious, ambitious and utterly devoid of humour. Perhaps it was a desire on the part of the Department to ensure that any possible neglect or misconduct on the part of its employees be fully disclosed at once, that prompted them to assign this person the task. Certainly his stare and inquisitorial style of interrogation had the effect of making even a blameless operator feel vaguely guilty. After a cool and unenthusiastic handshake, the interview got underway.

It turned out to be even less fun than I had anticipated. Still very much pre-occupied with the quality of first-aid which I had rendered—as this was always my greatest concern, I was astonished at the lack of interest shown in this aspect of the proceedings. Instead, I was mercilessly grilled on every minute detail of the placement of my and other vehicles, and on the traffic control at the scene. When it was over I felt as if the Department held me responsible for everything that had gone wrong that day. It was my first encounter with that type of individual and with the type of investigation based on the premise that, sooner or later, everyone ends up in court. Although it was rather unpleasant, it was another valuable lesson. Years later, instructing a class of wardens on protection of an accident site, I vividly remembered standing by the rockcut in a hot July sun, sweating while I tried to recall everything that I had done or failed to do.

In addition to the accidents, there was always a steady complement of illnesses and health problems affecting people who happened to be in, or travelling through, the district. Old age, excitement and altitude were a deadly combination in some instances. Late in the afternoon of a bright summer day, a busload of senior citizens rolled up in front of the Icefields Chalet. After a moment the door swung open and an attractive young tour guide stepped out and waited to help the passengers.

One of the last persons to step rather stiffly down onto the pavement was a tall, gaunt old man from Saskatchewan. The leathery face and big, work-worn hands proclaimed him to be a retired farmer, which in fact he was. His wife was a round little woman with soft, silver curls. Squinting a bit, they gazed around at the shining mountains, while their spectacles adjusted to the light. This trip to the mountains was something they had promised themselves for five years.

After being shown to their rooms and served a light tea, they were taken for a tour of the glacier tongue. At one point the Bombardier actually stopped and they were allowed to step cautiously onto the ice at a point where the meltwater swirled in a spiral down into the depths. It was like nothing they had seen before. In the evening while blue shadows crept up the sides of the mountains, they were served a small steak supper in the dining room of the Chalet. They finally retired to their beds after a couple of hours of bridge. For the retired farmer, it was somewhat past his normal bedtime.

Although he had been weary when he went to bed, the old man did not sleep well. He woke a number of times during the night and was slightly alarmed to find that his heart rate was up. Finally, at about six o'clock in the morning, he decided to get up and go for a walk.

As he stepped out, the top of Snow Dome was turning from rose to gold and the rising sun threw long shadows across Sunwapta Pass. He decided to walk along the base of Wilcox Ridge. The old man's stroll was rewarded almost at once by the sight of a bull moose grazing quietly in the meadow east of the Chalet. Soon after this, he noticed the bighorn sheep further up the ridge and decided to climb up for a better look. His shoes slipped in the mosses and loose rock, and the gorse bushes entangled his legs. He soon grew very short of breath and had to stop to rest. His heart was beating very fast, and although he longed to get closer to the sheep, he now realized it would be foolish to press on. Somewhat shakily, he made his way back to the Chalet. There was just time to clean up and pack before breakfast. By nine, they were back in the shaded confines of the big bus, on their way to Jasper. The old man noticed that his breakfast seemed to be lodged just below the breastbone—not moving.

When the bus stopped above Dead Horse Canyon for picture taking, his wife took the camera and joined the others at the edge of the parking lot. The old farmer stayed in his seat, grappling with what appeared to be a growing case of indigestion. When she took her seat beside him again, she was concerned to find him bent over in obvious discomfort. With a gentle hiss of brakes, the bus started the long descent into the Sunwapta Valley.

As they rolled along the foot of the Endless Chain Mountain, the pain in the old man's chest increased alarmingly. It was a steady, relentless pain which gave no quarter. Convinced that it must soon ease up and go away, he did not complain; after all, what could be done anyway? Grimly he wrapped his arms around his waist and hung on. He could not take any interest in the scenery, and it seemed that the voices of the other passengers were fading away into some dim, obscure place.

By the time the big bus crossed the bridge at Poboktan Creek, this passenger was in serious trouble. The pain in his chest was so enormous that it claimed his entire attention. By now he was bent completely double, forehead pressed against the seat in front. He could not have said if his eyes were open or closed, the world around him was simply a dark red haze. All sense of sound had receded to nothing: His entire world was centred around the monster in his chest. The wife, in mounting concern, held one of his hands in hers, her fingers on his pulse. In the aisle, the tour guide stood by them and the driver glanced at them uneasily in his rear-view mirror.

A few miles further on, the old man's wife could no longer feel a pulse. The driver happened to look up and, when he met her terrified eyes in the mirror, he knew a crisis was at hand. He brought the coach to a careful stop in front of the Sunwapta Falls Teahouse.

I had been on my way into town when I stopped in at the Teahouse to see how things were going. I noticed the coach at the front door. I was urgently greeted upon entering the lobby and escorted to where the old man was lying on the floor. I didn't fancy the look of the old fellow a bit; if ever a man looked about to die, this one did. However, he was still getting about one breath out of three and there was a faint heartbeat. I knew I'd better make that phone call while there was still time.

Somehow, in trying to order the ambulance, I found myself speaking to one of the doctors in Jasper and here the trouble started. The doctor wanted to know if the patient looked like he was going to live long enough to warrant sending the ambulance—no point rushing all the way out there if it's just to bring in a body. I wished myself anywhere but where I was, which was on the forestry telephone on the north wall of a very busy tea room with the poor missus standing there by my shoulder.

I stick-handled the situation. Although the patient was having a great deal of difficulty, there was still a chance he could be saved. As I spoke, I thought, "Doctors are lucky; they rarely have to operate on the floor of a crowded tea house. They get to work behind closed doors, with all the tools and facilities and, if things go wrong, a carefully prepared message of condolence is ready for the people waiting outside."

The ambulance was an ancient Volkswagen bus, barely able to make it up some of the hills south of Jasper. It took a good three-quarters of an hour to reach Sunwapta Falls. The old man was dead long before that. Now no one wanted to touch the body. All attention was directed to the wife in shock and grief, and it fell to me to drag the heavy old fellow behind the stove, through a very narrow door, and into an empty staff bedroom. A most macabre business!

When the ambulance arrived, we wrestled the body onto a stretcher and secured it at the rear of the ambulance. Halfway into town, on a steep downslope, the stretcher somehow slipped its moorings and careened to the front to where the driver, who was already feeling spooky, nearly had a heart attack himself.

After getting home for a late lunch, I decided to put in the afternoon checking the action at Honeymoon, Buck and Osprey Lakes. All three were open for fishing, and I had no doubt at least one fisherman would have been happily contravening park regulations while I was busy struggling with heart attacks and corpses. I loaded my green fibreglass canoe, the Mary Jane, checked to be sure I had my book of angling permits and headed down the road again. As I drove, my mind turned to a subject regarding fishing regulations that I had been pondering for some time.

Protecting park resources is part of the warden mandate but so is public relations. As a result, the wardens were encouraged to use a good deal of discretion in dealing with visitors. The problem arose in trying to decide when and when not to lay a charge for an unlawful act. I used to refer to such acts as illegal until the day that I went to one of the Mounties for advice on a possible charge. That officer, sensing an opportunity to twit me a little, haughtily informed me that an "ill-eagle" was a sick bird, and after going on at some length, told me to make up my mind whether I had an unlawful act on my hands or merely an indisposed fowl!

Although not inclined by nature to be soft on law breakers, I eventually reached the conclusion that the soundest criteria to use when in doubt, was to determine whether or not any real damage had been done to a park resource, in this case fish. And secondly whether the offender knew better or should have known better. Indeed, I reflected, the majority of blatant offences were not committed by visitors anyway, but by locals, which put a slightly different light on things.

My first stop was at Buck Lake. As I drove into the little parking lot and prepared to unload the canoe, I noted a rather disreputable and down-at-the-heels van tucked away in the trees to one side. The old vehicle had a kind of furtive look about it, as if it knew that its owner might be up to no good. It carried local plates.

Arriving on the shore of the little lake moments later, I paused to look things over. The first impression was one of utmost peace and tranquility. The water was inviting in appearance, the surface reflecting the green, sun-dappled forest which surrounded its shores. Some distance beyond, the Endless Chain Mountain towered magnificently into the summer sky, a few fleecy little clouds floated just above the ridge top. Against the lower slopes, an osprey circled over the lake of the same name. Everything seemed in order in this little corner of my district, this bit of paradise on earth. In order, that is, until my eye caught the flicker of flame among the trees, on a point of land which extended out into the lake from the left-hand shore. Although the day was warm, there appeared to be a large bonfire blazing away there, with three or four people moving around in the vicinity. I knew the ground well. The point was covered with tinder-dry caribou moss and dry pine needles.

With alarm bells beginning to sound in my head, I hurried to put Mary Jane in the water, when my attention was again diverted, this time by a most curious sight. There were about a dozen or so small, whitish balloons bobbing around on the surface of the lake. Odd, elongated balloons, like huge fingers. Giving the canoe a shove, I paddled over to the nearest one. Arriving alongside, I gingerly closed thumb and forefinger over a small nipple-like protuberance at the top and lifted it from the water. The contraption, which greeted my wondering gaze, was an inflated rubber condom tied shut at the opening and trailing about four feet of fishing line. At the end of this line was a gang hook baited with what had until recently been a live minnow.

I whistled to myself while I scrolled the fishing regulations up in my mind's eye. The following lines appeared "No one shall, while in a national park, fish by any method other than angling. The use of minnows or other live bait, is strictly prohibited." Next, a mental review of fire protection regulations: "No one shall, while in a national park, light or maintain a fire, other than in a stove or fireplace provided."

I looked over at the campfire, noting that a small rowboat was now pulled up on the shore. I paddled over to the next balloon and found very much the same thing, except in this case there were three lines, each with a single hook. All three had been baited with minnows. I dropped this one into the canoe as well and looked thoughtfully at the crew around the fire.

They seemed to be watching me and were probably planning a get-away. They could jump in the rowboat and try to push by me on the lake, perhaps even tip me over. Or they could run around the shore to the van and take off. I cursed myself for not having taken down the license number. On the other hand, they could scatter into the bush and try to outwait me, or simply remain at the fire and play innocent and dumb. As for me, I didn't really have much choice but to proceed to the fire and hope to apprehend at least one of the culprits.

At least there was no doubt in my mind whether to charge them or not. They were contravening several park regulations at once, and they were endangering the area with that fire as well—not to mention those sleazy "safes." The "Chief" would see red when he heard about this one. Patting my shirt pocket to make sure I had my notebook, I set my Stetson squarely on my head and paddled swiftly and decisively to the far shore.

As it turned out, there had been a considerable amount of indecision amongst the group as to the best course of action to take when I appeared. Some were for leaving, and some were for staying, and one fellow felt they should put the fire out but couldn't decide what to use to carry water with. All of which was made more confusing by the fact that they had been into the beer since ten in the morning. Finally the strategy was settled by the eldest in the bunch, a beefy, grey-haired individual of middle age, with a large belly, small mean eyes and several days stubble on his chin. This party was mainly his idea and my appearance was putting him in a bad mood. He also had to maintain face in front of his younger colleagues.

"To hell with the 'effing warden," he said truculently, opening a beer

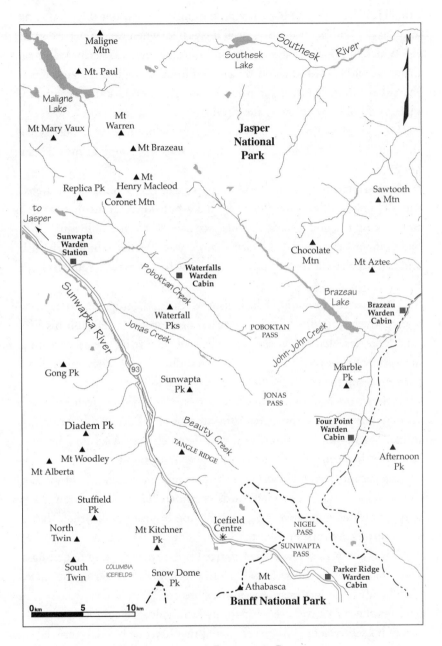

SUNWAPTA AND BRAZEAU COUNTRY

can. "He can't prove we have anything to do with that out there," waving at the lake, "and as for the fires, well it was here when we got here. Piss on it!" Which he appeared about to attempt until he tripped backward over a dry stick, and landed squishily on a pile of freshly caught trout. And it was there that I found him, apparently relaxing, fly undone and beer in hand, just a good old boy enjoying the park.

He greeted me jovially. "Hiya, ossifer, come on in. Have a beer? Give the man a beer, boys. Hell, I know this guy," with a wink at me. "He's a good shit."

"Good afternoon, gentlemen," I said pleasantly, declining the proffered can. "Doing a little fishing?" I indicated a bulgy-eyed trout that seemed to be trying to climb out of the man's coat pocket. That individual, who had managed to convince himself that he was effectively hiding the fish and had been about to deny any fishing, now had to make a sudden about face.

"Why sure, we're doing a little fishing," he said, struggling to his feet, apparently surprised to discover a dozen or so trout underneath his person. "Hell yes, that's okay, isn't it? Lake's open, ain't it?" he asked with a great show of concern, as if anxious at the thought that they might have been breaking the law.

"Oh, it's open all right, but I'll have to see your fishing licenses."

The man seemed somewhat affronted by this but, after considering for a moment, pointed at one of the younger fellows. "Ask him," he said, "He's got the license." When it was produced, it proved to be a provincial angling permit. The red lettering at the bottom clearly stated "Not valid in the National Parks." "Old Grey Curls" was incredulous. "You mean to say that permit's no good here?" he said, shaking his head in disbelief. "Since when isn't Jasper Park in Alberta?"

I was about to reply when I noticed one corner of the fire getting a good start on the caribou moss. "Here you fellows," I said to the three, "Somebody better get busy and put this fire out."

Right away "Grey Curls" was in my face again, trying to save a smidgen of his self-esteem. "We never started that fire," he bawled, very red in the face. "Put it out yourself!"

"I never said that you did start it," I replied pleasantly, "but it's also unlawful to maintain a fire and furthermore you can be charged for failing to put out a fire when instructed to do so. It's up to you. Make up your mind."

The three men looked at each other uneasily. My voice had developed a rough edge and they realized they could be in a good bit of trouble. They scuffed their feet. "What can we carry water in?" one asked.

"There's a canvas bucket in my canoe," I said, "You can use that. And there's all these empty beer cans, too."

As they busied themselves at getting water, obviously relieved to be doing something useful, I turned to the leader again. Now came the hard part. "OK, Mister," I said, "Who owns the fish?"

"Oh hell, I guess I do," he said while stamping around angrily, "Anyway, so what?"

"So they're illegal. If you don't have a Parks fishing license, I'll have to see some other ID."

"Grey Curls" was fast losing it. His big fishing party was a mess and he was looking like a fool, all because of this pipsqueak in the green suit. A vein stood out on his forehead and the red little eyes were meaner than ever as he staggered over and bunted me with his beer belly. "You're a real smart-ass, aren't you," he snarled, shaking a big, dirty finger under my nose. "Comin' in here makin' all this fuss over a few stinkin' fish, spoiling our day. Bloody wardens anyway! Here's some ID," hurling his wallet at me. "Take that!" he said, falling heavily on his back, completely beside himself. "Here, take the fish too," he roared, slinging a soggy trout at me. "Take the effing boat too, why don't you. I don't care!"

I decided I had better give the big fellow some time to cool off and I knew better than to pick up the wallet, so I turned away and met the watering crew struggling up the shore. These three were practically sober and keen to appear as reasonable as possible. I was even able to get a sheepish admission out of them as to the set lines and condom floats. By the time the fire was completely out, I had all the evidence and information I needed to proceed with charges, even including the name and address of their sullen, but now much quieter, leader. Bidding them all good evening, I climbed into the canoe and paddled slowly away.

When I got home, I poured myself a large Scotch and leaned my behind against the kitchen counter while I gave Glennys a rather impassioned rundown of the day's events. And some time later with another

Scotch in hand, I went out to the corral, where shadows were lengthening, and told most of it all over again to Old Slippery.

Finally the autumn arrived. The endless traffic began to thin, the fire hazard moderated, the days grew shorter. In the early dusk of a September evening, a handsome lady came calling at our back door. She wore a glossy black and white fur coat and had long black gloves on her dainty hands. She had dark, seductive eyes and a slinky way of walking. She was a classy act. Soundlessly she climbed the wooden steps of the back porch, paused and looked around.

The first item to claim her interest was the dog's partially-empty supper dish. Whatever it contained seemed to be to her liking and as her enthusiasm increased, she lost caution and allowed the bowl to rattle. Glennys took a look and rang me on the phone which connected the house with the workshop. "Be careful coming over," she said, "There's a skunk on the back porch!" A few moments later the beautiful animal disappeared.

As usual, we were delighted to have a wild visitor—a visitor from the wilderness, as wild visitors of the other kind were not so welcome. As usual, we could not help trying to encourage further acquaintance. Next evening, after making sure everyone was inside, we placed an egg in the dog's bowl and settled down to watch. At precisely seven, the lady in her striped coat arrived, climbed the steps and discovered the egg. She knew at once what it was and what she wanted to do with it. The performance that followed was marvellous to watch. Lifting it from the dish, the little animal gently rolled the egg across the short porch. Then with wonderful dexterity, she juggled it down the steps, tumbling it between her hands in an act that the eye could scarcely follow. Once on the ground she moved her prize across the boardwalk and into the shadows before settling down to make it her supper.

For about a week, the skunk returned each evening at exactly the same time, taking her egg down the steps and out of the circle of light before consuming it. Then she disappeared for her winter sleep. She came back briefly in the spring and for awhile we worried that she might be planning to hang around all summer. So far all the visits had been without incident but, with tourist season approaching, the danger of an unfortunate encounter was imminent. Somehow the lady sensed this and with the innate grace and good sense which had marked her every action, she took her leave. Like the very best kind of visitor, she left only pleasant memories.

When winter arrived in the Sunwapta District, some problems did abate. The tourists went home, the bears went to bed, and only a handful of hardy souls continued to scramble around on the mountains. I began to unwind a little, as did most highway wardens at that time of the year. I put a stove in my workshop in the garage and got back to drawing and painting, which I had always liked to do in my spare time. As well, there were small carpenter jobs that needed attention and sometimes I would build a rocking horse or some other plaything for one of the boys.

This winter, however, was to be marked by a new duty which, although seemingly routine, would nevertheless produce some difficult moments. For many years there had been an ongoing debate over what to do with the Icefields Parkway during the winter months. When I first joined the Service, the road was closed and allowed to snow in. When I had assisted at the Saskatchewan Crossing even Bow Summit was allowed to close. It was always a stirring sight in the spring, to see the big snowblower ploughs chewing their way through the drifts, sending a white plume of snow into the blue April sky.

The thinking had changed by the time I worked my way through the two backcountry districts and returned to the highway posting. Now Parks kept the road over Sunwapta Summit open all winter using work camps at Mount Coleman and Tangle Creek. Even so, the concern for motorists who might get into difficulty at night in the high country persisted, so that the authorities felt compelled to close the road during the dark hours. This was done by means of a gate at Camp Coleman, on the south end, and at the Poboktan Creek Park Warden Station on the Jasper end.

The first winter that this plan was put into effect, the gate was erected about 400 yards north of the station, and was manned by an attendant. My involvement consisted of checking and clearing the highway of all vehicles each evening before the gates were locked, and occasionally going down to settle disputes that arose when some irate motorist was giving the attendant a bad time. This happened in spite of the large and obvious signs south of Jasper that were aimed at travellers.

This year, for one reason or another, the attendant's position was done away with, and the gate moved to the north end of the bridge, right by our house. Now it became a real headache. Hardly a day went by that people didn't arrive at the gate, after hours, demanding to be allowed through. The very fact that our house was right there, encouraged motorists to pull into the yard and come thumping at the door, even in the dead of the night. Whether or not they had actually missed the warning signs, as many claimed, hardly anyone was prepared to backtrack 45 miles and wait another day. So the arguments went on. Urgent reasons for special consideration were presented, including weddings, important meetings and jobs waiting. Ill and dying relatives were invented by the score. When I wasn't home, my wife had to deal with all these people, many of whom were belligerent and sometimes drunk.

At first, I tried to accommodate those who really seemed to have an urgent and legitimate need to travel through and, on a number of occasions, I would get permission from the chief park warden or the superintendent of the park to allow a motorist past the gate. The system soon broke down as such procedures usually do. It meant endless judgement calls, and became an irritant for the superiors. Eventually, we decided simply to say "No," period!

As with any situation where the law must be upheld in a lonely place, there were elements of danger. I was alone at the station when a blizzard moved in on a night late in November. I must have neglected to latch the back door upon retiring, because I was awakened at two in the morning by the sound of someone in the kitchen. Looking outside I made out a car in the yard, swirling flakes dimming the headlights. Pulling on my jeans, I went through the house and found a wild-eyed young man standing in a puddle of melting snow in the middle of the kitchen. The pupils of the man's eyes were dilated black, and he waved his arms threateningly while gazing wildly around. I decided the visitor was badly frightened and possibly spaced-out on drugs as well.

When I tried to calm the fellow down and reason with him, I gained the impression that the man had left town late at night on impulse but, for what seemed to him at the time, an urgent reason. As the miles went by and the storm worsened, he became frightened. By the time he reached the gate he was panic stricken and had forgotten his purpose altogether. Actually, this one was fairly easy to turn back; his reason for wanting to travel now was as vague as it had been imperative originally.

The next problem was that the car was nearly out of gas. Had he been allowed to go on, the man would have become stranded in a few miles. I got the Jerry can that I kept filled for these contingencies and put five gallons in the guy's tank. The tires spun wildly in the snow as the car slewed onto the highway and headed north. It was lost from sight almost immediately, but I did not go back to bed for some time. Some people had the unnerving habit of simply parking a mile or so down the road, then coming back later to monkey with the gate or do mischief in our yard. It made for many sleepless nights.

One group arrived after dark, long after the highway was closed on a cold February night. Three big, burly men were in a huge dump truck, which came to a stop just inches from the gate. The horn blew imperiously as I walked out to meet them. The driver, a pig-eyed ruffian in a greasy red sweater, leaned out the window.

"We need through the gate," he informed me loudly.

I said, "The gate will be open at seven o'clock tomorrow morning."

"That ain't good enough," a voice yelled from inside the cab, "We need to be at a job in Golden by seven!"

I was about to say I'm sorry, but I didn't. You never say sorry with guys like this. Instead I repeat that the road is closed for the night, and I explain why. I told them there are no exceptions to the rule, and point out that they had passed a huge sign just south of Jasper which told them all about it, had they paid attention. At the end of my little speech I turn and walk away. Both truck doors fly open and three pairs of heavy boots hit the pavement.

I whip around just in time to come face-to-face with a red sweater, which covers a huge and surprisingly hard beer belly. The belly bumps me in the chest, knocking me back a good three feet. The next thing I know, I'm being propelled rapidly backward by all three truckers, to the accompaniment of various obscenities and demands for the gate key. With the open door of the workshop just behind me, I jump up on the step, hoping to make a stand, but it doesn't work. "Beer Gut" punts me halfway across the workshop and then they all try to push through the doorway at once, waving their arms and shaking their fists.

Once inside, what had been a ludicrous, even comical performance outside, quickly turns ugly. Within moments, I am backed into a corner behind the stove with nowhere to go and no help at hand. Without any idea what might happen next, I simply stiffen my back, fold my arms and refuse to give in. Suddenly, to my complete amazement, the atmosphere changes. A look passes between them, there are mutters about "Best be going," and "We can go by Valemount."

It is only after they have turned and are headed for the door that I am able to see the house. There, framed in the kitchen window is my wife steadily pointing a .38 Police Special and following the hasty retreat of three very ugly guys. Minutes later the big truck roars away in the night, and peace descends once more on the little station beneath the pines. It had been the most serious confrontation so far.

Because the gate at Poboktan Creek was solidly built, and Glennys and I were determined to uphold the regulations, our end of the closed road was never violated. That could not be said for the south gate which closed the highway at Camp Coleman. Here, there was no park warden station and the camp itself was separated from the road by a band of trees. As a result, this gate was broken through a number of times, with the perpetrators then ending up on the wrong side of the gate at my station. If it was nerve wracking to have vehicles arriving in the middle of the night wanting through the gate, it was even more upsetting to have them arrive from the south during closed hours. This almost always meant that an infraction had occurred and the party had to be apprehended.

I was aware that a surprisingly large number of people who broke park regulations were also habitual lawbreakers, sometimes dangerous ones. Stolen cars arrived at our gate a number of times, and at least one person was wanted by the police. Therefore, I had my .38 pistol under my coat on a cold morning that I walked out to greet the latest blockade-runners on the wrong side of my gate.

The dark coloured car, of uncertain age, was nearly hidden by exhaust fumes and vapour rising from the frozen creek. There appeared to be two male occupants. I walked up to the driver's door, my easy manner belying my inner tightness. I managed to get the operator's license and queried the men as to how they came to be there. They were quiet and uncommunicative. I suspected they might have more on their minds than merely a broken barricade. Telling them I would be back in a moment, I went to the house to do a little checking.

After the rather complicated business of getting someone in town to phone around to the Banff side and then relay the information back, I was able to ascertain that the gate at Camp Coleman had indeed been crashed in the early hours. The vehicle in question was believed stolen; the authorities were looking for the driver and his companion.

Having returned the pistol to the dresser drawer, I was preparing to escort the two men to town when the situation was complicated by another vehicle arriving at the gate, which was still closed. There were four male occupants in this one, in various stages of intoxication. They were not happy at being turned back and I suspected that they might not be entirely persuaded. The suspicion was confirmed when, leaving for Jasper moments later, there was no trace of their vehicle. Obviously they had ducked off the road somewhere, probably waiting for me to go past.

It was another difficult situation. Worried for my wife's safety, I radioed instructions for her to latch the door and not to have anything to do with the four if they arrived back in the yard. Back at the station, Glennys made sure the boys were in the house and locked the doors. Then, with the pistol back out on the table in front of her, she took up her knitting. The minutes ticked by.

The tension built. Every few moments she glanced up, expecting to see the old car coming into the yard. When an empty tin can toppled over in the garbage pail, it startled her nearly out of her wits. Before realizing what she was doing, the loaded gun was in her hand. Slowly she laid it down, and said to herself, "That's it! Enough of this foolishness. I've come to no harm before and I'm not going to let these guys scare me." Resolutely, she unloaded the revolver and put it away. The four men never did come back.

Incidentally, it was also Glennys, in her newfound determination, who devised the most effective method for dealing with nuisance visitors. The very next time anyone approached the house during closed hours, she threw open the window and tore into them.

"What the hell do you think you're doing here at this time of the night?" she demanded angrily. "Didn't you see the signs telling you the road is closed? Can't you read?"

The startled motorist turned and drove away without a word. Intrigued by the effectiveness of this departure from normal park warden public relations, we tried it again on future occasions. It worked every time.

On the Trail of a Misfit

There were many days that I wished I could have returned to my old district on the Brazeau River and I watched rather wistfully as a succession of newcomers came and went to the backcountry. The station at Poboktan Creek was the commonly used trailhead for outfits going into the Brazeau, the other trailhead being Parker Ridge Cabin, south of the Columbia Icefields. Whichever route the backcountry park wardens used, we kept tabs on them, helping to pack up when they were heading out and often giving them a warm meal when they arrived back in civilization. For the most part, these beginner wardens were sturdy, self-reliant types, carefully picked for their ability to travel alone in the wilderness.

The chief park wardens were cautious in choosing these men, mindful, if they chose the wrong type, of the dangers to the district, the horses, and the individual. The process was made difficult, however, because it was the custom to assign rookie wardens to the backcountry. Normally, the new man would only be given a few weeks of general duty around town before being sent out to sink or swim on his own. This meant that the old chiefs had only a short time to assess the capability of the beginners. Naturally, most had a résumé indicating satisfactory performance in some related type of experience or they would not have been on the eligible list for a district. Even so, many were sent out based on what was perceived to be their potential to make good, rather than their proven ability.

Most of the time the decisions proved to be happy ones but once in awhile a misfit slipped through the cracks. For many, the big problem in the backcountry was loneliness. Some people, myself included, revel in the freedom of being alone in the wilderness. But for others, the lack of human companionship can be a terrible thing. There is no one to provide advice, no one to tell your troubles to, no one to converse with. One may sing or sit in a corner and whimper, rage and rant; it could matter less to the mountains. There simply is no one there and won't be the next day or the day after. For those individuals who are not happy by themselves, this complete aloneness can be pure hell.

If they were in tune with their surroundings, they would realize that they were actually surrounded by company, much of it congenial. There is the little chickadee singing his brave song on the window ledge, waiting for a handout; the red squirrel, busily scolding from the roof of the tack shed; the bighorn sheep, grazing peacefully on the mountain, and a host of other friendly, cheerful souls in close proximity. But the stranger does not recognize them. Brought up in the false and arrogant belief that only humans have souls or personalities, he simply sees all these denizens of the wild as part of a hostile environment and takes small comfort in their presence.

The other problem is the silence. The cabin is silent, the meadow is silent, the woods stand quiet, and the mountains that never forgive, look down in silence. For those who are not used to being alone, the lack of any human-made sound adds to their sense of solitude, and, for some, it is a terrible, nerve-wracking thing. They do not realize that the wilderness is speaking to them with a multitude of voices—quiet, musical voices with wonderful stories to tell. The wind, breathing a warm sigh against one's cheek, brings news of melting snows in the high country; or rising fitfully, tells of an impending storm. And the river, silent where deep and dangerous, noisy in a cheerful way where the crossing is safe and shallow, thunders a warning upon approaching a rapid waterfall. As for the birds, each family, and there may be a dozen different families out there, is carrying on an excited conversation about everyday things. But the unfortunate misfit, longing for the babble of his fellow humans and all the senseless roar and clatter that they create, is deaf to the beautiful sounds around him. And so he believes himself to be all alone and he is miserable.

Naturally, everything gets worse in the winter. In summer a patrol of the Brazeau might be a couple of weeks and there were the horses to provide some company. Then in the fall, it was the practice to put extra men on the park boundaries during hunting season to watch for poachers, which meant company for the district wardens. It was on the long winter patrols, a month at a time with nobody but a pack of wolves for company, that reality set in.

Through the long, dark nights in those lonely cabins beneath the cold stars, a man had too much time to think. Fears and doubts, plus the sheer brute labour needed to travel and survive, would wear him down. In the end, if he didn't have the right stuff he would begin to crack and his mind would turn to schemes for getting out.

Those who would eventually fail were the ones who allowed their fears and worries to get the upper hand and drifted hopelessly into lethargy and ennui. At first there would be an effort to keep up some pretence of patrol work, but as winter set in and the days became shorter, so did the trips. Cabins would not be properly provisioned in the fall, nor firewood cut, making the prospect of winter patrols even less attractive. Signs of poaching activity, if noticed at all, would be timidly investigated and soon abandoned for lack of evidence. Lying in a snowdrift all night on a wind-swept ridge, waiting to apprehend a bunch of hard-bitten sheep hunters, is no task for the faint-hearted.

Eventually, these types would be driven to falsify their diaries and month-end reports, in an attempt to cover up the fact that they weren't doing the job. And finally, the whole sad pretense would come to light. The trigger might be an accident with the horses or while away on foot. Sometimes it was unwillingness to return to the district after holiday leave and in rare cases there were even simulated mishaps, designed as an excuse to return to the highway.

Such a one came along while we were at Poboktan Creek. Somehow he got to an interview, talked his way through it and pulled the wool over the eyes of a couple of chief wardens. The next thing he knew, he was alone on the Brazeau River in the middle of 500 square miles of wilderness, in a situation he couldn't handle.

This warden, whose name shall remain anonymous, probably made his first trip out to the district in early summer with a senior warden, before being turned loose on his own. I recall that he was a smallish individual with a nervous way of talking too much. He seemed to make out well enough with the horses and as I was inundated with the usual flood of road kills, runaway campfires and rescues, I really didn't have too much to do with him until the onset of winter.

He left our station at Poboktan Creek on a day in November for his first snowshoe trip, and was planning to come out via Nigel Pass shortly before Christmas. This he did and I picked him up at Parker Ridge and gave him a ride to town. The nervous chatter seemed worse than usual but this is not uncommon when men have been "out in the bush." After the holidays, he wanted to return to his district by way of Nigel, so I took him back and dropped him off at the Parker Cabin, not expecting to hear from him again for a month or so. To my surprise, I received a message two days later asking for a pick-up.

I found the man in a very agitated state. He was pacing around the cabin, talking to the walls and I noticed what appeared to be scratches on one side of his face. According to his story he had started off for Nigel the previous day and had been following the creek near the summit when he slipped and fell over a cliff of some sort. As further proof, he made a considerable show of a very large tear in one leg of his new blue jeans. Something about the whole scene didn't sound right but he insisted on going back to town, so I took him in and left him to sort things out at the chief warden's office.

Driving back to the station, I kept mulling the thing over until I realized what was wrong with the picture. It was the torn jeans. New denim is extremely hard to rip and I could not understand how he managed such damage to his clothing in a fall and still walked away from it. I decided to check it out. Going back to Parker Cabin, I put on my snowshoes and started off in his tracks.

Immediately after leaving the cabin, the regular trail descends a steep hill and then crosses Nigel Creek, after which it follows the east side of the stream up to the pass. Our man never even crossed the creek. After going down the hill, his snowshoe track followed the west bank for a few hundred yards and then swung around and back to the cabin. The whole trip didn't take 10 minutes. There was no evidence of an accident of any kind. The whole story was made up.

Now I had to make a decision. Normally one does not rat on a colleague. But, as far as I was concerned, this wasn't a colleague, he was still just some guy trying to get established in the warden service. The thought that I might someday have to rely on him in a dangerous situation was a scary scenario that I wanted to avoid. In the end, I called the assistant chief, who incidentally was the one who hired him, and suggested he check it out for himself. As is often the case when one delivers bad news, the assistant wasn't very happy with me but there was no disputing the evidence. The would-be warden was given other work.

The details of his last trip, from the Brazeau Headquarters to Parker Cabin, are not available and he did not remain long with the service. It appears likely that he had a difficult time, and may even have been badly frightened by whatever happened to him. While purely fictional, the following is intended to illustrate the kinds of fears and mishaps that can beset the timid or inexperienced mountain traveller in the winter.

Let us imagine that we are with him on the morning of his departure. He was up at six to cook himself a breakfast and make up his pack. He took a Thermos of tea and some SPAM sandwiches, the spare set of long underwear and sock, his monthly diaries and game observation cards. Then he debated long and hard over whether or not to carry the rifle. It was his wont always to have the gun with him if he was going any distance from the cabin. On the other hand, he knew that most park wardens viewed their rifles as unnecessary weight in the winter, particularly once the grizzlies had gone to bed. He hated the thought of appearing silly for lugging the thing along for no earthly purpose. Finally his timidity prevailed. He could always stick it out of sight somewhere at the trailhead cabin before his pick-up arrived. The shells should be right on top of the pack, just in case, so he placed them carefully on the foot of his bed, ready to be added at the last minute.

After the breakfast dishes were done, he forced himself to take time to tidy up the cabin. He had begun to convince himself that once in town, it might be possible to remain there for the winter, so he disposed of all scraps of partly used food. Finally, he took the remainder of a rather heavy loaf of homemade bread and set it on the front porch for the whisky jacks. They had been his only company through the dreary weeks. Glancing around, he noticed the old, grey blanket still hanging by the door—the one he used to stretch across it at night to keep the frost out. That would look better folded across the foot of the bed, he thought. The phone rang just as he had made the last fold and as he ran to answer it, he tossed the blanket hastily on its place.

The call was from his wife and having given her the news that he was

Original Sunwapta Patrol Cabin

coming out, the urge to be on his way quickened. The remaining chores were performed hastily and soon he was on the porch with his pack and snowshoes. While closing the shutters the warden was briefly embarrassed by the quantity of yellow snow at the back of the cabin. He should have taken the trouble to be a little tidier; however, it was too late now to worry about that. He strapped on his snowshoes, shouldered the pack, and turned to the trail.

At the far edge of the pasture he stopped once to look back. The cabin stood quietly in the growing light of morning, a wisp of wood smoke drifting from the chimney. The whiskey jacks were making a great fuss over the last chunks of bread. He wondered if they would be hungry without the daily handouts, until it occurred to him that they had probably packed enough groceries away in the last six weeks to last them and all their friends until springtime. This thought cheered him. He turned his face to the trail again, crossed the frozen river, and started the first hard climb of the day.

Ten o'clock found the warden above the falls and entering upon some fairly level country, but the going was heavy. Early winter snow makes for tough travelling. It hasn't settled yet and hangs on all the scrub willow and bog birch. Because he had been staying so close to home, there was no track beyond the two miles he had tramped the day before.

As usual, there had been a great deal of activity of which he had been unaware. Shortly after leaving the cabin, he came across a fresh moose track which had made holes in his snowshoe trail from the day before. After about three miles, he came upon a track he could not at first identify. The imprints were of a large, heavy animal, obviously a predator of some sort. There were four claws on each foot, and the length of stride was about 18 inches. He believed it might be the trail of a lynx or bobcat, and assumed the animal was carrying something in its mouth, an extremity of which frequently dragged in the snow. He wondered if the lynx would attack if surprised at its meal. For a moment he was tempted to take his rifle off the pack and carry it by hand, but shrugged away the notion, telling himself not to be a fraidy-cat. It was just as well for his state of mind that he did not recognize the drag mark as having been made by the heavy tail of a mountain lion.

Squirrel tracks were everywhere, crossing and re-crossing the trail and occasionally those of a deer. After awhile he came to a point where the way led to what was, in the summer time, a ford on the upper fork of the Brazeau River. He decided to travel the river ice; it was level, and the snow only a few inches deep. He had gone barely half-a-mile when he found wolf tracks. There were at least six of them, moving back and forth across the ice as they hunted. The warden shivered involuntarily, imagining their dark forms gliding along through the timber on each side of him. Once again he nearly unpacked his rifle, and once again talked himself out of it, quickening his pace instead.

At about eleven o'clock he looked up to see two caribou almost directly in front of him. They gazed at him curiously, a cow and calf making their way downstream. After a momentary pause the mother resumed her course, very carefully picking out a little detour around the man and his snowshoes. At the point where they were about to pass, she stopped for a moment and looked at him very carefully. He could see the wet, black nostrils, dilated as she tested the scent, and her breath made little puffs of vapour in the cold air. When she moved on the calf did exactly the same, copying each footstep and pausing to eyeball him at the same spot.

For several minutes, while this was going on, the park warden had remained motionless, fascinated by the chance encounter with these handsome animals. It was when he started off again that he made a startling discovery. Each snowshoe weighed a ton! They dragged so heavily on his feet that he nearly fell flat on his face when he tried to move. Looking back he could see that his tracks for the last ten steps were filled with water. The river was flooding under the snow.

In a panic lest the ice were about to give way, he scrambled to one side and threw himself upon the bank and in the few minutes which it took to realize exactly what was going on, approximately 40 pounds of wet snow froze solidly to each snowshoe. It solidified on the straps of his harness and all around the frames, but worst of all, it froze in every joint and cranny of the webbing. He tried knocking them together, but that did nothing except get rid of a little excess snow. Then he tried picking the ice off by hand but that didn't work. He was nearly weeping now with frustration. Precious time was wasting. In fact, before this happened, he had almost gotten around to thinking that he might make it out in one day. Finally, he settled down and decided to build a small fire and try to solve the problem in a calm and reasonable manner.

It took over an hour to free the snowshoes of ice. The method that he finally devised was to hold a shoe near the fire, being careful not to scorch the webbing. Then, as the ice began to loosen, he picked at it with his penknife, breaking it away in little pieces. As it was nearly noon, he unwrapped his lunch and ate as he worked. While he was thus occupied, he became aware of a soft, mewing sound in the trees above him. It was a seductive and slightly cynical sound, like the soothing murmur of a hooker while she removes the wallet from your jacket. Glancing up, he was astonished to see a whiskey jack peering at him from a nearby tree, one speculative dark eye on him, the other roaming around the landscape. The bird fairly oozed a benevolent interest in his work and general well being. He was amused until he realized that a second operative was perched not three feet from his sandwich. He quickly covered the remains of his lunch. He wondered how the hell these guys always knew when it was mealtime? Was this the cabin crew or a different pair? It was hard to tell.

Shortly after one o'clock, he strapped the snowshoes back on, shouldered his pack with the rifle tied across it and set off again. The whiskey jacks swooped in behind him and policed the area quickly and efficiently. They had a leisurely trip back to the cabin in the bright afternoon sunshine, making the whole voyage in less than half an hour. Then they spent the rest of the day stockpiling the leftover dry bread, hotcakes and scraps.

The early part of the afternoon went well, travelling through the parkland dotted with low, shrubby lodgepole pine. It was just before three in the afternoon when he found himself on the river flats in front of the midway shelter cabin. There was heavy snow on the roof and the front step. It would be colder inside than out; it always was. He looked at his watch. At his present rate of progress, two hours of daylight would put him over the pass. Then he would be able to see the light of passing vehicles on the highway and there would be nearly a full moon as well. If he were lucky and caught a ride, he could be walking into the little basement apartment in Jasper by nine o'clock. After the weeks of loneliness, it was an inviting prospect. They would be surprised to see him a day early!

"The hell with it. Here I come. Highway or bust!" He declared, and stepped bravely off to what would become one of the worst nights of his life. The going soon became more difficult. The trail led through spruce where the snow was heavy and there were a number of watercourses to cross. The deep shadows under the timber were in chilling contrast to the friendly, open atmosphere of the pine country. In stubbornness born of ignorance rather than confidence, he refused to turn back.

Dusk was already settling into the valley bottom when the park warden came to the frozen pond below the headwall that formed the eastern side of the pass. Off to the left, high above, two peaks cradled a small basin of permanent snow, cream coloured in the last rays of the sun. It was very still, standing there in the shadow of the big spruces; the only sound was the whisper of his parka as it moved to the beating of his heart.

Over towards the centre of the pond a raven lifted laboriously off something dead. It moved over him on heavy wings and then all was still again. Up in the peaks, cream turned to rose as the sun began to set. He shivered suddenly, and moved across the lower outlet of the pond and up the ridge to the left.

This ridge ran parallel to the wall for some way, separated by a gully that became shallower as it rose. The ridge was shale—windswept. After awhile, he removed the snowshoes and sidestepped upward, using a shoe in each hand, like a pole. Climbing so, head down and deep in thoughts of getting home, he missed the point where the trail swings right across the head of the gully and goes over the rocky lip of the pass.

When he realized his mistake, he moved over to the other side, and began to follow a ledge that promised to lead him back in the right direction. The ledge climbed and became narrower. Before long the traveller arrived at a point where the path vanished altogether for three or four feet, but appeared again on the other side of a small crevice. In preparation for jumping the gap, he tossed the snowshoes across, in order to have both hands free, then held his breath at the possibility that they might slide away. They held. "Thank God!" he exclaimed. "I guess luck's with me."

With a clumsy half-step, he jumped. His left foot landed in the snow just short of the ledge. Here his mukluk found concealed beneath the snow not the rocky ground he had been expecting, but the smooth surface of a frozen waterfall. Within an inch of safety, he shot downwards and with a wild cry fell off the cliff.

After 15 feet, he smacked into the waterfall again, getting a smart rap on the chin, and 10 feet further down he landed in the bottom of the gully. The weight of the pack drove his shoulder painfully into the rock. He lay there for awhile, whimpering through clenched teeth. There was a taste of blood, though he wasn't sure if he'd broken anything or not. Some moments later he began carefully to move, both arms, then legs, then to a kneeling position and finally struggling out of the pack, he got to his feet. At least nothing was broken; he gathered the blood in his mouth and spat painfully.

Turning to the pack, it struck him at once that his rifle barrel was full of snow. Shaking it was to no avail. There didn't seem to be any way that he could clear the thing. Suddenly he realized it was getting dark. Floundering along in the bottom of the gully, in snow up to mid-thigh, he finally found the proper trail and climbed to the lip, carefully back along the ledge to retrieve his snowshoes. In the very last of the daylight he struggled back to a little hollow just above the saddle of the pass. Here he tramped out a small space and settled down to get reorganized, and wait for the moon to rise.

The fact that he now had sense enough to do certain things possibly saved his life. Digging the spare set of long woolies from his pack, he took off his outer garments and put on the extra underwear. Then replacing his clothes, he added the sweater. There was still a sandwich left from lunch, but when he tried to eat, the injured mouth made this difficult. Finally, he soaked the bread in the remnants from the Thermos and swallowed it that way. While he was thus engaged over the pack, it occurred to him that the wire rods, which ran down each side of his Trapper-Nelson packboard holding the canvas to the frame, could be used to clear the barrel of the .308.

Doing this cheered him considerably, and combined with the effect of the tea and food, went some way to restore his badly shaken spirits. As he carefully repacked, something nagged at the back of his mind. It seemed that some familiar item was missing, but he was too tired to concentrate. Propping the packboard against the side of the hollow, he sat on the snowshoes and leaned back against it. Then he pulled down his earflaps, pulled the hood of the parka over all, and settled down to wait, eyes half-closed.

After awhile he must have dozed off, because when next he opened his eyes, it was to gaze around in amazement. The moon had risen behind the peaks at his back, and the entire mountain across the basin was brilliantly lit. Moving his wondering eyes up the slopes, each hollow and ripple of the snow was defined in light and shadow. Higher yet, the bare rock seemed almost close enough to touch where the moon shone on the ramparts, while the crevices and couloirs were mysterious in purple shadow. Finally, at the very top, the cornices gleamed silver between moving fragments of heavy cloud. This cloud mass loomed all along the western sky; many of the further peaks were already disappearing in a cloak of darkness. Heavy cloud cover, or perhaps a storm, was something he hadn't counted on. He wished now that he had stayed at the halfway cabin. How foolish he had been to try to do the trip in one day!

Getting stiffly to his feet, his gaze fell on the frozen pond behind and below, just in time to see a dark shape glide from the shadows of the spruce. Moments later a second wolf emerged from the timber on the opposite side of the pond, trotting across the moonlit snow. As the warden watched in consternation, five more of the sinister grey shadows appeared, converging on the spot where animal remains stained the ice. It was a sight he wished he hadn't seen. In spite of all the blowhards who scoffed at the idea, wolves did sometimes attack people. He remembered Jack London's story, *Love of Life*, which he had read as a boy; suddenly he pictured himself crawling weakly through the snow, exhausted, while a starved, slavering wolf inched closer at every step!

This time he was going to load the rife, no question about it. His eyes still glued to the scene below, with trembling fingers he undid the fastenings of his pack, searching for the box of shells. They weren't there. He dug deeper, then frantically began pulling things out of the pack. When he reached the flashlight, he turned it on, and looked at everything carefully. There was no ammunition. Then, as he stood staring at his pack in disbelief, he remembered. The shells were lying at the foot of the bed, in the cabin, under the blanket from the door. As he swore helplessly over his latest misfortune, the flashlight began to fade. Panicking again, he shook it violently. For a moment the bulb burned brighter, then went out altogether. With a despairing epithet he hurled it over the cliff.

The presence of the wolves spurred him to move on. Glancing to the south, in the direction of the highway, he noticed the headlights of a vehicle moving slowly up the road. Only a few miles to the safety of a cabin and possibly even a ride to town. Hurriedly he tied on the snowshoes and eased the pack straps over his sore shoulders. He stepped onto the trail just moments before the leading edge of the storm front cast a shadow over the moon.

During the next twenty minutes, during which he may have travelled a quarter of a mile, the light grew progressively poorer. Then the snow began to fall, lightly at first, blurring outlines and hampering his vision. If he had had a long acquaintance with the trail he might still have been able to proceed, but he had only been over it once or twice before, and that when the ground was bare. Now everything began to look the same, and after awhile he realized that he had lost the way. As he had been on a sidehill, it seemed logical that he might have drifted to the down side but, after working his way uphill for several minutes, he was still unable to get his bearings. It wasn't a black darkness that enveloped him, but a baffling greyness—a world without edges or contours. He was in a grey void with no landmarks and no sense of direction.

Suddenly the snow gave way beneath his right foot and he lost his balance, falling heavily against the base of a balsam fir tree, giving his shoulder a painful knock. Where he had been confused and disoriented a moment ago, he was now almost upside down in the hollow at the foot of the tree, held down by his pack and nearly smothered in loose snow. Panicking again, and not even sure which way was up, he began to fight hysterically, with the result that he dug himself in even deeper. In the end sheer exhaustion made him stop. His heart was beating wildly and he was both gulping for air and choking on snow. Finally, by a lucky chance, he was able to reach his face with his left hand and claw away some snow. Then for several minutes he simply lay at the bottom of the hole.

After awhile, when his heart and breathing began to return to normal, he realized that he was no longer in danger of suffocation and he tried to think. Lying very still, he noticed that cool air carrying snowflakes was striking his left cheek. Twisting his head in that direction enabled him to breath freely, and by moving his hand around cautiously he was able to clear more space, finally realizing that he was simply lying in a depression full of soft snow and not hopelessly buried. The next task was to work his arms out of the pack straps, then reach up and unfasten the snowshoes. Now he was ready to try to get to his feet. After some floundering he was reminded of the presence of the tree beside him. Turning to it, he reached up and managed to haul himself to his feet.

Totally exhausted, he stood for several minutes, breathing hard and thinking. Everything seemed to be against him. There wasn't very much he could do but bundle up and try to last until daylight. At least it wasn't too cold with the snow coming from the west—not like a norther. For the second time that night, this time with his back to the tree, he arranged his gear for a bivouac and tried to rest and stay warm.

He spent some time like that, and was actually beginning to doze, when from out of the dark came a long, spine-tingling wail. The warden's eyes flew open and he stiffened against the tree. Low pitched at first, the ululating cry drifted up the scale then hung quivering in the night. While the last note still lingered, two new voices rose in duet, again beginning low, then rising to a high pitched howl. Within minutes three more wolves had joined the savage chorus.

There is something primitive and terrifying about the howl of a wolf. Hearing it, even in broad daylight, ten thousand years of evolution are swept away and man becomes once again a naked thing crouched over a tiny campfire, peering into the dark, while his hand reaches for a stick or stone. The warden's reaction was no different. He crouched beneath his tree, while the hair rose on his neck and his hand clutched futilely at the empty rifle. Petrified with fear, thoughts raced wildly through his head. How close were the wolves? Had they followed his trail over the pass and were they even now on their way down, to circle his little camp? It was impossible to tell.

As he sat, desperately trying to gauge their distance, a seventh wolf raised its voice. It was a voice to make even a brave man quiver. Much deeper and more powerful than any of the others, filled with a terrible menace; it dominated the entire choir.

Other wild animals stirred uneasily in their resting places, gauging the distance between themselves and that terrible voice. As for the man, sitting in his hole in the snow under that little tree, something shrivelled up inside him. He sat, arms clutched around his knees, and stared into the darkness, and stared, and stared, and stared.

Shortly after midnight, two of the wolves came up the trail and checked him out, trotting silently to within 30 feet of the sitting figure. They smelled the fear of the man, but sensed that he was alive and therefore could be dangerous. Presently they turned and drifted away as silently as they had come.

The park warden's eyes closed, and without realizing it, he slept. Later in the morning the wind picked up and snow came in swirling gusts. It covered the pika in his burrow and fell upon the rock beneath which nestled the ptarmigan. It covered the wolf tracks and the figure beneath the balsam fir and everything was part of a vast and formless swirling darkness.

He awoke, shivering, in the very early dawn. He could not recall ever feeling so cold; it was as if the frost was deep inside him, at the very core of his being—a terrifying feeling. In fact, he was suffering from severe hypothermia. He wondered if he could stand up. When he did stagger to his feet his limbs felt numb, the only feeling being in those places where he had hurt himself the day before. For a few minutes he stood swaying, beating his arms around his sore shoulders to restore some circulation. Then without a backward glance, he shouldered the pack and stumbled off in the direction of the highway. Fortunately, he had been wearing all his gear during the night, so it all went with him. Many people in similar circumstances leave behind articles of clothing and other critical items.

It was also fortunate that the morning was not really cold. After twenty minutes of travelling, he got his circulation back and by the time he got to Parker Cabin, he was able to start a fire and make some tea. Two hours later, he was home and the trip was over. Although he may not have formed the thought at the time, so was his sojourn on the Brazeau.

Back to the Brazeau

When the decision had been made to relieve the Brazeau park warden of his duties, I was instructed to make a patrol through that district. Although it was a long, lonely winter trip, I was delighted at the prospect of travelling my old haunts again. Furthermore, it meant three weeks of marvellous freedom. No roads, almost no phone calls, no VHF radio. Just miles and miles of magnificent park land: the moose, feeding quietly in the spruce by the beaver dams, the herds of elk in their winter meadows, flocks of bighorn sheep on the sunny hillsides, the wolves, grey shadows floating through the quiet pines. I could hardly wait to get started. I tidied up loose ends on the highway, made sure Glennys and the boys were in a carry-on mode, and two days later was on the trail.

In the next three weeks I would travel over 200 miles, reaching the farthest corner of my old district. I had promised the chief warden that I would call once, from the radio at the far end. The "Old Man" no longer worried about me, though he had sent search parties out before when this loner was overdue, only to find me gliding along some inviting bit of high country on my beloved Head Skis, self-sufficient and happy.

I had packed my Trapper-Nelson #3 packboard very carefully for this trip, my mind ticking off the items from long practice. For clothing: extra socks and long, medium weight underwear, a sweater, a small wax kit, repair parts for my skis, some leather lace, needle and thread, aspirin bottle of naphtha for cleaning my skis en route if the temperature changed. For food, I carried dried fruit, some cheese, half a loaf of town bread, canned sardines, a bit of rice, tea, packages of dry soup, a can or two of bully beef, a piece of side bacon. Bottles and heavy containers were all replaced by lightweight packaging. Also packed were: a piece of candle and matches in a waterproof container, shaving articles and toothbrush, a wide roll of white adhesive tape, a small Thermos. There was nothing that could freeze. I carried a small photo of my wife; her picture would be propped against the salt cellar on many a lonely supper table. I did not need sugar, or salt, or sweets, but I did take a small can of baking powder. I depended on finding flour and possibly spaghetti or macaroni in various cabins.

In addition to this, I took with me a small sketchpad, drawing pencil and an art eraser—also my diary and pen and, as always, a book. Even the book had been carefully chosen to provide reading only for the length of time I would be out, no more. When everything was packed, the Trapper-Nelson weighed 46 pounds, exactly one-third of my own weight. It would grow a little lighter each day.

As I clamped the front throws of my Ramy-Securis harness that morning, I was wearing double-walled ski boots, very light dress socks inside a pair of woollen stockings, long underwear, warden winter-issue pants, and handsome canvas spats, or leggings, which closed the gap between the ski boots and trousers. For a parka I still preferred the old one with the canvas back and the red, down filled liner. On my head I wore my second best winter-issue fur hat—RCMP style. The park officer badge, with the beaver above the number 35, was brightly polished and gleaming against the dark fur.

As I waved good-bye to my family and the station, I was sobered by the knowledge that there were many tough miles ahead, beginning immediately with a two-day climb to the pass. But deep inside a quiet exultation began to grow. I was heading home to the valley I knew so well. Once over the pass, I would feel the sense of freedom and complete aloneness again. After a week I would be moving down the river, at one with the elk and sheep and trees, completely in my element. For awhile I would not care if I ever came back.

The first day was uneventful, hard slugging all the way. I reached the first cabin at three o'clock in the afternoon, thoroughly tired out. After fetching water, I made tea and laid down for a short rest. When I got up, I climbed on my skis again, and broke three-quarters of a mile of trail beyond the cabin. Daylight was fading when I got back. There was time to clear the roof of snow and split a few blocks of wood, and then it was dark.

Before making supper, I phoned the station and talked to Glennys. There, the little gas-powered electrical generator had quit shortly after I had left in the morning and the mechanics had been out in the afternoon and gotten it started again. The water line was still okay. The little boys were in their bath. Everything was normal.

As I was still in my own district, the cabin was well stocked and I had a good dinner, even rounding out my pack with a few last minute additions. After the dishes, I cleaned the Heads and put on new wax for the morning, a mix for climbing in cold to moderate temperature. I wrote up the daily diary. My comments dealt with snow conditions and game observations: two deer tracks near home, one moose near the big bend, marten tracks around the cabin. Next I made two sets of fuzzy sticks, one for morning and one set for the next visit. I carefully remade my pack, leaving only last minute items to be added in the morning. Then I made a piece of toast and jam, poured a last cup of coffee, added fuel to the airtight heater, and climbed into bed. Just before dozing off, I rewound the old alarm clock by the bunk, but I didn't set it. I hate alarms the same way I hate loud telephone bells, sirens and radio calls. After years of highway work I had become conditioned to respond to these sounds with an instant adrenaline flow and an accelerated heartbeat. No matter what time the alarm was set for, I would wake in time to shut it off, simply to avoid the nervous flash.

In the morning I was up well before daylight, repeating all the moves learned from years on the trail. Everything was at hand; there was no wasted motion. While the coffee was heating, I shaved, as I did each day of my adult life. Then the Heads went outside on the porch in time to adjust to the temperature, but not long enough to take on the frost. Daylight was coming through an overcast sky when I shut the door behind me and tied on the skis. Beginning with the closing of the shutters, I would spend every minute of the day on the Heads. By eight o'clock, I was on the trail, moving slowly and steadily towards the pass.

I reached the summit at noon and stopped in a sheltered gully in pale sunlight for tea and a sandwich. On these stops, I would set the Trapper-Nelson upright on the tails of the skis, one wooden post on the outside of each, while I sat on the pack. After lunch I applied a little candle wax to the bottom of the skis for the afternoon run down the south side of the pass. Then the pack went on again and I was away, gliding easily now on hard snow, using every advantage offered by the terrain.

By two o'clock I was at the lower edge of the basin, standing on a huge snowdrift looking down into the big old spruces that hid the Jonas Shelter. It was here that I had stopped to repair the snowshoes, and cut my hand so badly that first winter on the district. I was feeling very much at home now, looking forward with excitement to the next few days in friendly country. I had lost a few pounds since leaving the highway, and body and skis were operating smoothly with little strain. Also, the weather seemed to be warming, although overcast now from the west. A sudden gust of wind stirred the spruces down below, making dollops of snow fall from the branches. Feeling good, I made a showy little hop-Christi off the drift and then immensely pleased, sat low over the tails of the skis and swished down through the snow among the spruces.

The old cabin was nearly buried: at one corner I could actually step onto its roof. There was no indication that anyone had visited the place since fall game patrol. Once inside, I inhaled the familiar smell of oakum, the tarred fibre originally used for caulking ships' hulls. At one time, someone had decided to try the stuff for chinking cabin walls. The aroma was pungent, but at least it was preferable to the usual smell of packrat piss. Furthermore, the oakum made excellent fire starter, if a person didn't mind stealing a bit from the walls here and there. One corner of the cabin was blackened where someone had accidentally set a row of chinking afire and nearly burned the place down.

There were no fuzzy sticks in the wood box, no kindling and very little split wood of any kind. This caused me to curl my lip a little in disgust at someone's lack of foresight. Fortunately, the next day was an easy run, so I was able to skip trail breaking and use the remaining daylight to cut firewood and clear the roof of snow. The one stove was a long, low type of heater with a flat top and could handle a good-sized log split in half.

With the lamp fuelled and lit I inspected the cupboard and was pleasantly surprised to find Kraft Dinner and canned meat—still good, and canned butter and biscuits. By eight o'clock that evening I was stretched luxuriously on the bunk of wooden rails, on an ancient mattress, covered by grey army blankets smelling strongly of oakum. The Heads, waxed and ready, stood trimly by the door; the alarm clock wound but not set. I settled down to my pocket novel in deep contentment while high above in the pass the snow snakes slithered silently over hump and hollow, making secrets of my trail.

By 10:00 the next morning I was on the shore of Brazeau Lake; it appeared to be solidly frozen, with a light covering of snow. One-half to two-thirds of a mile of straight running would take me diagonally across the lower end, striking the far shore just above the bridge. It was very tempting, particularly when one considered the alternative—an hour of tough slogging along the trail to reach the same place.

There really was no decision to be made, however. There never had been since the bright April morning of my second year on the district. I had been heading out at that time, looking forward to a few days in civilization, and had opted without thinking for the shining hard pack that stretched so temptingly across the lake. It had been an earlier pair of Heads that day, and I was still glorying in the ease of movement compared to the old wooden Peterboroughs. About two-thirds of the way across, head down and just a givin' her, I was startled by a soft hiss and sense of settling beneath my heels. Digging in hard with the poles, I made three quick strides and turned my head.

Beginning at the point where I had heard that gentle hiss, my trail for 30 feet had vanished. In its place was an area of black, still water about the size of someone's front lawn. Not the milky green water of overflow, but the jet black of one hundred feet of deep lake water. The wind crust that had carried me across had disappeared.

It had been a sobering experience. I ranked it along with the time I had caught my ski on a bit of windblown shale just before leading six other park wardens off the edge of Brewster Rock in a whiteout and the time that little Tuffy and I outran the silvertip at Saskatchewan Crossing. Later when I had told the story, old hands nodded sagely and agreed one should never trust a mountain lake under snow. But it was peculiar that no one ever told you these things until after you nearly did yourself in. Instead, they drove you to the trailhead, saw you off and went back to the bars and coffee shops to speculate on when, if ever, you might return.

I firmly believed that a man could count himself extremely fortunate if the Lord allowed him one chance, one life, to learn each lesson on the trail. I had no intention of ever squandering whatever lives were left to me in making the same mistake twice. Resignedly I swung right and in three feet of snow trailed a cow moose and her calf through the timber. So far there had been no sign of any human travel on the trail since early winter. The whiskey jacks met me on the little open ridge above the riverbank, about half a mile from the main cabin. They flew on either side, one a little ahead and one behind, swooping silently between the lodgepole pines. When I reached the old familiar clearing, they both perched just ahead of me as I paused. Each cocked an eye around the meadow and then, head on side, regarded me as if to say, "Well, there it is Chief, remember the place?"

Indeed I did, so many memories. I remembered the day in late June when I had brought the horses over the pass through the last of winter's snowdrifts, arriving at the cabin late on a warm and sunny day. The pasture was already green with soft new grass and early summer flowers. That was the day that the two black packhorses were just so overcome with the joy of it all that they threw up their heels like orphans at a church picnic, and scattered their packs all over the meadow and spooked the bay mare. Such memories.

There was a time during the first winter on the district when I got caught at headquarters for nearly a week in temperatures that never rose beyond 35 below zero Fahrenheit. The old cabin had been roofed with tarpaper and the roofing nails came through the boards a quarter of an inch. Each morning when I rose in the ice-cold dawn, the nail points were thick with white frost like hundreds of un-winking stars in the dark sky. By 10:00 am, the warmth of the stove and the rising sun warmed things enough that the frost would melt and a brisk indoor shower would ensue for 15 minutes.

In the afternoons, when the outdoors became bearable for a couple of hours, I would walk up on the mountain slowly, taking careful breaths of the frost-filled air. Here I allowed the sheep to become used to my company, sitting casually on a rock while the ewes and young of the year grazed by me and finally around me. Each day the sundogs hung yellow on either side of a sun without warmth; at dusk the bitter cold clamped down, the spruce trees cracked like rifle shots in the starry nights.

I smiled when I recalled the old billy who hung out on the ledges on the lee side of the sheep range. For fun, I used to climb above the goat, while staying out of sight, then move out to the edge of the hill and allow myself to be seen. This always gave the old guy a problem, because he simply could not abide having anyone above him on the mountain. Even more embarrassing was the prospect of his having to hike up past that person, obviously admitting that he had been had. You could see the wheels turning in his head. Finally, he would slip around below me and pick a route up the hill behind me. By peeking over one's shoulder at the right moment, the old fellow could be seen skulking along about 40 feet away, eyes straight ahead, pretending to be invisible!

A few minutes later, by again glancing surreptitiously, the animal could be observed, with puffing flank and cheek, on a ledge up above and looking anxiously down. At this point, if one played the game, the thing to do was to continue looking downslope in seeming bewilderment over the miraculous disappearance of an old goat. After another short pause it was okay to look for him. Fully composed now and suitably ensconced on the high ground, he could be openly viewed in all his splendour, long white beard flowing in the breeze. Then casually, as if only mildly interested, he would glance downward. And in his eye was the benevolence and disdain of an old king once again secure upon his throne!

During this reminiscing, I crossed the little meadow to the cabin. An hour later, I had the place opened up and both fires going to take off the chill. Actually, the cabin was quite tidy; the only item that puzzled me was finding a box of .308 cartridges under a blanket on the foot of the bunk. The place felt like home, yet not like home. For one thing, the presence of the former warden was strong when you were inside and that bothered me.

I took the axe and water pail, and snowshoed over to the south corner of the meadow. This was where the old cabin had stood when I was on the district. It had been a large, comfortable one-room affair, with white-washed walls and red and white curtains at the windows. In one corner had been a large brass bedstead packed in by a married pair, and at the opposite end of the cabin, a double stand-up cupboard.

For some time during my first year or two, a centrefold featuring Kim Novak in a short pink nightie graced the wall above the bedstead, and caused a visiting assistant chief warden to make this disparaging comment. "Is this a bedroom or an office?"

Gazing at Kim after the inspector had left, I pondered the point. For one thing, she was very easy to look at. For another, I hadn't expected any more visitors for months. One or two horse outfitters might pass through in the fall, and from November to June—no one, no one at all. Kim stayed. In spite of the loneliness or perhaps because of it, I had been very happy in the old cabin, with the big pine trees standing around and the river running by.

On dewy summer mornings, Shorty would be on his picket over by the gooseberry bush, and I would take the old horse, rumoured to be 32, down to the meadow to jingle the outfit. Shorty believed himself to be a marvellous tracker and would thunder down the trail with his nose to the ground—a perilous performance. Unfortunately, his eyesight wasn't what it used to be, so he usually ended up galloping right past the bunch. Those clowns, of course, stood around all pop-eyed and quiet as mice. They would have let him run on without saying boo. Old Shorty would always be surprised and a little crestfallen when reined in and shown where everybody was. He was just too speedy, that's all. A fa-a-ast tracker! On a frosty morning in November, with the horses gone, the elk would be right by the hitching rail, jostling to get at the salt cradled in the old stump. The friendly cabin would smell of hot coffee, bacon and pancakes with wild gooseberry jam.

I laid over at the new cabin for a day; long enough to ascertain that the previous occupant hadn't travelled more than two miles in any given direction since snowfall. Next day, I closed up and started down the valley. The weather was pleasant, the sun actually warm, as I made my way across the meadows downriver from the cabin. Travelling in this direction, the mountain range rose to the left, a band of timber between mountain and meadow then, beyond that, great stretches of open winter range nearly clear of snow. Sheep were often seen, while the lower pastures were liberally trampled by elk and moose. The Heads slipped quietly along making the most of every animal trail, every downslope.

I never hurried in the backcountry nor did I waste any time. Route selection and economy of movement were the key to good travelling—the saving of one's energy for tougher days. Having left the telephone behind,

I was now experiencing my accustomed change of mindset. There were miles of rugged country ahead; days of solitude and silence save for the sighing of the pine trees, and the quiet murmur of the river beneath the ice. There would be stormy nights spent in cold cabins with the packrats for company, heavy trails with only the odd wolf track beneath the quiet, frozen timber, crossings of swift and green, dark waters. In all those days and miles, there would not be a single trace of any human, save myself. So I adjusted. The mind put civilization away as a thing not needed or even desired. The pine-covered slopes became home, the birds and animals my companions.

One also became more careful as the distance from the road increased. You ate carefully—going hungry rather than touch a can of possibly tainted food. You were more conscious of the danger of fire in the cabins. When equipment needed attention, it was repaired at once, before it became a problem. On the trail, every move was calculated, every step balanced and coordinated. Snow was gauged for carrying capacity. On the rivers one listened for the sound of water beneath the ice, avoiding, like the plague, anything that sounded hollow. Always one looked and listened: to the wind, to the snow moving off the cornices, to the position of the sun, to the amount of daylight left.

And always, one moved the skis neatly and with precision. No runaways,no falling through the ice, no running under snags, no blundering into open water, and above all, no stress beyond what leg and harness and ski could handle. Help was far away.

A person kept clean and tidy. Being removed from civilization was no excuse for becoming slovenly; in fact the opposite was true. Those park wardens with reputations as the best travellers were usually men who shaved every morning. Socks and shirts and underwear were washed on the trail and good personal hygiene carefully observed.

And so I travelled on. Eleven o'clock found me picking my way through a frozen swamp. It was not ideal country for skiing. The distances between the hummocks were too short to allow a proper stride and, half of the time, one foot was on a hillock while the other lagged in a trough. It was while I was thus engaged that I happened to raise my glance. A very distant thunder reached my ear and looking higher yet, I saw the arrow-straight trail of a jet against the bright blue sky.

Standing there, my ski a foot or two away from a pile of frozen moose droppings, dead snags of black spruce all around, I mused on the incongruities of life. Here I was, measuring the day in ski-lengths, using all my skills and strength to cover 12 or 15 miles, while 40,000 feet above were other people sipping wine in great comfort, while they traversed over my entire valley in a matter of seconds. When they reached their destinations they would be whisked to sumptuous hotels or summer beaches, while at approximately the same time, I would be arriving at a dark, snow-covered little cabin, marten tracks on the porch, my drink for the day somewhere in the next gully, under the ice. It was two different worlds. With a sigh I shifted the pack straps on my shoulders and pushed on.

By two o'clock I was at the door of the line cabin at Mount Arête. The huge, black iron latch triggered the memory of arriving on another day, when it had taken all the strength in my two hands to raise the latch—a day when I would not have travelled had I known how cold it was. I had been upcountry and was on my way back to the main cabin, when a blizzard overtook me at Isaac Creek. For three days I was cabin bound, so when I awoke to a clear sky on the fourth day, I decided to push on. Not having a thermometer at the cabin, I was unaware that the temperature that morning stood at −52°F, but I was not long on the trail before I began to realize that it was very cold. Although the sun shone brightly, I could not keep my hands and feet warm; when I tried to hurry, or exert myself, the frigid air bit my throat and lungs.

Alarmed by the severity of the cold that day, I had attempted a short cut over the great slough, only to find open water in the timber at the far side. It was incredible! Icy as the water was, it steamed in the frigid air, coating my skis with ice and hampering my way with evil, sinuous channels, which I either had to bridge somehow or lose precious time in circumnavigating. That day became a nightmare. I moved mechanically, the cold eating deeply into my body. The slightest accident would have done me in. When I had gotten inside the cabin, it was all I could do to light the stove, then crawl into the blankets where I had shivered for nearly an hour.

The next day was still bitter cold and I felt ill in a strange, premonitory way. The world around me seemed dark, even in the sunlight. I shivered often, unexpectedly. After awhile the temperature moderated to 30-below-zero Fahrenheit. and I moved on again, but something was not right. I was weak and dizzy, and had to stop frequently to rest. I couldn't keep warm, and there was a frightening sense of worse to come. It did. Three weeks later, I had begun to cough; a dry cough, accompanied by a foul taste. It had lasted until spring, and by that time I had grown accustomed to seeing scraps of dead lung tissue in my sputum.

Continuing on my present patrol, I arrived at Isaac Creek next day. Here the country was at its friendliest. A number of tributaries branched off to the west, each one a fascinating adventure waiting to be experienced; on every side, ideal winter range for sheep and elk, while down along the creek beds, mule deer browsed quietly in the winter sunshine.

Across the river to the east stood the odd, flat-topped mountain named Tarpaein Rock. Nearly 25 years after leaving the district I would find the source of that strange word in Wells' *Outline of History*. I would be greatly intrigued to learn that it was originally the name of a cliff on the outskirts of ancient Rome, from which it was customary for corrupt officials to be pushed—having already suffered a fall from favour. On this day I was many years away from reading Mr. Wells' fascinating world history and the name of the mountain puzzled me. No one that I had asked seemed to know its meaning.

When I walked into the big, bright cabin at Isaac Creek, I smiled to see that the hands of the old alarm clock, which had probably not turned a tick for three months, stood at exactly ten past two, the same hour as shown on my watch. It was a phenomenon that had occurred countless times during my days on the districts and it always gave me a neat feeling of somehow being in tune with the universe.

I spent a pleasant day of layover at this, the secondary headquarters of the district. In the morning I made a side patrol up the creek from which the cabin got its name. In the afternoon, I washed clothes in melted snow water and made baking powder biscuits. Also, because this place was well stocked with many years' accumulation of dry goods, I carefully replenished my pack with dried fruit, soups and other lightweight staples. Finally, I gave the Heads a thorough going over. The next five or six days were going to present some rough travelling and dubious accommodation.

When I set out on the morning of the eighth day the mood was different. The open parklands of the middle part of the district were behind me and I was heading into flat country, heavily timbered. Because of the tree cover, the snow was basically untouched by wind and sun, the winter's accumulation lying in much the same condition as it had fallen. I was also out of the area populated by game, and with the exception of an occasional moose, there was no track to break the monotony of deep untrammelled snow. Nor was the weather very encouraging on this day. The short January thaw had disappeared overnight and a cold air mass from the north engulfed the valley. A chill wind persisted under leaden skies and, by noon, dry cold snow was sifting down through the tall timber.

I ski on in a world of grey: grey skies, grey tree trunks rising like spectres in their white shrouds, only to be lost in the gloom above. I am still three or four miles from the next cabin, with early darkness approaching, when a lone wolf howls somewhere up ahead. Like the lament of a lost soul, lonely and melancholy beyond description, the call of the wolf drifts through the frozen woods, then dies away while I stand transfixed. Suddenly at the very perimeter of my vision, where trees and snow blend into a never-never world, a shadow moves.

I stop to look and listen. Nothing stirs save for the almost imperceptible swaying of snow-laden boughs, the only sound is the whisper of graupels on the hood of my parka. I am barely underway, however, when I see another apparition, a grey silhouette gliding from tree to tree. A moment later, glancing back, I actually see two wolves cross my trail and I realize I am surrounded by the pack.

And that's how we travel the rest of the day: the wolves criss-crossing the valley floor in their hunting pattern, keeping me in the middle, matching their pace to mine. That night, in my cabin, and mighty glad I am to have a cabin, I try to convince myself they will be gone by morning. As darkness fell they melted into the landscape, vanishing as mysteriously as they had appeared.

My lodging for that night was a relatively new place, having been built during my own time on the district. I vividly recalled the old cabin that I had encountered on my first patrol down the valley. It had stood in the timber and faced north, which always depressed me. It had two small windows, barred against the bears. The floor had been of round poles; the bunk was also of wooden rails, no springs of any kind; the pole roof had been covered with black roofing, patched many times. An ancient Watson

Jack fire pump, 1925 vintage, had been stored under the bed along with another fire pump—a cranky Paramount Cub. The inside walls of this holiday inn had been tracked with years and years of accumulated packrat urine, as were the table, cupboard and the chairs. The pungent smell of these varmints had been so overpowering that after an hour of trying to clean up, I had developed a headache that drove me outside.

I had spent many a night sleeping on a few spruce boughs, wrapped in half-wet horse blankets. These arrangements were preferable to a night spent in the bedding of that particular old cabin. In an era of ancient, lumpy, disreputable mattresses, that one had been particularly noxious. The pillows were equally bad. One of them had apparently had coal oil spilled on it, which made a change from the essence of packrat. It had undoubtedly been the most depressing, cheerless hole that a man could face at the end of a long day.

Finally, on that first visit, I had opened the door wide and fired the entire contents of the shack out into the yard—mattress, pillows, chewed-up blankets, rusted and dubious looking cooking ware—the whole bit. Then I had hauled water, filled a tub upon the stove and boiled a blanket that I had hung on a tree to dry. Next I had poured a generous dollop of Pinesol into the tub and, using a mop fashioned out of a pole and old rags, had done my best to swab out the cabin. It was exhausting work after what had already been a hard day on the trail. That night I had cooked wieners and beans over an open fire in front of the cabin and, under the November stars, had gone to sleep right in the middle of my household goods with the one clean blanket between myself and the unwashed smelly ones. With the help of another park warden and an assistant, a new cabin was built the following year.

Now, on the present trip, I enjoy the luxury of a clean board floor, clean cupboard and decent pots and pans. As the storm whispers outside the door, the austere, single-spring bed and new blankets look like heaven. Supper is a dish of Kraft Dinner with baking powder biscuits and coffee. After doing the dishes and making fuzz sticks for the morning, I sit down at the wooden table to make out my warden diary. As might be expected, the wolves are today's hot topic. Then it's time to relax on my bunk with a John D. MacDonald paperback. After awhile I doze off, the Coleman lantern hissing away companionably where it swings on its hook above the table. As it burns down, the light and the sound fade, and in my dreams I'm on the trail again, the graupels pattering on my parka—just me and the wolves.

The next day marked the last outward lap and, in many ways, the most exciting part of my patrol. On this day I would cross, or try to cross, the turbulent river named after the Earl of Southesk. After following it for some miles, I would encounter the Cairn River and travel it to the pass with the same name. It would be a long day, much of it uphill, but interesting in terms of changing terrain and the possibilities of seeing wildlife. The sky was clear and the cold biting as I set off in heavy timber. I soon found the wolves' tracks ranging east into the province at the place where I had to turn west.

This point was one of those places on the east slope where the mountains meet the flat country—a notorious storm path. In the summer, mighty thunderheads massed on the summit of the Cairn until midday, at which time they would roll down the valley. Down in the timber of the Southesk, one would be aware of the heat, the stillness and the palpable feel of electricity in the air. Riding quietly under the heavy timber canopy, it was not possible to see the sky ahead but, as the sunlight faded, there was a sense of impending violence and drastic change in the weather. One instinctively looked to the packs, put on the slicker and shortened the hold on the lead rope. A thunderstorm on the Southesk was an awesome experience. There was no chance of thunder today—no mosquitoes, either. I adjusted the scarf over my face, swung my arms and skied into the cold, blue morning shadows.

After awhile the trail led out of the timber, onto the riverbank. I stopped and surveyed the scene through ice-rimmed lashes. It didn't look good. In the summer, the river at this point was very fast—the current could knock a horse off its feet without it even being belly deep. A man was in trouble once the water reached above his knees. Now, having frozen over numerous times since the fall and just as promptly flooded again, a sinister looking channel of black water, at least six feet deep and five feet across, slid menacingly between the icy banks. The vapour of open water was clearly visible, as far as I could see, in both directions.

I said a couple of bad words. They were not uttered loudly or with great vehemence but with great depth of feeling. A setback like this on a long trip and a short day was bad news; the cold made everything worse. I skied along the south side of the channel, heading upstream. Rounding a bend a half a mile further, I came to a place that was now frozen across. I stopped and thought. In the summer, this part of the river was a deep pool—slower moving. Lifting the earflaps on my fur hat, I strained to hear the water. It came to me in a muted gurgle from well below the level of the ice. I studied the scene carefully for several minutes, noting that the ice was slightly concave. Finally, I pried a rock from the bank and tossed it hard onto the surface ahead. It didn't break through, but the sound was ominously hollow. Regretfully I turned away and proceeded to siwash up the steep bank to my left. It would be necessary to climb up and around the pool and try again somewhere else. There are old park wardens and there are bold park wardens, but there are no old, bold park wardens. The mountains don't forgive and neither do the rivers.

After nearly an hour of scrambling over rocks and deadfall on the south side of the river, I reached a point where it was no longer practical to continue on in this way. I descended once more to the river itself. There was still no safe and sound crossing area in sight. If I were to terminate the patrol, the decision would have to be made soon, as it was by now ten in the morning. Taking one last look up and down the stream, I noted a spot where the channel appeared to be no more than four feet across. Approaching cautiously, I found the ice apparently resting on water and it seemed firm right to the edge. Taking off my pack, I turned to the bank and pried loose two rocks, each as large as I could carry. Standing about a foot from the edge, I hurled the rocks hard at the ice across the channel. They bounced solidly, the ice held.

What was needed was a bridge of some sort. Turning once more to the woods on the bank of the river, I used my trail axe to loosen a couple of pieces of driftwood. These I laid gently across the open channel, side by side. When all was in place, I sidestepped carefully across, one ski pole firmly planted on each side. Although the crossing took only a few seconds, it was a very interesting time. Gazing down into swift, black water directly beneath one's feet, on a 20-below-zero F. morning, does wonders for the concentration. Each move has to be made with utmost care.

Safely over, I picked up the trail again, threw my shoulders into the packstraps and pushed on. Half an hour brought me to the crossing of the Cairn River, near its junction with the Southesk, and by noon I was on top of the high ridge which separates the two waters until their confluence. The sun was warm now and the worst of the trip was behind. As well, the eminence of the ridge over the valley below gave me a sense of mastery over past travails. The successful river crossing provided particular satisfaction.

Picking a sunny corner away from the north wind I built a tiny fire with twigs over which to thaw the two inches of garlic sausage, only a little bit mouldy, and two frozen hotcakes from breakfast, stuck together with strawberry jam. Even this small task had to be performed carefully. Dropping the pancakes off the end of the forked stick meant the end of lunch, and charring them too much invariably produced heartburn. I was not surprised to find myself being watched with great interest by a pair of whisky jacks. Their concern over the fate of the pancakes was at least as great as my own and my culinary efforts were applauded by little murmurs of approval. They were each rewarded with a mouthful.

By late afternoon I was in the basin just below the waterfall, which marked the beginning of Cairn Pass. Here, the cabin stood on a piece of high ground on the south side of the river, above the falls. In the summer, the slopes on either side were green with alpine grasses and mountain flowers, wonderful habitat for elk and moose, and higher yet, the sheep and goat. Even now the valley was criss-crossed by game trails of all kinds, and travelling was easy. Also, the weather had warmed and a hint of west wind came from the darkening clouds over the pass. I was thoroughly relaxed now, for although I was at least 70 miles from the nearest road, this was friendly country. Taking a deep breath of high country air, I turned sideways to the hill and sidestepped the last climb for the day.

The inside of the cabin was already dark when I creaked open the door, and the quick scuffle in the far corner indicated that not all the wildlife in the area was outside. Treading carefully, I felt my way to the cupboard, found the matches in a tobacco tin, lit one and located a piece of candle. Using another match to soften the bottom end, I stood it upright in the lid of the tin and took a look around.

Cairn was an old cabin; the log walls were black with years of wood smoke, dust and packrat trails. The whip-sawed boards of the floor were also black and patched in many places by pieces of tin—attempts to thwart the comings and goings of generations of rats. Over in the east corner, a new tunnel marked the exit of the animal I had surprised. Making a quick survey of the outside of the cabin before complete darkness, I noted the heavy rails nailed across the windows; grizzlies frequently visited the place, trying to get at the mice and rats. On the second railing up of one window, someone had nailed a piece of stovepipe and on the other side of the cabin a similar length was attached to the third rail. Across the lower half of the small window at the front, a heavy, iron cross-cut saw was fastened—teeth up.

The friendly peaks had vanished now in darkness and an alien wind touched my cheek. In the open doorway, the candle flickered wildly. I filled a bucket with snow, grabbed whatever loose wood I could find and threw it inside, then kicked the door shut. It was time to establish my territory for the night. Having gotten a fire started in the rusty old stove, the next priority was to find a source of light. The results were disappointing. There was a Coleman gas lamp, about half full, but the mantle had been destroyed and I was unable to find any new ones. There was an old kerosene lamp, but no fuel. I did find one more candle, about four inches long.

By six-thirty, the first piece of candle was already half gone, and my plans called for one more night in this place. Some essential things needed doing. Putting snow in the teapot, I heated a small basin of water and scrubbed mouse and rat sign off the table and counter top. Then I made up the bed, laying my parka over the pillow in order to avoid direct contact with this dubious piece of bedding. Next I found a spare tin lid and nailed it over the current rat hole.

Over a drink of over-proof rum and snow water, taken in celebration at having reached the turn-around point in the patrol, I thought about supper. The choices were oatmeal, Kraft Dinner and rice from the cabin stores, and a frozen can of bully beef from mine. A memory occurred of a ski trip with Alf Burstrom, when that doughty traveller had achieved wonders with rice and bully beef in a frying pan, so I decided to resurrect the famous dish. In the dim light I almost missed the brown kernels among the white. When I recognized the dark droppings for what they were, rice and bully beef lost its appeal; I dined instead on Kraft Dinner and baking powder biscuits smeared with bacon grease, accompanied by strong tea of a unique flavour. By eight o'clock I was in bed with the candle out and dozed off almost immediately.

Exhausted as I was from the exertions and anxieties of the day, I would have likely slept until the cold awakened me in the early morning except Mr. Packrat came back. Between nine and ten, with the fire in the stove dying down and the cabin quiet, the animal tried to re-enter by way of its tunnel in the floor. The scrabbling woke me. "Is that little prick inside or out?" I wondered. Satisfied that it was out, I was about to doze off again when the rat scrambled through a hole just under the peak of the roof, dropped onto a shelf on the wall, and plopped heavily onto the bed. I was electrified. With a knee jerk, I fired the rat into space and clawed for the matches and candle. Pulling on my parka and climbing into my ski boots, I discovered my adversary in the far corner under the bed. The little monster was gnashing its teeth and thumping the floor with its tail. After a general melee involving the use of a broom, pieces of firewood, and assorted pots and pans, the rat decided the party was getting too noisy for him and departed through the open door.

I climbed up to the hole under the roof with some difficulty and hammered a chunk of wood into the opening. It was while poking around on the fire-hose shelf that I found a small, leg-hold trap. Pondering the possibilities afforded by this discovery, it occurred to me that the stove pipes nailed to the outside window rails had been put there for the very purpose of catching rats, whose habit it was to run around the top sides of the cabin logs, rather than flounder about in the snow. I set the trap in the centre of one of the pipes and went back to bed. The outlines of the railing and stovepipe were faintly visible through the window. After a few minutes, the rat went up the corner logs of the cabin, set off along the centre log and came level with the second rail across the window. Here it did a kind of double-take, hesitated ever so slightly, and skipped up to railing number three. It then crossed the window and disappeared around the far end of the cabin.

I leapt to my feet, tip-toed outside in my socks and moved the trap up to the third railing. The rat came by on its second trip, hit the third rail at high speed, did a fancy somersault and landed on the second rail, thundered through the empty stovepipe, and went around the corner. I didn't know whether to laugh or cry. After a bit of both and some very strong language, I managed to get back to sleep. Up on the pass the dark wind moaned, and the snow snakes slithered over the buried trails, sifting here and filling there. The fire gave its last spark; the rat subsided and I slept on.

Full daylight, which arrived at about 8:30, showed a bleak and wintry day. I fried one of the few remaining strips of bacon and toasted the baking powder biscuit, again using the bacon grease on the biscuit for want of butter. The fresh pot of coffee also tasted better, the "rodent-al" flavours of the night before having been tossed into the snow.

After cleaning up the cabin and rustling up enough wood for another night, I stepped onto the Heads and started out to circle the pass, looking for game. On the pass, the wind had changed again and winter had returned overnight. The sky was grey and very light snow fell, gusting occasionally from the north. It was very lonely and quiet, even the whiskey jacks seemed to have deserted me for more congenial surroundings.

Striking up the main trail, I soon found fresh moose tracks, including three recent beds in a little side valley of spruce and balsam. Midday found me on the summit, the long, rather monotonous valley of the Medicine Tent River stretching to the northwest. Here, I found the imprint of a snowshoe track. On closer scrutiny I could actually see where the park warden of Rocky River had circled briefly, before plunging back into the sombre forest of his domain. It did not occur to me to regret that I had missed a possible contact in this faraway place with another human being. I simply studied the tracks with clinical interest, as I would a sheep or elk sign, and mentally filed them away for recording in my diary that evening, along with notes about the snowpack and other observations. As I swung to the south and worked my way up into winter goat range, my thoughts turned to the prospect of heading back to civilization. My feelings were mixed.

The change of mindset, which had begun some days ago, was now complete. While the comforts of home and the company of other people were still attractive, the urgency to return to civilization was gone. Instead of growing increasingly anxious to see familiar faces again, I viewed the world of roads and cars, home and office, bar and coffee klatch, with growing detachment as the miles stretched on.

On the south side of the pass, up above the grassy little meadows where the horses grazed on summer evenings, I came across the scant remains of a dead ewe. A proliferation of predator tracks, including coyote, cougar, wolf and weasel, led me to the site where little remained except a greenish depression left of the paunch, a few pink scraps of bone, a small set of horns and one little hoof. Many of those who had previously come to dinner here would return again in the appropriate pecking order, hoping against hope that some slight morsel might yet remain.

The most recent visitor had been a young wolf. He was not a large animal, but fit and handsome in his light-grey fur flecked with a reddish tinge. Originally a member of a pack which ranged the Brazeau and Southesk Valleys, this one frequently ran alone. He preferred solitude to company. This had resulted from being seventh in line for meals and taking a lot of harassment from the more dominant members of the pack. As for sleeping, due to not having a mate to curl up with in the snow, he found his bed no chillier for being on his own. Most days, he enjoyed his independence.

At this moment, the wolf stood on a rocky goat trail about a quarter of a mile away, and well above me. The tracks he was investigating were rapidly taking him out of his preferred territory. Unlike the wolverine, who seemed equally at home in any elevation, wolves tend to shun the high country. About to change his plan, he sat on his haunches beside a big boulder and searched the surrounding country for signs of movement. Across the valley, to the north, nothing moved except the snow in the north wind, curling over the summit, drifting down the empty slopes. Farther up the basin, in sparse fir and balsam, three moose browsed in their winter yard. Hundreds of pounds of warm, red meat, but unobtainable at present, only food for thought at this time. Later, with luck, one might weaken or die.

Directly below, the watchful yellow eyes discerned a wisp of smoke from my dwelling and noted the scurry of a little rodent with a long tail along the cabin wall. Even at his hungriest, and he was always hungry, he could not fancy one of those pungent little varmints. As the north wind ruffled his collar, he curled his bushy tail around his feet and shifted his gaze to observe me in the clearing where the ewe had died. Off to one side, a wolverine paused in its tracks at the scent of a man and, further over yet, a snowshoe hare puttered around in a patch of willows, oblivious to all these things and unseen except by the yellow eyes. And the wolf on his chilly observation post felt a certain superiority in that he saw all these creatures and none had seen him. Since leaving the pack he had proved that he could survive and he would continue to survive.

Ever watchful, ever careful, content with little but happy to be free, he would go on for days, weeks and months. If in the morning a new and shining valley stretched away before his eyes, and new adventure beckoned, he would turn that way as surely as flowers seek the sun. Intent upon the hare, but keeping the whereabouts of all the other players filed away in his head, the young wolf uncurled his tail, straightened up, and drifted silently down into the snowy dusk.

We were kindred souls, the wolf and I. Two loners on that winter pass—at home in the snow, the rocks and the wayward wind.

When Bears Come Calling

It was two o'clock in the morning on a dark and stormy night when the bear came tapping at the kitchen window. I had just ridden in from Poboktan Creek that afternoon and I had placed the remainder of a slab of bacon in between the window and the outer screen to keep cool. Although we did have a small generator at the station, we had no fridge. Glennys and I were light sleepers after years of listening for horse bells, packrats and other nocturnal sounds. What we heard suggested something or someone trying to break into the kitchen.

Jumping out of bed I grabbed my rifle from where it leaned against a corner of our bedroom and headed for the disturbance, while trying to remember where I had put the shells. Running for the window, I managed to throw it open just as a very large, black bear ripped off the screen. His jaws closed on one end of the bacon, as I seized the other end. During the tug-of-war that ensued, I recalled leaving the bullets for the .303 in my saddle pockets that were out in the barn and so couldn't do much with the rifle except whack the old bear over the head.

In the end, he got the bacon, but our little skirmish goes to show the difference between blacks and grizzlies. I would not for a moment have tried to pull something out of the mouth of a grizzly, as the grizz, after the first smack on his head would have had my arm along with the bacon. For one thing the black, although a strong animal, is not nearly as powerful as his cousin and their personalities are also very different. As a boy growing up in Banff, I used to listen to the residents sitting on their porches of a summer evening telling wonderful stories about bears. The black bear is a comic, with a well-developed sense of humour; whereas anyone who has ever looked a grizzly in the eye at close quarters, knows he is a very serious fellow indeed!

Incidentally, it appears that having the rifles and the ammunition in separate locations may have been a common failing of mine. Glennys recalls a horse trip to Grizzly Cabin, with me in the lead and her bringing up the tail, five or six pack horses in between. After awhile we pass a large pile of grizzly sign by the side of the trail, so fresh the steam is still rising. The horses are very antsy, and she gets a bit nervous herself, so she hollers up at me, "Where are the shells for these guns?"

And the answer goes back, "I don't know. In one of the packboxes, I guess!"

It seems that food is almost always uppermost on a bear's mind. When a little bear goes mooching along with that downtrodden look which they do so well, like an Oliver Twist in a fur coat, chances are he's thinking about food. Food on picnic tables, food in tents, food in garbage pails and at roadside handouts—especially roadside handouts.

There was a mother bear at Honeymoon Lake who had raised generations of little camp thieves and highway beggars. Evenings and early mornings they worked the campground, afternoons they did the highway. I finally decided the situation needed taking in hand. The chief park warden had been receiving reports of long lines of traffic being held up in the vicinity of Honeymoon Lake, prompting him to remind me that there was a regulation about feeding bears. I took my ticket book and climbed into the big green Ford and drove north. I was feeling harassed and cranky.

When I reached the lake my resolve hardened. There were about forty cars parked in the right hand lane; mama and kids were working their way systematically down the line. Things really were getting out of hand. I pulled up at the rear of the line and watched the performance. I didn't have long to wait. From a car about eight lengths up, a box half full of overripe cherries sailed out a rear window, landing in the ditch. The bears were into it at once. I placed the Stetson firmly on my head, took my ticket book and marched resolutely along the line of cars. I knew I was walking into what could be a tricky situation, but I had sounded forth the trumpet as it were, and could nevermore turn back. All eyes were on me.

The first problem was to retrieve the crate of cherries. The circuit judge of the day had made it very clear that he would not even listen to a charge of bear feeding unless the evidence was there. When I reached the edge of the pavement just above the bears, I was making up my mind as to the best approach. Bluffing a mother bear with cubs is a risky business. I decided to simply go in quickly and quietly and take the box away before she had time to figure out what was going on. It worked. The bears nearly beat me back to the truck but I got there ahead of them, threw the box into the cab and slammed the door. That took care of the evidence. Now the ticket. As I went back to the offending car, I noticed mama and the kids slouching along behind me. They did not look happy. Obviously I was no longer their friend and protector. In fact I was a spoil-sport and a scrooge. I'd wrecked their bonanza.

It was also obvious by the looks directed at me from the various vehicles that the bears were not alone in their opinion. Well, tough bananas, I was going to be even less popular in a few minutes. Squaring my shoulders, I greeted the driver politely and asked for identification. The occupants of the car looked at me incredulously. Was this park warden actually going to give them a ticket for throwing a bit of food to those poor, hungry little bears? Yes, he was! As I stood by the car writing up the details, I became aware of two little paws resting on my right hip. Then two little paws landed on my left hip. My first reaction was to give whatever was down there a friendly pat on the head, but I immediately checked that impulse. I looked down carefully. One pan-handling, little bear moocher stood on each side, looking up.

Very slowly, I looked over my right shoulder. Mama bear was standing at the rear of the car, about eight feet away. She was motionless, watching me intently. There was something very serious in those dusty, little brown eyes. She was waiting for the slightest wrong move. Suddenly, everything was very quiet.

I took a deep breath. Keeping hands and elbows high, I finished writing, tore off the ticket and gave it to the driver. "Please note, you are requested to be in Jasper Court at two in the afternoon, on Thursday." By the time I was done, the cubs had dropped down and all three bears were ambling up the road. I got back in the truck and shakily drove away.

Other than cautioning the campers at Honeymoon Lake and discouraging motorists from feeding bears along the road, I was limited in the means at my disposal to eliminate the problem. If I destroyed the mother, it meant destroying the cubs as well, because they would not get through the following winter. Furthermore, it seemed to be an overly drastic solution, and would undoubtedly attract a lot of bad publicity. A culvert bear trap was being used to relocate problem bears but this also posed difficulties. In nearly every case involving a sow with cubs, the mother would enter the trap first and spring the door, leaving the cubs on the outside.

With a tranquilizer gun still some time off in the future, this situation had no solution at all. Secondly, many park wardens were hampered by lack of a suitable place in their own district to take and release a problem bear. As a result, their neighbour wardens kept a wary eye open for any nefarious attempts to smuggle bears into their district. More than one such endeavour was headed off at the pass in the early dawn.

However, when a big male bear broke into the back door of the Sunwapta Teahouse, I knew I had to take action. Shortly before my arrival on the district, a tragic incident had occurred here in which a black bear had fatally mauled a little girl. Although incidents as serious as that were uncommon with blacks, the owners of the Teahouse were terrified of any similar occurrence. I knew that the chief park warden's phone would keep ringing until I got rid of the big bear, one way or the other. For starters, I decided to go into Jasper and pick up the culvert trap.

While I was there, I went to see the wise old warden who was in charge of the town district. There are tricks of the trade to live-trapping bears and the old man was acknowledged to be the master of them all. The secret of his success lay in a vial of clear, colourless liquid which he kept hidden in the recesses of the Wardens' Equipment Building. The stuff in the vial was beaver scent and, of all the ways to attract a bear, it was the most effective. It took a considerable amount of begging and grovelling but I finally got the old boy to give me a few drops of the precious potion. The next visit was to the butcher store for a large stew bone and then I was on my way to the Teahouse. Here, I backed the trap into a quiet area at the rear of the bungalow camp and tied the stew bone to the trip lever inside the culvert. Finally, taking care not to waste a drop, I rubbed a bit of the rank, yet sweet-smelling, beaver lotion on each side of the opening at the rear of the trap and went home to await results.

By morning, I had a bear and was able to get permission to haul it into the Whirlpool Valley for relocation. I backed the trap right to the edge of the river before turning my prisoner loose. Sweaty and sick from his confinement and rough ride, the big bear plunged gratefully into the cold waters of the Whirlpool River. Climbing out on the far shore, he shook himself vigorously, gave one anxious look over his shoulder, and disappeared into the tall timber. Some bear stories do end happily.

While the black bears kept everybody busy along the highways and in the campgrounds, the grizzlies prowled around in the backcountry, making random hits on warden patrol cabins. In the 1960s, the Chaba River Patrol Cabin sat on a knoll beside a pretty little lake, about eight miles west of Sunwapta Falls, in Jasper National Park. Unfortunately, the cabin was poorly built. It was of a frame construction, rather than logs, and badly put together. Although there were no mice under the floor, as there were in the old log cabins, the tiny attic was teeming with them. And we know what mice attract.

I got a phone call, late on a summer afternoon, from my neighbouring warden at Athabasca Falls. Harold was a big, weather-beaten old man, with a dry sense of humour. He began by asking me if I had been out to the Chaba cabin recently or if I had plans to visit there in the near future. I replied negative on both counts. The deep voice rumbled on, and told that he and some friends had been out there on a fishing trip that afternoon. It was his day off, and there was something about a bit of a mess and then his voice trailed off. I began to suspect the friends might have had a bottle along by the sound of Harold's voice. Sensing that there was a message here, I listened carefully, but he was either losing his voice or else toying with me for some reason of which I was not aware. Finally, after rambling on a bit more he suggested that I, "Should maybe go out there sometime. Looked like there might be a packrat in the cabin, or something." And then he hung up the phone.

Intrigued, I took my .22 rifle and drove out to the Chaba next day. As the green Ford four-wheel drive bumped slowly along the ruts and splashed through various mud holes, I pondered the matter of packrats. They were bad news when they got into a cabin, chewing their way into cupboards and urinating on everything. Their motto seemed to be, "If I can't eat it, piss on it!" And yet, supposedly they were under the protection of the National Parks Act like all the other wildlife. Strictly speaking, the proper thing would probably be to catch them in a live trap and dump them off somewhere. But like the bears, they had a bad habit of showing up again somewhere else. Musing thus, I turned the last corner in the trail, pulled up in front of the cabin and was totally unprepared for what I saw.

Shock and awe would hardly describe my feelings. The door and half the front wall of the cabin had been ripped away and tossed aside, the porch littered with battered tin cans and torn food wrappers. Getting out of the truck, the first thing I picked up was a half empty can of tomatoes, the tin deeply punctured by powerful teeth.

Inside the cabin was a scene of havoc. The stand-up cupboard beside the stove had been torn from the wall and tipped over, cutlery and groceries pillaged and broken, the stove pipe knocked over with pieces and soot scattered about. The double bunk had also been upset, the blankets and pillows ripped. The floor and walls were stuccoed in fanciful designs of strawberry jam, feathers and soot. Imprints on floor and furniture indicated a sow grizzly with one or more cubs. Finally, adding insult to injury the wrecking crew simply exited through the back wall in the grand manner favoured by grizzlies, scattering two-by-fours right and left and leaving the cabin open at both ends.

Some packrats! I hoped Harold was enjoying his little joke. I rescued what little I could from the mess, and left the cabin as I had found it. A hasty patch-up job would simply invite the bears in all over again. On the way back to the highway, I decided to have my assistant spend a few days at the cabin.

My helper at the time was a quiet-spoken, middle-aged warden, fairly new to the service. Although pleasant and willing enough, he had so far not distinguished himself in any particular line of endeavour. What I had noticed, with some irritation, was that very often when I returned from a patrol, Bert would be sitting snugly in my kitchen keeping my wife company. Other than a propensity for polite chatter over tea, I really had no sense of the man's mettle. I decided this was as good a time as any to find out what he was made of.

With this in mind, I informed him that he would be going out to the Chaba River for three or four days to do some cabin maintenance, and make a few foot patrols of the area. I sensed a raised eyebrow but he quickly recovered, acquiesced in his usual agreeable manner and proceeded to gather his gear. As I helped him load lumber and other building supplies, I made mention of rats and general disrepair, but did not go into specifics. I did make sure that he had a good rifle with him and plenty of ammunition.

I took him out in the truck next evening. It was a warm, ominous kind of atmosphere, with black clouds and thunder brewing. As usual, Bert chattered away during the whole trip. He was still at it as we turned the last corner but, at the sight of that devastated shack, he stopped in mid-sentence, his jaw hanging slightly agape. He remained uncharacteristically quiet as we unpacked his stuff, and talked about the repair work that needed doing. There was no mention of bears. It was nearly dark by the time I was ready to leave. Bert was standing in front of the cabin, deep in thought, his little pile of bedroll and belongings at his feet. Just as I went to climb into the truck, he spoke.

"I say," he called softly and I swear I saw a twinkle in his eye, "Do you suppose those pack rats might be back?"

Cool guy. He stayed in that damn cabin, wide open at both ends, all that dark and stormy night and the next day. He went to work and did a fine repair job.

Among all the mountain rescues, road kills of wildlife and other disasters which occurred the following summer, there was at least one other marvellous bear story. That was the year in which I was provided with a crew to rebuild the trail up Poboktan Creek. The foreman in charge of the crew was Herman, a lanky old Swede, dour and short spoken most of the time. They had been on the job about a month, and were camped near Waterfalls Cabin, 12 miles from the road, when I got a telephone call at suppertime. It was the foreman and he seemed in a rare state of excitement. In words that fairly tumbled out, he told me that he had gone through a nerve-shattering experience that afternoon and could I possibly bring him a mickey of rye, for medicinal purposes? It was that time of the summer when daylight lasted until nearly eleven o'clock, so after supper I saddled the grey gelding, put a bottle of whiskey in one saddle pocket and rode up the trail.

Arriving at the camp, I was quickly ushered into the foreman's tent, where the immediate order of business was to ensure that I had in fact brought the mickey. The old man was still highly excited, and it took a good few pulls at the rye before he trusted himself to relive the events of

When Bears Come Calling

the afternoon. Anyway, it appeared that the crew had been working up-country from the cabin. Herman had been ahead of them, locating the trail through an old burn, when he bumped into a sow grizzly and two cubs. When the sow immediately gave chase, the first decision that had to be made was whether to run uphill or downhill. Herman remembered something to the effect that grizzlies were slower going down than up, so down the hill he went.

"Pass the rye."

The direction now established and the race fairly under way, Herman sneaked a look over his shoulder to see how he was doing and what he saw nearly stopped his heart. The old sow was coming on like a freight train and closing fast. With her mouth wide open, he calculated her teeth were two and a half inches long, and she roared like a lion! It must have been a truly fearsome sight. He figured if he was Wyatt Earp or Wild Bill Hickok, he could have whipped out his .45 and shoved it right down her throat, but he wasn't either one of those two gentlemen and besides he didn't have a gun anyway. So he kept on running.

"Youst a nip more of that rye, thank you kindly. Man, that hits the spot!"

What worried him now was that he was rapidly approaching the bottom of the valley, at which point they would have to start going uphill, and the bear could be expected to make even better progress than she was already. Not that the old girl needed to do any better, she had the race pretty well in the bag as it was.

One last desperate stratagem suggested itself. Ahead of him, down slope, was a schoolmarm, an old burnt snag that divided into two trunks about four feet above the ground. Making his skinny self as skinny as possible, the old man launched himself through the two forks and landed running. When the jaws of death didn't close on him in the next few seconds, he looked back to see the bear wedged securely in the cleft. Taking advantage of the respite, he beat it back to camp, and after his heart rate slowed enough that he could talk, he had phoned me.

The old fellow got excited all over again as he related the story, and I noticed it took nearly the whole mickey to calm him down once more. It turned out as well that he lost his false teeth in the race and the bear stepped on them. He went back later and found them— "They won't chew meat worth a damn but, by yimminy, they can still chew beer and rye! "

Herman claimed to have nightmares about the sow for the rest of the summer and I had to make frequent mercy trips up the creek to deliver medicine for those shattered nerves. I didn't really mind. It gave me a chance to check the work and got me away from the accident-prone highway for a few hours.

Halfway between the house and the barn at Poboktan Creek stood a small, one room cabin for the use of the Brazeau warden when travelling in and out of his district. One morning when Glennys and I were staying over, we had an incident with a black bear which, in retrospect was quite hilarious. Unbeknown to us, the old bear had been quietly poking around outside while we were having breakfast. After washing the dishes, the cabin being without plumbing of any sort, Glennys took the dishwater outside and pitched it around the corner at the same moment that she saw the bear. Dashing back in she exclaimed, "My God! There's a bear." I, not thinking very clearly, ran outside and around the corner, where I immediately came face-to-face with something in a black fur coat and a near-to-scalded rump! Fortunately, everyone came out of that one with no serious damage.

I think the most heart-stopping moment I ever experienced in bear country occurred a couple of years later, after I had become the town warden of Jasper. That incident started out as an uneventful foot patrol around Twenty Mile Circle Trail, west of Jasper townsite. I was travelling light, not packing a rifle, a decision which began to weigh on my mind when I found fresh grizzly sign on the trail in the late afternoon. By evening I was at the far end of the circle, with darkness coming on and in a pouring rain. Although I had been planning to sleep out, the prospect became less and less attractive, as this was in the 1960s and we did not have the light, rain-proof gear available today. I decided to check out an old cabin. The place had no door, and was a foot deep in pine needles and packrat litter. On top of that, someone once had left a box of dynamite blasting caps on the table, and a rat had busied himself hiding these caps in all the chinks and crevices of the cabin. This made clean-up an interesting business.

However, the old cabin was fairly leak-proof, so I spent the last few hours of daylight cleaning out most of the litter, and making a bed of spruce boughs in one corner. While I was working, I noticed a number of gas and kerosene cans stacked against the outer wall, at the back. As there was no lamp of any kind in the place, I did not check contents. Lack of a lamp also meant that after a rather damp supper of beans and coffee cooked outside over a smoky fire, there was not much to do but climb into my bedroll and prepare for sleep. It was very peaceful lying there, listening to the rain. There was no telephone to worry about, no two-way radio, and best of all—no people. After awhile I snuggled deeper into the covers and dozed off.

It was about two in the morning when I awoke. The rain seemed to have stopped. It was very, very quiet in the cabin, and pitch dark. I could just barely make out the open doorway. Lying there in the dead silence,

I began to think about the grizzly tracks I'd seen the previous afternoon. There had obviously been a number of bears going up and down the trail, but one in particular was a very large animal. The great claws had been sharply etched in the damp earth. I hoped that brute wasn't anywhere around. The thought had barely crossed my mind when one of the gas cans at the rear of the cabin fell over with a loud clunk.

My heart missed a beat; in fact, it nearly stopped altogether. This was the worst fear come to pass. Trapped helplessly in an old shack, miles from anywhere, in the dark with no gun, and a monstrous grizzly right outside. I lay paralysed, waiting for its shape to darken the doorway. I must have lain there for five minutes scarcely breathing when another sound occurred. It was the rustle and scrabble of a packrat climbing up the back wall of the cabin and across the roof. For once in my life I blessed that smelly little rodent; I was so relieved I would have gladly kissed his ornery, whiskery little face!

Part Two

Jasper and frontcountry;
law enforcement in
the Hippie era.

Desk Patrol

The Sunwapta District was the worst posting I ever had so I was relieved when I was offered a move into the town of Jasper. There are times in people's lives when they need a change, even if it only means a different set of problems. I was at such a point. The chief park warden may have felt this, for it was part of his job to be sensitive to such things. Or, it may simply have been that he wished to explore my potential for junior administration. Whatever the case, it was a welcome move for me, as I felt that the only constructive thing I had accomplished, since that hectic day of my arrival, was to have the trail rebuilt up Poboktan Creek. In retrospect, the rest of the time seemed simply an endless series of responses to emergencies of various kinds. By this time, there were also our three young boys to consider. Glennys was already teaching the eldest at home, which added to her work load as well. Therefore, it was with a sense of relief that we packed up for Jasper.

My new position was that of office warden and dispatcher. I worked in a small upstairs room in the old fieldstone building, which originally served as the park superintendent's house before it was converted into the administration centre for the park. The chief warden and his assistant shared a larger room which connected with mine.

The job commenced inauspiciously enough. I went to Stores to draw a new uniform, in order to look as spiffy as possible for the office. The new issue included a Stetson hat, a very stiff Stetson which felt alien upon my head, whether placed forwards or backwards. The thing would have to be worn for some time before it ceased feeling like a square box.

At any rate, Monday morning soon arrived. I gave the badge on the front of my new hat a final polish, placed the hat firmly on my head and marched to the office. Upon arriving at my new domain, I was somewhat disconcerted to find the failed, backcountry park warden using a typewriter over in one corner of the room. It was a meeting both of us would have preferred to avoid and several strained minutes went by while I waited for some sign of recognition from the chief warden. Finally, the assistant came out to introduce me to my new duties. He was a stocky, mild-mannered man. Although quiet spoken, his black eyes rarely missed a detail. Now he stood in front of me, carefully appraised me from head to toe and then mildly inquired if I habitually wore my hat back to front on Mondays?

Fortunately, after this dubious introduction, things picked up. In addition to manning the VHF radio and the telephones, the new job entailed drafting reports and correspondence for the chief park warden and the superintendent, plus various clerical and administrative duties for which I found myself well suited.

I also continued to play an active role in search and rescue, and other emergency activities, in my role as dispatcher. After so many years in the field, this was a new perspective. I was now the one who alerted and directed my colleagues to the reported accidents, fires and drownings. It was not a job to be taken lightly. Park wardens on patrol proceeded to potentially dangerous situations on the strength of the information provided by the dispatcher. As the bond of understanding and confidence grew between the chief park warden, myself and the men in the trucks, it became natural to assume that my instructions represented the wishes of the chief. Poor judgement would quickly erode the confidence of my fellows, and reduce my effectiveness. It was a role in which my field background in a variety of settings and difficult situations proved a valuable asset. In many instances I was able to form a mental image of the situation being reported, which in turn enabled me to suggest appropriate responses.

I was also fortunate at this time to be working under one of the finest chief wardens in the annals of the Service. One thing this gentleman, and he was a gentleman in every sense of the word, was extremely good at was the ability to visualize something which might be happening many miles away. It was a skill essential to planning the appropriate response to an assumed or potential accident in the mountains, and he was a master of the art.

The key to planning a successful rescue lies in determining as accurately as possible the circumstances leading up to, and after, the accident. Based on local knowledge of the terrain and weather, and information regarding the make-up and experience of the missing or overdue party, the rescue leader bases his plan on what appears most likely to have happened or to be happening. Combining this with a keen understanding of human behaviour, the chief could sit at his desk and, with uncanny accuracy, form a picture of events in some remote corner of the park.

The following incident was a typical example of how his mind worked. Promptly at eight o'clock on a Friday morning in September, the duty warden in Jasper townsite checked the overnight travel registration for the park. At eight-fifteen he advised the chief park warden's office of an overdue party on Mount Columbia, west of the Icefields. A call to the Sunwapta Park Warden Station confirmed that the vehicle described on the registration was still parked in the Icefields parking lot. When he had all the available facts, the chief got to work.

"OK," he said. "A party of four. I don't know three of these guys, but I know Charlie to be a good mountaineer. He's done that trip before. So he went out on Monday, and should have been back Thursday evening. But it stormed like hell yesterday and the Icefields would be in a complete whiteout. My guess is Charlie just holed up at the foot of the mountain and stayed put. Send a couple of park wardens up to the top of the headwall with binoculars," he told dispatch, "and alert the necessary people to be ready for a possible rescue on Mount Columbia, leaving the Icefields Chalet at daylight tomorrow."

At two in the afternoon, the park wardens on the headwall reported a party of four skiers approaching from the direction of Mount Columbia. At four in the afternoon, Charlie and his party, accompanied by the wardens, arrived at the Icefields Chalet. The chief allowed himself a small smile; he was bang on as usual.

Occasionally, when hands were scarce and the need was urgent, I would be sent out to take care of a problem myself. Many of these call-outs took me back to my old highway district, such as the morning that a serious collision occurred near the station at Poboktan Creek. This time the worst injury was a woman with a suspected skull fracture. For some reason, the creaky, old Volkswagen van that served as an ambulance in Jasper National Park was not available that morning and the next best vehicle was the assistant chief warden's station wagon. Although not equipped with a siren, and carrying only a standard first-aid kit, it at least had a revolving red light.

I very nearly had a collision of my own about a mile out of town, when, relying too heavily on the emergency light, I found my way blocked by an old man who pulled onto the road directly in my path. After getting by that one with a bit of skill and a great deal of luck, I proceeded to Poboktan Creek, where I found the semi-conscious woman laid out on the warden's living room floor. We made a bed for her in the back of the station wagon, and loaded her into it as gently as we could. Then, with another member of her party sitting by to steady her, I drove carefully back to town.

Arriving at Jasper, we were stopped by a Canadian National (CN) freight train parked at the level crossing south of town. It was a problem that all of the park wardens and Mounties were familiar with and it seemed it usually materialized on the occasion of an accident or fire. Furthermore, getting the railway to separate the train was an exercise in frustration. Moses parted the Red Sea with less time and effort than was needed to get the CN to move a train. On this occasion, agonizing minutes passed, during which the unconscious woman laid out in the back of the station wagon vomited and nearly choked on her own effluent. Messages flew back and forth between the park warden, the dispatch and the CN Station. Finally, I was able to get through and deliver my patient to the hospital.

Of all my duties in the office, which included coordination of fire, weather and hazard data for the park, it was the drafting of correspondence that I enjoyed the most. Unlike the majority of my colleagues, I took pleasure in analyzing a complex file or chain of events and then drafting a report, which carefully summarized the situation, and recommended action. Over the years, I was to hone my writing skills at a variety of levels in the parks hierarchy and in the service of various masters. From each I learned one or two valuable lessons and, as my ability increased, so did my enjoyment in the art of letter writing. However, it was during the first few months of my tenure in the Jasper warden office that this aspect of the position was to cause me great frustration, and led in part to a denouement which could have cost me my career.

The first lesson I learned, under the superintendent of the day, was that you never said you were sorry, to anyone—ever. If a tourist wrote to the park complaining about losing a tailpipe in a pothole on the Pyramid Lake Road, you expressed no regret nor did you admit that there might be a pothole in that road. If someone else complained of a bear wrecking his tent—same thing. It might be regrettable, yes, but it was probably because the camper had food in the tent, etc. It was the attitude which I, being of a compassionate nature, found hard to understand, until I realized that it was probably a defence mechanism used by that particular superintendent, to protect the Department against possible claims. An acceptable response was one which proposed some sort of solution to the problem, without admitting any negligence on the part of the National Parks Service.

At first I manfully struggled away at my new duties, realizing that I had much to learn. After awhile, however, even though I was now able to satisfy the chief warden in most things, I still could not get my letters through the superintendent's office in their original form. It seemed as if the "Old Man" was determined to beat me to my knees for some reason. What I have not mentioned so far is that I not only drafted correspondence, I was also expected to type it. Although I had taken typing lessons as an option in Grade 7 and had enjoyed it, (mainly because I got to sit beside Jane A. who was blossoming into ripe young girlhood that year) the truth was that I never got much past the two-finger hunt-and-peck method. Now, seated before the old Smith-Corona in the warden's office, I had to pick up where I had left off years ago. The suspense of waiting for me to strike the next key drove the chief park warden to distraction. Having gravely observed that my letters were a thing of perfection because each letter was placed with loving care, he would firmly close the door between our offices. The strain of keeping up with my new job, as well as drafting and typing letters, began to tell on me. Although I came early, stayed late and began a life-long habit of working on weekends, I still could not keep my basket clear.

Over the years there have been three well-known administrators in the National Parks Service This particular superintendent, who affected a green ink pen as a personal trademark, was included in the roster. As I struggled with my workload, the superintendent would continue to ruin entire pages of carefully typed correspondence with one irritating stroke of the green pen, sometimes for nothing more serious than the omission of a comma. Then, dark spectacles in place and hand-rolled cigarette stuck to his lower lip, he would carefully ascend the stairs and gently lay the day's rejects on my desk. I began to dread the smell of "Buckingham Fine Cut," which invariably heralded one of these visits.

☆　☆　☆

As I settled into my new job, I soon made the acquaintance of the other people in the park administration office. And, as would be the case throughout my career, I grew to like and respect these good folks very much. There was the older lady who kept the files and who, upon request, could not only quote you the number of every file in the office, but describe each letter in it. I eventually became pretty intimate with some of these files myself, particularly "Number 212; BEARS."

And, there was the old man at the front wicket where the licenses and permits were sold—a careful, conscientious bean-counter in the Old Country tradition. And a gorgeous girl in accounts, whose legs must have been made on a Saturday, because even God would have wanted a day off next to admire such handiwork. And the chief accountant who, in his role as keeper of the park's purse strings, aggressively denied all requests for funding.

One of the staff with whom I developed a particular camaraderie was the chubby, jovial and energetic second accountant. Here was a man who applied himself assiduously to his work from eight to ten in the morning, at which time he would leave his desk for 15 minutes of coffee and cheerful networking though the office. Then he would hit the books until noon. After lunch, the same pattern prevailed, with the three o'clock break for coffee and kibitzing.

Now as the second accountant roamed the hallways on his twice-daily rounds, it frequently happened that he would turn a corner to find me approaching from the opposite direction. One day, upon encountering each other thus, both of us simultaneously made a motion with the right hand, as if drawing and aiming a pistol. It soon became a game, to see who could outdraw the other in the many cornered hallways of the old park administration office.

One morning before getting up, I lay planning my day's work when it occurred to me that it was about time for some innovation in my daily contest with my friend. I went to work early that day and took with me one of the boys' water pistols and my own service revolver. Moving quietly in the still deserted office, I laid the water pistol on the accountant's desk, then went upstairs and placed the revolver in my own centre drawer. Then, the trap set, I dove into the task of redrafting the usual pile of green-inked rejects from the previous day.

Deeply absorbed, answering two telephones and the VHF radio, as well as writing letters, the 10 o'clock break snuck up on me and so did my friend. Looking up at the sound of a furtive footstep, I just had time to note the gleeful countenance of the hallway bandit before a squirt of cold water hit me between the eyes. Round one to the accounting section! Caught off guard, I was determined to be more alert for the rest of the day.

It turned into a long, drowsy summer afternoon. The chief warden and his assistant decided to go for a drive to see what their park wardens were up to; the wardens sensing this, drove off to various hidey holes and pulled the bushes in behind them. Everyone kept radio silence, so as not to give away their whereabouts. In the office even the phones fell silent, and the dust from old papers hung glitteringly in the rays of sunlight coming through the west window.

I was wide awake, however. Finally, I heard what I had been waiting for, covert footsteps on the stairs. I glanced at the clock: three o'clock, exactly. Sensing that I was about to get my man, I slid the Colt .38 quietly out of the centre drawer and checked to be sure it was empty. Then, timing my actions to the approaching steps, I levelled the gun across the desk at the exact second that the superintendent walked through the door.

The "Super" had on his green-shaded glasses. The usual hand-rolled cigarette clung to his lower lip, and, as usual, the lapels of his dark business suit were flecked with ashes. In his hand was a sheaf of correspondence, each page of which had been visited by the green pen. He approached to within a foot of the desk and was about to lay the papers down, when he noticed the gun. His hand stopped in mid-motion.

For several moments, neither of us moved a muscle. The office was very still. There was no one else upstairs. The phone didn't ring and the VHF radio was silent. A fly, crawling over the desktop, stopped to check out a lunch crumb.

I was in shock! I couldn't believe that I was sitting at my desk, in the chief park warden's office, pointing a revolver at the superintendent. I wanted to put the thing away and pretend it had never happened, but I couldn't move. I was paralysed. I also knew I was washed up as a warden. There was simply no logical explanation for what I was doing. Whichever way it ended, I was finished. Maybe worse than finished. I sat and stared helplessly at the green spectacles and the green spectacles stared back.

The superintendent probably couldn't believe what he was seeing either. His eyes flickered briefly to my face, looking for evidence that this was all some ridiculous joke, but my features seemed carved in stone. My hand was steady and the .38 was aimed at a spot two-inches below the "Super's" tie. It never wavered.

After a few seconds during which not a work was spoken, the superintendent seemed to make up his mind about something. He glanced once or twice at the sheaf of letters in his hand and then began inching backwards through the doorway. Just before leaving, he looked over his shoulder and the unlit cigarette on his lower lip bobbed a couple of times, as if he would speak. Then he was gone, taking the papers with him.

I carefully placed the Colt .38 back in my desk drawer. My hands were shaking and I realized I was covered in cold sweat. I spent several anxious days and sleepless nights, waiting for the summons that never came. Several times each day I found myself on the verge of going downstairs with some sort of explanation, but nothing I could think of made any sense. Finally, when a week had passed without mention of that crazy afternoon, a very faint hope grew in my breast that the "Old Man" might be going to ignore the incident. Perhaps he had returned to his office that day and wondered if he had really seen what he thought he'd seen. Maybe, just maybe, for some reason, the superintendent had decided to pretend it never happened. In fact, after awhile I almost convinced myself that it hadn't happened. Except for one inescapable fact—from that day forward, not one of my letters ever came back upstairs.

Farces of Law and Order

Although nothing was ever said to me about the pistol incident, it might have had something to do with the fact that I soon found myself back on the street, as town warden of Jasper. Possibly the "Old Man" felt that what he perceived to be my somewhat confrontational style was better suited to breaking up pot-parties at Lake Annette than clerking for the chief park warden. Whatever the reason, I was relieved of office duty, assigned a sexy new International half-ton truck, complete with party hat, and instructed to maintain frontcountry law and order. It was to be an interesting time.

The first case in which I became involved had to do with a tall, cadaverous and rather unappealing old man whom we shall call Mr. Smith. Mr. Smith arrived in town, on a late summer afternoon, locked on the inside of the men's lavatory on a Canadian National Railway passenger train. Having ridden the throne all the way from Edson, he was finally extricated by an irate railway policeman at Jasper, and kicked off the train. After taking an hour or two to locate his bearings, Smith began to take an active interest in the park. The first area to catch his attention was an interpretive display, which occupied a small office about a block away from the park's administration building.

Among other items, the display featured two large, glass-fronted cabinets containing shelves of insects and flower types indigenous to the park. When I arrived at the scene in response to a request from the dispatcher, I found two agitated female attendants hovering behind the Information Desk, while Mr. Smith was busily re-arranging the butterfly section of the insect display. After a few minutes of conversation, I decided that Smith was weird enough that the Mounties might want to have a look at him. The trip from the interpretive display to the RCMP detachment was fairly short, which was fortunate because Smith was about a foot taller than I was and, when interrupted in his work, of a cantankerous nature.

Once in the detachment office, however, the old man became much less belligerent and increasingly nervous. After a brief interrogation during which he provided rather unsatisfactory answers, he began to sweat profusely and begged for some water. I was intrigued to see Smith down at least a dozen glasses of water, one after another. It occurred to me that the man might be suffering a chemical imbalance of some sort, which could account for his erratic behaviour. In the absence of any charges being laid, the old fellow was finally released late that evening, with the stern injunction to behave himself. I went home with the knowledge that one more crackpot had just been added to a town which already seemed to be crawling with drunks, hippies, potheads and other assorted troublemakers.

Mr. Smith surfaced again before the next week was out. Still deeply interested in park operations, he took it upon himself to re-arrange a number of traffic counters which were being used that summer to determine traffic flows in the downtown area. Smith uprooted the counters at night and carefully re-set them in what he obviously believed were better locations. This had been going on for some time, and the people in charge of the survey were extremely frustrated. Finally, I picked Smith up while I was on an early morning patrol. Following this incident, serious thought was given to removing the strange old man from the park.

After some delay, during which he pulled various other capers, arrangements were made for him to go to the Oliver Institute at Edmonton for psychiatric observation. A Mountie was to escort him there. Smith was by this time well known to the local Mounties and park wardens, and his departure was cause for a mild celebration. A small group gathered to see him off. The old fellow entertained everyone to the last. Smith took a lively interest in all the preparations for departure, insisting that the signal lights on the police car be tested to his satisfaction and checking to see that all windows and doors were properly secured before leaving. As the car pulled away he smiled and waved at all the nice officers that he had come to regard as friends.

My next case had to do with the blonde in the pink nightie. At the time that I was town warden in Jasper, persons wishing to register out for an overnight trip in the park were able to do so at a self-registration stand outside the fire hall. One of my duties was to go through these forms every morning so that we could check on overdue parties.

I am thus occupied at about 7:30 on a sunny June morning, when I sense someone tip-toeing down the alley behind the hall. Stepping around my truck for a better look, what to my wondering eyes should appear but a near-naked lady in a very short, see-through, pink nightie. She's a good enough looking gal in a fleshy sort of way, but her blonde hair is tousled and she has a rumpled look, like an unmade bed. Her eyes are as big as saucers, and her chubby bare feet hardly seem to notice the stones as she starts across the intersection in the direction of the old hospital. I look up and down the street. Something is about to happen; I can feel it, something violent.

Developments aren't long in coming. The blonde is barely across the avenue when a blue half-ton truck comes screeching along and slams to a stop halfway through the intersection. The door flies open on the driver's side and a heavy-set guy with dark, curly hair leaps out and starts after the woman. Seeing this, she makes a change of direction and beelines it for the RCMP office, which is actually closer than the hospital.

She's making good time, having nothing on to slow her up, and under different circumstances the sight of all those creamy curves pumping and swinging along would make for some fine viewing. The man, who I now recognize as a local railroader, is obviously in a towering rage and when he catches up to her there's going to be hell-a-popping! I take a quick peek at my watch and begin to sweat a little. It is not yet 8:00 am, and I know that the Mounties are not usually on deck before eight, which leaves it up to me to do something. I know that the curly-haired railroader outweighs me by 50 pounds, plus his having the added strength of the berserk. Running into him is going to be like running face-first into a buzz saw.

It must have been an odd sight for anyone passing by that morning. A naked lady, hotly pursued by a purple-faced railroader; close behind them the town warden who, while he appeared to be trying to catch up, was actually running hard in one spot!

Panting and keeping a prayerful watch on the barracks, I saw the door open just as her pursuer knocked the blonde into the petunias under the office window. To my immense relief, two Mounties stepped out and after an initial moment of surprise, during which the man got in a couple of good thumps, proceeded to separate him from the terrified girl.

One of the policemen, a tall gentlemanly officer, was visibly outraged. "What's the matter with you?" He said sternly. "You can't beat a lady up right in front of the Police Office in Jasper!"

And the guy, who was jumping up and down and still purple in the face, yelled, "Lady my ass! And what's so 'effing' special about Jasper?"

I wiped my brow, and walked slowly back to my truck. Another Sunday was underway.

Later on that morning, I was sitting, in the backroom of the RCMP detachment, choking down some RCMP coffee, when a young constable burst excitedly into the room. He was carrying a waste paper can and with more enthusiasm than good taste, emptied a stack of bloodstained paper towels onto the middle of the table amidst the coffee cups and ashtrays. One of the Mounties had a girlfriend who worked at the hospital and on the previous evening she had mentioned that there was a patient in one of the wards, in whom the police might want to take an interest.

It seems a middle-aged man, bleeding profusely from the crotch, had been delivered to Emergency that afternoon. A tourist had picked the patient up in the campground at Mount Robson and brought him in. According to the nurse, the family jewels were missing. Having been apprised of this interesting piece of information upon arrival at work in the morning, the sergeant had dispatched the young constable to Mount Robson to investigate.

Now, while the company hastily pulled back their cups, the constable described having found the campsite deserted but liberally sprinkled with blood. Reaching into the waste paper can, he produced Exhibit A—a stained butcher knife, and Exhibit B—a partly dried human testicle. Pushing some cups aside, these interesting items were laid out for perusal. Close examination showed the knife to be rather dull and the testicle much the worse for wear.

Although there was some lively conjecture at the time as to what might have happened at the campground, the ensuing investigation turned up a sad story. The man was the father of three daughters, two of whom he had allegedly impregnated. Upon finding out that the third one was also in the family way, the sick soul apparently decided to go away on a camping trip and castrate himself. He might have succeeded, but for the excessive and unexpected bleeding. In the end he lost his nerve and had to seek help.

As the 1960s got underway, frontcountry wardens began to notice an increasing number of transient youths drifting into the national parks in the summertime. At first there did not seem to be anything unusual about this. Towns like Banff had been a mecca for many years to young people of both sexes. They came for summer employment and the hiking, swimming and parties away from the constraints of home. After awhile, however, certain characteristics of the new wave became noticeable.

For one thing, they looked different. The men wore their hair long, often in a ponytail, sometimes with an Indian-type headband. Many sported earrings, something the park wardens noted with interest. Their clothing consisted mostly of leather jackets or bush shirts and scruffy jeans; they were barefoot, or in sandals. It often appeared that they were emulating historical characters, such as the more famous buccaneers of earlier times, or perhaps Daniel Boone or Buffalo Bill.

As for the girls, their appearance was even more curious. Like the boys, they wore their hair long and straight, with no styling and very little adornment. Boys' shirts and cut-off jeans were popular with some, but many others wore long, ankle-length dresses, which became known as granny gowns. Where spectacles were required, they wore steel-rimmed granny glasses and they went barefoot or in sandals. Brassieres were conspicuous by their absence. The girls also appeared to be harkening back in their dress code to an earlier time of different values, when the world was a simpler, and possibly kinder place. These youths, who began showing up during the mid-1960s in considerable numbers, seemed to be walking to a different drum than that of the kids of the 1940s and 1950s.

Another noticeable feature was the disregard for material things. They did not have cars, preferring to hitch-hike across the country; communal groups sometimes travelled in old converted buses—buses which usually carried a number of young children and pets as well. Very few had any money, at least none they were inclined to spend. Every second person had a guitar. They were not popular in cafes and shops, and signs began to go up in many places of business—"No Shoes, No Service!" Nor were they particularly interested in work. Those who did find jobs seemed to prefer manual labour; they spurned anything that smacked of white-collar competition and promotion.

But the thing that initially brought these young people to the attention of park authorities was their refusal to pay for regular campground use. During the day they lined the roadsides leading into and out of park towns; at night they congregated on public lawns and beaches, and in picnic shelters. Many had small tents that they pitched wherever the mood struck them. Others built shelters with cardboard, plywood and tin. On summer mornings in the sixties, the frontcountry in many national parks looked like a refugee camp.

And the superintendents went forth and were upset by this affront to their orderly parks, and they went back to their offices and demanded to know of their chief park wardens, "What the hell is going on?"

And then the chiefs were upset and called their park wardens in to find out what the hell is going on and the wardens got together in their favourite coffee shops and asked each other, "What the hell is going on? Who are these people anyway?" We decided to find out.

What we found, at first, was that many of these youths were quite well spoken and better mannered than their bizarre appearance would suggest. The majority were college or university students, both Canadian and American. When questioned as to their identity and immediate plans, they were usually polite, but vague. One sensed a passive resistance to authority, more so in the case of the police than the park wardens.

The hippies, as they were becoming known, were at first ambivalent in their attitude toward the wardens. The reason for this had to do with the platform of the movement. These young people were part of a movement and one of their tenets was a belief in the protection of the environment. So, while on the one hand, they were obliged to resist the wardens as simply another form of authority; on the other hand, they felt compelled to relate to us as warriors in a common cause. Thus, the wardens were able to maintain better communication, for the most part, than their colleagues, the Mounties.

Furthermore, while marijuana was almost as common as beer in the hippie camps, drugs were primarily a police concern rather than a warden problem. So, for the first few summers there was a certain tolerance between the park officers and the hippies. We encouraged the kids to camp in places where they would not be too conspicuous, and the hippies for their part were reasonably polite and refrained from calling the wardens "Pigs," except on those occasions when they felt unduly provoked.

Had a person taken the trouble to nurture the trust of one of the more eloquent and believable leaders of the movement, to the point where they would willing elucidate their philosophy, this is what one might have heard:

- "We no longer accept the beliefs that have traditionally kept society organized, and we reject the system of rewards that have encouraged individuals to operate within society.
- "Nuclear weapons, in fact all weapons, are an abomination, and should be destroyed.
- "We are by no means atheists, but the religions we subscribe to are often the older religions of the east."

And as a direct consequence of the Vietnam War and the draft that was needed to support it, the American kids said:

- "The new life style can find no place for patriotism in the old sense, and respect for the military has been replaced with contempt."

And from one of the statuesque young women who thumbed for rides at the side of the road, while her wild-looking partner hid in the ditch, so as not to frighten away a potential pick-up:

- "Children we love, as we do the inevitable pets found in our group.
- "We reject the brassiere as a stigma of middle class confinement, and we go barefoot because shoes are a drag."

And finally:

- "While some of us may wear shabby clothes, as a mark of our disrespect, most of us are meticulous in personal cleanliness. We know that it is essential to good health."

Had we been privy to some of these ideas, sensibly expressed, we might have understood the hippies a little better.

It is illuminating in this regard, to note the young women's reference to disrespect. This disrespect was the product of a convergence of moods, disaffections, ecstasies and unconventional conclusions arrived at by a youthful segment of society, which held the older generations largely to blame for everything that was wrong with the world. It was expressed by deliberately defying conventions as applied to music, politics, sex, religion, drugs, and dress. Aimed as it was at nearly all forms of government, police, and even parents, the rebellion inevitably turned into disrespect for authority of any kind. Unfortunately, it was the notion of disrespect which most appealed to increasing numbers of restless youths who didn't give a fig about world peace but welcomed the opportunity to defy parents and policemen.

As the attitudes between the hippies and the rest of society began to harden, the result in the national parks was that the hippies lumped the wardens who were protecting the parks in with the rest of the establishment; therefore, wardens also soon rated little respect. As for the wardens, who after all had a job to do, we were becoming fed up with the hassles and verbal abuse from people we were beginning to view as a lot of radical Marxists. We were really losing patience with the increasingly bizarre behaviour of the hippies, often exacerbated by the use of drugs. So outrageous was some of the behaviour that there were not even laws in existence that could be applied.

Like the night, about 2:00 am, that a young assistant warden and I are patrolling the highway east of Jasper. It's getting set to rain and blacker than the inside of a cow. We're about four miles east of town when I sense something on the road in front of us. I don't really see it. I slam on the brakes and we bail out to find two guys, under a grey blanket, sleeping on top of each other, in the middle of the driving lane! We whip off the blanket, and there's a great cloud of marijuana smoke and these two apes come clawing their way up, all spacey-eyed. As soon as they see the truck, they grab their belongings and make for the back, thinking we're going to give them a lift someplace. Well, my partner and I are pretty shook-up at having come so close to being liable for manslaughter, and when we get over being shook-up, we get mad. Between us we make it very plain to these guys that the only lift they can expect from us will be off the pointy-end of a boot. After delivering a thorough dressing-down, I told them that if they had nothing better to do, at least, for God's sake, climb over the curb rail and lay on the grass! Well, they did climb off the road while we stood there, but I had a feeling about those two. I made my partner a small bet and we carried on down the road.

Sure enough, coming back a half hour later, we find these two clowns in exactly the same position as before, right on the road. This time we don't fool around. While my partner gets them up and organized for a move, I get on the blower to the constable on duty and, 15 minutes later, the guys are booked and in cells. We're a little vague at this point as to what they were booked for, not having found anything incriminating on their persons, but we promise to let them know as soon as we have it figured out. Actually, the men were quite docile and seemed more inclined to sleep than argue.

Not surprisingly, we were unable to unearth a law that forbade sleeping on a highway in Alberta. We hunted for over an hour and all we could come up with was a statute which prohibited "stunting on a highway" which, at that time, turned out to be a Voluntary Appearance type of offence. So these guys were each given a ticket and turned loose. The next day they hiked into British Columbia and threw their notices to the wind and that was that. So much for the farces of law and order.

Marijuana was common in the hippie community but there were other drugs around as well—strange and frightening drugs, the most terrible of which was lysergic acid diethylamide (LSD). This mind-bending chemical had unpredictable results, inducing euphoria in some individuals, raw terror in others. The latter frequently hallucinated, one common phenomenon being the illusion that various body extremities, like hands and feet, were melting away. Many became violent in their fear, and their strength at those times was the strength of the berserk. A lot of young people, seeking an out-of-body experience, never found their way back in. Even when they did, there was no guarantee of safety. The effect of the drug could re-occur over time, without warning.

LSD could be slipped into a drink, and given to an unsuspecting person. One Calgary police detective even fell victim to this vicious practice, through no fault of his own. According to the story that made the rounds, his car had stalled on the way to work one blizzardy winter morning. As he was standing bent over beneath the hood, a van pulled up and the driver offered him a ride to work. The detective gratefully accepted the offer, and climbed in. As they got underway, his benefactor motioned to a Thermos bottle parked between the front seats, and offered the detective a cup of hot coffee. Shivering with cold and not suspecting foul play, the policeman again accepted gratefully and consumed a cup of the brew.

An hour or so after arriving at his office, his colleagues were astounded to see the detective going crazy. In order to prevent him from committing mayhem, he was forcibly detained, taken to a hospital for treatment, and kept under observation for some time. When he was able to tell about the morning's events, it was concluded the Thermos had been spiked with LSD.

My first opportunity to observe the terrifying effects of this drug occurred on an afternoon, when I stopped in at the RCMP office for a coffee. As it happened, there was no coffee that day. All available members of the detachment were being engaged in subduing a madman in one of the cells. It seemed that early that morning this individual had almost killed the sergeant. It had been about 8:00 am when the commanding officer (CO), a sergeant who was rather short and portly, unlocked the front door of the office. He was alone at the time, when a wild-eyed young man burst in. The young fellow had a small Collie dog which trailed closely at his heels but, of which, he seemed unaware. His complaint was that someone in authority had taken his dog away. He claimed that he had been given the run-around at the park's administration office and his visit to the police was a last, desperate attempt to obtain justice and get his little friend back.

As he spoke, the tall hippie became increasingly agitated and when the sergeant disclaimed any knowledge of the missing dog, it became obvious that the young man thought he was lying. In a surprise move, he seized the sergeant by the throat and bent him backward across the edge of the high counter that was used to separate the working area from the office entrance. Thus caught off guard, the Mountie tried to extricate himself, only to realize, with growing panic, that he was powerless in the young man's grip.

Fortunately, just as it felt as if his spine must surely crack, two young Mounties came racing down from the upstairs sleeping area and pulled the madman off their shaken commander. Meanwhile, the poor little dog dithered nervously at the heels of his master, who was still unaware of its presence. So it was that when I dropped in for an afternoon coffee break, I heard the screaming and struggling in one of the cells. The young man's father had been located in Edmonton and to everyone's amazement had offered to send an ambulance all the way to Jasper for his deranged son. In order to affect a transfer from the cells into the ambulance, the attendants had called ahead to request that the patient be sedated in advance. The rumpus I had walked into was the result of the Mounties' efforts to hold the man still while a doctor administered a needle. The young guy was screaming that he knew what they were trying to do, which was to put water in his veins so he would die. In his terror and rage, he actually lifted four hefty policemen off the floor at once. It was my first encounter with that demoniacal drug. I was impressed, but not favourably.

As usual, the Mounties and the night duty warden responded to all the senseless goings on in the park with their own particular brand of nonsense. One member strongly advocated gargling with peanut butter first thing in the morning in order to be mentally conditioned for the vicissitudes of the day. Another claimed that consuming a lightly boiled orange for breakfast worked wonders for him, and yet another tried to get all his colleagues to have raw egg sandwiches for lunch. It was in this climate that the Rubber Rooster Act was born.

It all started one drippy night when a young policeman strode portentously into the detachment office and took up a position in the centre of the room. There he assumed a dramatic pose with this legs braced and one hand mysteriously concealed within his jacket, reminiscent of Napoleon reviewing his demoralized troops on the retreat from Moscow. As the other Mounties in the office became aware of their colleague standing there, obviously about to produce a surprise of some sort, the tempo of the typewriters slowed perceptibly. Within moments there were just a few random pecks, then one last clack and silence. All eyes were on the young constable. Even the sergeant, noticing the silence in the bullpen, ventured cautiously from his inner sanctum, to see what was going on. These days you never knew. The only people nuttier than those out on the street, were the ones in the detachment. When the suspense was at its peak, the one at the centre of attention glanced carefully to the right and left, then slowly drew forth a gruesome looking rubber replica of a naked, skinny, featherless, yellow and purple chicken. Holding it at arm's length, he dropped the horrible thing on the floor, where it flopped and quivered and jiggled about for all the world like a freshly decapitated rooster.

In the hilarity that followed someone said, "Hey, that's quite an act!" and another said, "Yeah, a rubber rooster act!" And finally, "Hey, that's what we need for law enforcement around here, a Rubber Rooster Act!" It took only seconds for their feverish and overactive minds to seize on this idea. Here at last was a chance to devise some legislation, albeit bogus legislation, with which to combat the crazy hippies. They couldn't wait to get started. The night warden was told to go out and keep the park safe, while his more learned comrades turned to the serious business of drafting sections and subsections, penalty clauses, whereas and wherefore stipulations, and all the rest of that wonderful stuff which makes the law so impressive.

In deference to their little buddy, the park warden, the first sections to be drafted made it unlawful to sleep on the driving lane of a highway at any time. From there they went on to regulate against all the erratic, irresponsible, irritating, disruptive, disgusting and irrational kinds of behaviour that one could possibly encounter—all with appropriate penalties. When I came back shortly after midnight, the back room of the detachment was a shambles of half-smoked cigarettes and abandoned coffee cups. The Mounties' ties were off and they were showing signs of fatigue, but they had completed 96 sections. The last one had to do with dragging a mattress behind a moving vehicle. Someone had reported that this was becoming a popular pastime at Cow Bay, Nova Scotia, and the guardians of law and order were determined not to let it get started in the mountain parks. Needless to say, the Rubber Rooster Act and its regulations never made it to the courtroom, which was too bad. It would have been a lot of fun.

As the decade drew to a close, there were literally thousands of Canadian and American youths roaming the country. At the newly proposed Pacific Rim National Park on the west coast of Vancouver Island, they camped on the beaches and didn't wear clothes. On the Queen Charlotte Islands, where another new park was still little more than a gleam in the park planner's eye, the hippies slid like shadows into the ancient cedar forests and disappeared from the world. Future park wardens would find fantastic shacks and tree houses, little garden plots and children's toys; they'd wonder at how the squatters had arrived, what they grew and how it was to be a hippie child in those rain-drenched haunts of mystery and shadow.

Meanwhile, in the more developed national parks, a little mystery and shadow would have been useful to hide some of the mess caused by hundreds of random camps and shack-ups. Finally, to try to bring some order to the situation, it was decided to create a number of free campgrounds, where they could do their hippie thing without bothering family campers. At least they would be more or less contained. The area chosen in Jasper National Park was actually a very nice location by a small lake, just below the highway bypassing the townsite. Although the place would eventually grow to nearly 600 campsites, at first it was only about a tenth that size. Tent pads and fire circles were built, but there was no accommodation for cars, the idea being that the only legitimate clientele were on foot. There was no camping fee.

At first, everything seemed to go forward in good faith. The hippies loved it and in no time at all the place was filled up with bearded guitar pickers and girls with long hair and granny gowns. The park wardens and Mounties patrolled the area regularly on foot and the kids seemed genuinely grateful for a place to camp where they weren't hassled. The officers had to listen to a lot of stuff about ecology and the threatened environment, but to compensate, they were occasionally treated to a view of young ladies bathing "au naturelle" in the pond, as naturalness was another big thing at the time.

The honeymoon was soon over. Word of the transient campground quickly got around and it wasn't long before the place became a haven for dope dealers and refugees from all over the country. Strange incidents began to occur and the veil of innocence that had prevailed at first, became badly tattered and was soon tossed aside. Confrontations between campers and the RCMP became frequent and increasingly hostile. The Mounties finally made it clear that nothing short of murder would induce them to go near the spot. As it turned out, murder was one of the very few things that didn't occur there that summer.

The place had become a travesty of the original intent. The haven for innocent youth had become a den of iniquity from which various types of unwashed scum felt they could get a free ride and thumb their noses at authority into the bargain. It was a pain in any park warden's arse and of a particular pain in mine. I kept smiling on my daily walk-a-bouts, but there was blood in my eye.

I decided to take a stand one hot day in early August. On the way to work that morning I drove down the by-pass to have the usual quick check on the state of affairs down by the pond, when my attention was taken by a column of smoke rising 60 feet into the air, originating from somewhere over the guard rail. The smoke, as it turned out, was coming from a spot about halfway between the road and the campground and emanated from a fallen Douglas fir, most of which was on fire. Around the fire, still in sleeping bags, were five motorcycle-cowboys, their bikes parked on the grass. Judging from the litter, much of the previous evening had been spent consuming beer and beans. The offences being committed by the five were in close proximity to that troublesome campground area and of enough concern, in a period of high fire hazard, to warrant some action. It was as good a place to start as any. I got on the blower to the RCMP and within minutes a constable was on the scene.

Well, we entered in our most official manner, hats down over our eyes, commenting on the untidy look of the place, while tipping these guys out of their sleeping bags. Then the constable took them over to the detachment office while I took their bikes and locked them up in the campground. When I returned to the cop shop, he was booking them all for having an unlawful fire, littering, and vehicles off the road. Now, no one in mid-summer has time to baby-sit a bunch of yahoos like that, and you know darn well once they get loose, you'll never get them to court. So generally what you do is give them time to stew a little, and then you make it known that if one guy will take the rap for everyone, bail can be arranged for him, and the rest can go free. With a bunch of guys who know each other, this suggestion is usually welcomed; everyone kicks in to pay the buddy's bail, and they're off into the next province and out of your hair.

But this morning we were in for a surprise. It seems these five dudes had all met for the first time that night. There were no particular friendships and no one was willing to take responsibility for the group. Furthermore, on looking over the sum total of their effects, the balance was not even equivalent to bail for one. We had arrested this crew and it looked like we were stuck with them. Even so, I didn't realize we had a problem until about an hour later when the constable radioed for me to come back to his office. He briefed me on his predicament—seems it was one of those unique occasions when his CO was away in Edmonton, another member was off sick, and so on. The long and short of it was that he was the only Mountie around for the remainder of the day. Worse yet, he had been unable to find a baby-sitter to come to jail. As the police were not allowed to leave prisoners unguarded, he would be in a quandary when the next call-out occurred.

As we were pondering this dilemma, the park superintendent happened in. He had probably picked up from the radio that something was going on. His advice was to turn them loose. Well, the superintendent was a prince of a guy, but not overly strong on law enforcement. Furthermore, the constable and I believed that we could easily be sued for false arrest if we turned these guys loose. Then the Mountie came up with a solution. With a phone call to Edmonton, he arranged to have a paddy wagon sent up to take the prisoners to the city, where it was determined they could be charged with vagrancy. The going rate for that was said to be 30 days. Satisfied that things were once more in hand, I went back on patrol.

Anyway, it was noon when we received the information that, to speed things up and, no doubt because it was a mighty fine day, the police in Edmonton decided to fly up with the RCMP plane instead. For some reason, the new turn of events made me feel faintly uneasy. It seemed the whole thing was getting out of proportion and becoming a big deal. However, events were out of my hands by this time.

Well sir, just before two in the afternoon the plane arrives at the airstrip and somehow word must have gotten out, because every ding-a-ling in Jasper was there to see the show. I noticed the five prisoners are really making the most of all this publicity, waving to the crowd as they boarded the plane and clowning around generally. Their good humour doesn't do anything to improve mine. "Anyway," I say to myself as the plane heads off over the tops of the pine trees, "If these guys are gone from here for 30 days, that's five less to worry about."

They were gone exactly 24 hours. They went before a judge, down there in Edmonton at 10:00 am and he gave them one night in custody, already served, and turned 'em loose! They caught a ride back to the park. At 2:00 pm, they're at the administration building, demanding their bikes back. They've got a court order for that too. Well, maybe you think these guys aren't chirpy! Fortunately, I was saved the ordeal of having to face them again by way of hauling away an obstreperous bear at the time, but the duty warden tells me they checked their bikes over real close and discovered all kinds of scratches and damages which weren't there before. Anyway, they finally roar off in a shower of small boulders, heading west.

Just in case we might ever forget them, this one guy, whose old man was an MP down east some place, writes to the park shortly before Christmas and thanks us ever so much for the nice plane ride across the Rockies and all the amenities so kindly provided, at taxpayers' expense, while he and his buddies were on their summer vacation.

Night Patrol

It was 1:00 am and so quiet you could have heard an ant sneeze. I was in my patrol vehicle on a back road near Jasper and I could not recall ever having been out on such a dark night. There was no moon; the stars were obliterated by a heavy pall of smoke from forest fires in British Columbia. The valleys in the park were filled with it, hiding the mountains and the air smelled strongly of burning forests. The weather had been hot for days and the nights were close and warm. The park wardens were red-eyed from lack of sleep and their nerves were tense.

In the headlights of the truck the woods were dim and spooky. I stopped, turned off the engine and rolled down the window. The main valley was full of tourists, the big campgrounds were packed, the town was overflowing. But in spite of the fact that nearly 20,000 people were within a mile or two of where I sat, there was not a sound to be heard. The smoky darkness muffled all sound. I shifted uneasily and was about to restart the motor, when a loud crackle followed by a booming, sepulchral voice nearly startled me out of my wits.

The voice, which seemed to come from nowhere, said "This is the Shadow." And then it continued in tones of mystery and menace, "The Shadow knows all. He sees into the hearts of men, and knows the evil which lurks there!" This was followed by a macabre chuckle.

Baffled and badly shaken, I was further discomfited when I found myself suddenly in the glare of a pair of powerful headlights. The disembodied voice said "Gotcha!" just as the red and blue flashers came on. Trying to recover my composure, I stepped out of my truck and walked over to where a patrol car was nestled behind some bushes. A big, mischievous Mountie, grinning like a Cheshire cat, sat at the wheel.

"What the hell was that?" I asked indignantly.

"That—," said the policeman, with an impressive pause, "is my new toy. Like it?"

"I don't know if I like it or not. What is it anyway?"

"Well, it's a gadget called a woofer. We can use it to make a loud yelping noise, like this." And he turned it on, causing me to jump all over again. "Or we can use it like a loudhailer, to talk to people. I guess I almost gave some poor old guy a heart attack yesterday."

We were interrupted at this point by the police radio, wanting to know the constable's whereabouts, and requesting he return to the barracks. "Whoops! Gotta go old buddy," he said, easing the prowl car out of the bushes. "Catch you later. Don't take any rubber nickels!"

Then he was gone, and everything was smoky dark and quiet again. It was getting on my nerves. I decided to check out the action at the Sixth Bridge, a notorious party spot. There was a certain irony in the fact that I was the first townsite warden to find myself assigned to night patrol. To some extent, I had myself to blame.

Although a park warden's work day normally ended around 5:00 pm, it was generally understood that most town and highway wardens would put in two or three hours after supper patrolling their districts, especially in the summer. As the national parks became busier and rowdiness increased, these evening patrols tended to run on until close to midnight or later. Furthermore, while it was one thing to stroll the shores of a lake on a pleasant evening and talk to a few fishermen, it was something else entirely to find oneself embroiled with 60 drunks at a midnight bash. The traditional public relations role of park wardens, aimed at resource protection, was being replaced by the need for hard-core law enforcement. And hard-core enforcement, as any city cop will testify, is not fun. One former Jasper warden, now retired, put it this way: "Riding around the Brazeau Valley, counting bighorn sheep, had not prepared me for the day when a Vietnam draft dodger presented me with a knife at my throat!"

Thus it was that the changing nature of patrol work, plus the advent of unionization, made a number of wardens restive under management's benign assumption that a bit of evening patrol was all in a day's work.

It even threatened to become a peer problem, with some gung-ho types competing to stay out until the last dog was hung, while others longed to go home and put their feet in the creek. With no one officially on duty at night, it became questionable at what point a warden could, in good conscience, call it a day.

I began to advocate strongly for a scheduled night shift in the town district, to run from 6:00 pm to 2:00 am. So convincingly did I argue, that the chief park warden eventually acquiesced and promptly gave me the job. I might have seen it coming. Instead of being able to go home at 5:00 pm and hang up the keys, secure in the knowledge that someone else was being paid to mind the store, I found myself trouble-shooting until the early hours of the morning.

To give my colleagues their due, most of them continued to come out after supper, lending a hand with bears and campers until 10:00 or 11:00 in the evening. But the really messy problems with drunks and vandals usually occurred much later at night, by which time I was on my own.

Nor was the local party crowd very happy to find me persistently putting a damper on their night orgies, where hitherto they had pretty much had a free hand. To me it almost seemed as if relationships were deteriorating to the point of a personal vendetta between me and the Happy Gang. When our house was the target of a 2:00 am drive-by shooting, I began to get a little paranoid.

Approaching the Sixth Bridge across the Maligne River, I slowed the truck to a crawl—my stomach tense. When the picnic spot actually came in sight, I was surprised to see only a small, desultory campfire smouldering in the fire circle. Although there were four or five vehicles in the area, only three young people sat around, sipping beer and talking quietly. They were very polite when I approached, agreeing to extinguish the fire when they left and pick up their empties.

I stood around indecisively for a moment, then walked over to the old wooden bridge. Something was bothering me. It was too peaceful, too quiet. There were subdued voices from the shadows under the bridge, but I could not make out the words, nor could I actually see anyone. I assumed that the owners of the voices were probably making love on the river bank and decided to leave them alone. It never occurred to me that someone was preparing to set fire to the bridge, which proves that I wasn't yet paranoid enough; furthermore, I was forgetting that a good warden was a curious one. Lulled by the peace and quiet I wished the beer drinkers a good night, and went home.

At sunrise the next morning, after barely three hours of sleep, I was jarred awake by the telephone. Dispatch informed me that the Sixth Bridge was on fire. Scrambling into the truck, I switched on the red revolving light and raced for the bridge, only to find a grim-faced chief park warden surveying the charred ruins. A couple of empty jerry cans lay nearby.

I could have kicked myself. How could I have been so stupid not to have made a thorough investigation the night before? I knew that almost any of the other wardens would have taken a flashlight and satisfied themselves as to what was going on. But I, the night patroller, had let a few punks make a fool of me. I could only remember having been so mortified once before, when I chose the wrong route to a rescue on the Columbia Icefields. That incident had led to nearly a year of castigation from the chief park warden and the superintendent, and a virtual disassociation by nearly all the wardens in the park. The Service did not treat ineptness lightly. As I miserably stood there in smoky, early morning sunshine, I wondered if this would be the same.

To my credit, I had noted the license number of the vehicles at the picnic fire but, although an investigation was launched, there was not sufficient evidence to lay any charges. When the town's work camp burned to the ground a short time later, the bridge incident was eclipsed by the greater disaster.

Although there was no way I could have been expected to know there was an arsonist in the government bunkhouse, I was still smarting from the bridge deal, and I felt that the torching of the town camp was one more black mark in what was turning into a disastrous summer. My paranoia became notably worse after the camp episode, and reached its peak the morning a Molotov cocktail was discovered in the administration building on Monday morning. It had been thrown through an upstairs window but failed to start a fire. Nearly all these disturbing incidents occurred on dark, quiet nights when I, beguiled into thinking everything was under control, had retired at the appointed time of two hours past midnight. No one was apprehended.

In desperation, I began to work longer hours, remaining on duty until sunrise. By 11 am, I would be back in uniform, either completing the paperwork on the last night's incidents, or investigating some new disaster. Stress and lack of sleep made me nervous and short-tempered and the stomach pains, which had haunted me for years, became a permanent fixture.

Inevitably, I began to associate more and more with the Mounted Police, in spite of the fact that the wardens were often cautioned not to become second-rate cops. In truth, however, most of the late night incidents in the front country were wholly or mainly within the jurisdiction of the Mounties.

Working late at night at accident scenes, fires and various other difficult and sometimes frightening situations, we naturally looked to each other for support. I grew to welcome the sight of the purple and white patrol cars, in which there was always at least one strapping, stout-hearted member. And the police, for their part, appreciated having a park warden on at night, and soon gave me full and equal status around the coffee table in the back room of the detachment. A strong camaraderie developed, and with it came an introduction to police humour.

Policemen everywhere have developed their own brand of black humour, an antidote for the seamy, scary soap opera that constitutes their daily lives. The Mounties were no exception and they also went in heavily for practical jokes. I became the subject of their attention on a number of occasions.

The first one took me completely by surprise. At about 10 am, I was just leaving the coffee room at the detachment when two of the Mounties waylaid me and tossed me into the cells' area. Then all but one put on their policeman hats, with the visors pulled way down, and disappeared. The remaining Mountie gathered up some paperwork and busied himself on a typewriter at the far end of the office. My pleas for release, passionately felt and fervently put forward, were studiously ignored. I now found myself in a ridiculous position, standing in the cells in full uniform with my patrol vehicle parked outside.

The old RCMP office in Jasper was laid out in such a manner that a person entering the front door would be in a small hallway, with three doors in front of him. The one on the right opened into the sergeant's office, the one directly in front led to the cells, and to the left was the general office and workplace. Persons coming in to visit the main office, as several did that morning, were able to see into the cell block, before turning to the left. Fortunately, I had been given the run of the corridor connecting the individual lock-ups, enabling me to slink into the very furthest corner away from the entrance. Here I propped myself up in a corner, and prayed to be let out before my whereabouts was discovered. I was also painfully aware that my truck, parked outside the detachment was in full view of the chief park warden's office window. Given management's distaste at having wardens too closely associated with police, I could imagine the speculation which would no doubt be taking place in that office as the morning dragged on. It was a long, strange morning, in a long, hot summer.

Sometimes the Mounties would extend their practical jokes to include a whole gaggle of park wardens as when, on Halloween Night, they locked the gates to the government compound, catching several wardens and the chief on the inside. But, mostly they liked to concentrate on me. The Orange Triangle Joke was a case in point. This one developed over several days and was a masterpiece of planning and execution. As usual, the fertile mind and fine hand of Corporal (Mandy) Manderville, the detachment's second-in-command, was discernible.

The whole thing began the pleasant afternoon that I received a phone call from the stables at Jasper Park Lodge. The Lodge, it seems, was planning a do of some sort at the Sixth Bridge. An old-fashioned, horse-drawn wagon was to be part of the setting. "What were the regulations governing the movement of horse equipment on motor vehicle roads in the park?"

This was a new one for me. I phoned the detachment office where I had the bad luck, as it turned out later, to reach the incorrigible second-in-command. The corporal was, as always, efficient and helpful. "No problem," he said, when informed of the request. "Tell them to hang an orange triangle on the back of the wagon and they'll be fine."

"Are you serious?"

"Just as serious as a kiss above the panty line!"

"But why an orange triangle?" I wanted to know.

"Because that is the universal sign for slow moving traffic."

I thanked the policeman for his help, passed the information on to the Lodge and forgot about it. But the corporal didn't. That discerning individual had made the connection between slow moving traffic and myself. Those who were associated with me frequently noted my personal style of locomotion. It was something in between a shamble and an amble. It always got me where I was going, but sometimes not as quickly as others got there. Thus late in the afternoon, after a mountain climb, my colleagues would often be gathered by the trucks or pulling their boots off in camp, while I was still descending the slopes. There I was, meandering along, sampling wild berries and poking around just like a little old bear. In the tale of the hare and the turtle, I was the turtle.

At 10:10 am, several days after the phone call from the Lodge, two policemen arrived at the Area 1 Warden Headquarters. After ascertaining that I was present, they invited themselves into the back room for coffee. On one side of the room was a long table used for meetings. The policemen seated themselves one on each side and near the head of the table. Various park wardens wandered in, poured a cup of brew and sat down. When I came in, I took the remaining empty chair, at the head, as befitted the senior warden-in-charge. As usual, the conversation dwelt on the latest outrages in the "Hippie Campground," and the farces of law and order in general.

About halfway through coffee break, I was called into the front office to answer the radio; when I came back a few moments later, I sat down somewhat absent-mindedly to finish my coffee. I figured out afterwards, that it was while I was on the radio that a flat piece of orange-coloured material was placed carefully on the old, plum-coloured cushion of my chair. Although the down side of this object was very bright, the side facing up blended well with the cushion. It was also very sticky. So sticky in fact, that after the Mounties departed, in what appeared to be an exceptionally boisterous mood, the object adhered to my posterior while I went about my duties for the next two hours. My first clue came when I arrived home for lunch and my wife asked how long I had been running around town with an orange triangle stuck to the rear of my pants!

During the time that I was employed as office warden, town warden, and later acting area 1 manager, my wife, the three boys and I lived in an old log house at the "Meeting of the Waters." The house, which stood on a peninsula of ground at the junction of the Miette and Athabasca Rivers, had previously been condemned by the government as being a place unfit to live in. Once the owners had moved out, however, the Department refurbished it and began renting the house to wardens in the town district.

It was actually a very comfortable old place, with a huge yard, and a row of spruce trees shielding the buildings from the road. At the rear of the house, the mighty Athabasca rolled by in full view of the kitchen windows and Signal Mountain rose in the background. The boys would climb way up in the spruce trees and give their mother fits.

The first winter we were in the place, I was sure I had discovered a poacher, when I found a hole drilled in the ice of the Miette River upstream from the house. Sure enough, there was a line in the hole, and there, upstream was another! I found four holes in all, with set lines. That evening it came out that the enterprising fisherman was actually our eldest son. It had not occurred to the young fellow that fishing might be closed for the season.

That was also the winter that we discovered our new home was flood prone. At around 10 pm, on a dark December evening, we were astounded to hear water pouring into the basement. After hastily moving various boxes and other items onto higher shelves, we rushed outside to find the house surrounded by water—black, icy water that lapped at the foundation logs in a most alarming manner. As a family we had many years of experience coping with primitive and sometimes emergency conditions. The first thing we did was to move the government and family vehicles out to higher ground near Tekarra Lodge. Then Glennys took the three boys to their grandmother's house in Jasper for the night and I returned to my embattled home.

When the grey, cold dawn finally arrived, it was learned that the Athabasca River had formed an ice jam under the bridge at Old Fort Point, backing water up over several acres of ground, which included our home. General Works crews came as soon as they were able and dumped several tons of sand around the base of the house in an attempt to keep the water out. They also attempted to open, with dynamite, a channel downstream from the house. The sand ploy worked but the dynamite did not. With each explosion a huge geyser of water and slush erupted in the air, only to settle back into the river and freeze again within minutes. They did succeed in blowing several windows out of the house. After a day or two, with the sand holding and the water beginning to recede on its own, we moved back in, commuting back and forth to the road by canoe.

The following June, we were again inundated by high water resulting from rain and snow melt. By this time, the Department had constructed a sturdy two to three-foot dyke around the place, and we had fine-tuned our flood procedures. There was no serious thought given to moving out. In fact, it was kind of fun to paddle home at the end of the day and pull the road in behind you. Potential visitors, wanted or unwanted, could be heard screeching to a halt at the approach to our deep-water driveway.

The kitchen window of the old log house looked eastward over the river and toward Signal Mountain. It was through this window that Glennys and I observed a grizzly late one afternoon. It was early April, and the Athabasca River was at its lowest. Old winter ice still lay along the shore. The bear appeared coming out of the timber on the far side. As it approached the edge of the water, its attention appeared fixed on our house. What followed was recorded with the family camera.

Having swum the river, the grizzly climbed the bank on the near side and came directly toward the back yard, gaining entry through the open gate. The bear appeared to be literally following its nose, and that nose was pointing unerringly at the rear of the house. Or, was it something in the house? The thrill which this family always experienced at sighting wildlife turned to apprehension as the bear climbed up on the dyke. It was now no more than eight feet away, with nothing in between us and it but a thin pane of glass, and it was still on a beeline. At the last second the animal paused, and the big head swung from side to side, nose twitching. Then it tumbled down from the dyke and climbed a high fencepost a few feet away. The attraction was explained. It was after a large piece of suet which had been nailed up, many weeks before, for the birds.

Having devoured the treat, Mr. Bear turned without another glance and shambled toward the back fence. In true grizzly fashion, it walked right through the fence without even appearing to pause; boards and posts were falling left and right. Moments later, it was over the river and back in the timber on Signal Mountain. One more good grizzly yarn was added to the repertoire!

About 2:00 am on a miserable rainy night, I was poking around town thinking of heading home for a nightcap, when the call came in—accident on the east highway, near the airfield. Police were on the scene, ambulance was on the way. I turned on the red revolving light and went east, rain pounding on the windshield.

When I arrived at the scene I saw that a southbound car had swerved across the road and crashed into an island at the base of a highway sign. For a period in the 1960s, the park used to anchor road signs in islands of earth mixed with rock, surrounded by a rock wall. Those islands were thought to be in keeping with the surroundings, but for some reason they drew vehicles like a magnet. Inattentive or intoxicated drivers seemed inevitably to gravitate toward these stone piles. Eventually recognizing the problem, the National Parks Service removed the islands but in the meantime two more people had come to grief in their car.

When I got there, I found a few vehicles, including the police cruiser, parked on the shoulder of the highway. The Mountie was on the pavement, directing traffic and half a dozen other people were running around on the road, not really doing anything. It was pitch black, and raining hard; I climbed down into the ditch to examine the car. Here I found a young male person, seemingly unconscious, pinned behind the wheel. The man's face had been badly cut by glass from the shattered windshield and the amount of blood splattered around was impressive, although not necessarily an indicator of serious danger to the victim. What was alarming, however, was the manner in which the man would, every few minutes, struggle violently to free himself from behind the broken wheel buried deep below his ribcage. I suspected internal injury, a thing I had learned to dread. Each time the victim fought, he would be making the problem worse. The door on the driver's side was crumpled shut, the one on the passenger side could be opened.

I scrambled back up to the road and was told by someone that the Jaws of Life were on the way. Then, I became aware of what appeared to be a figure lying under a sodden grey blanket in the ditch, some distance behind the car. I pointed to this object and thought I heard the policeman say, "There's nothing you can do for her." Obviously then, the immediate concern was with the guy in the car.

Moving past the other people on the road, I was surprised to discover at least two park staff, whom I knew to have had first-aid training. "Why aren't they doing something to help the injured," I wondered. "What's the matter with them anyway?" The answer, as I realized later, was that training, particularly the antiseptic type of first-aid taught at that time, did not necessarily make a competent first-aider. Putting a clean bandage on a clean, well behaved person in the basement of the town hall, is vastly different from climbing into a pile of twisted metal and shattered glass, on a dark night, and laying hands on a bloody, vomit-smelling stranger. At the moment, however, I was concerned and irritated and I wasted no diplomacy on hauling one of these persons into the ditch and over to the wreck.

Here we found the injured man once again struggling behind the wheel. His face was white and sick-looking and shiny with sweat. I got quickly into the passenger side and placed myself carefully beside the driver. I then put my left arm around the victim's shoulders and held him strongly, at the same time grasping the man's right wrist with my own right hand. In doing so, I was exerting control, and in such a way that I could also monitor the pulse. It was shallow, feeble and rapid. On the chance that the fellow could hear me, I spoke words of comfort and reassurance. After a few moments the struggles subsided, but the man moaned quietly and from deep within. I carefully disengaged myself and made the reluctant first-aider take my place. After showing him how to take the same position, and how to monitor the pulse and breathing, I went back up on the road. "Do you good to get a bit of that blood on you," I thought savagely.

Free for the moment to think of other things, I remembered "Jungle Jim." "Jungle Jim" Atkinson had been a park superintendent who had informed me, on one occasion, that in his view, the most important attribute for a warden was curiosity. The longer I was in the Parks Service, the more I had to agree with that observation. Now I shone my flashlight along the ditch until it found the grey blanket. What the hell was under there that no one seemed to want anything to do with it? I decided I'd better find out.

I had peered beneath enough soggy blankets in other various places that it took a great deal any more to surprise me. Expecting the worst, I gingerly raised one corner and was startled to find a white face and two, enormous wide-open eyes. The terrified eyes belonged to a young girl and although in shock, she was perfectly capable of hearing what went on around her, probably even to having heard the remarks of the policeman. Furthermore, when I examined her, it appeared that her only injury was a broken upper arm.

My irritation increased. Leaving a victim like this unattended, in a dark, rain-soaked ditch, did not fit with my idea of patient care. I gently stabilized the injured arm, talking to her all the while. Then, I got the other first-aider to come sit with her. Moments later the ambulance and the Jaws of Life arrived and my part was done. Driving slowly home, I tipped my Stetson, one more time, to old "Jungle Jim" and his emphasis on curiosity.

At 7:00 am, the next morning—a Sunday, I was about to sit down to my bacon and eggs when the telephone rang. It was the switchboard advising me that a deer was impaled on a picket fence at 125 Street. These calls were bad news no matter which way you chose to handle them. If I went ahead and had my breakfast, the meal was ruined in any case by the anticipation of what lay ahead. On the other hand, if I removed the deer first, chances were I wouldn't want breakfast anyway. Sadly I pushed the plate away, finished my juice and put on my old coveralls. Making sure I had gloves, a piece of rope and my rifle, I drove into town.

In spite of the unpleasant task ahead I couldn't help but notice it was a beautiful summer morning. The rain from the night before had left a sparkle of droplets on every tree and bush; the Athabasca River rolled majestically down the valley, the sun glistening on its mighty bosom.

From force of habit, I took the bypass route in order to check out the Hippie Campground. The place looked quite peaceful and serene, most of the citizens having been up until 3:00 am and now sleeping it off. As I drove along watching for untended fires and new evidence of litter, a girl poked her head out of one of the tents. When she stepped forth a minute later, it could be seen that she was a tall girl with long brown hair, wearing a granny gown. After a brief glance around, she proceeded up the path to the little lake on the west side of the campground. Here, without the slightest concern, she dropped the gown and raising both arms high above her head, turned and stretched luxuriously, her breasts saluting the morning sun. She stayed there for nearly a minute, head back, eyes closed, dark hair hanging to her waist. Then with a sudden change of mood she relaxed, turned and ran splashing into the pool. Seconds later, she was out again, brushing the drops vigorously from her body and wringing water from her tresses.

The tent village was slowly coming alive now, but the girl went on with her morning toilette, as if she were the only person around for a hundred miles. Selecting a fallen tree in the sun, she sat down and propped a small mirror up beside her. There, completely at ease in her birthday suit, she combed her hair as the smoke rose from various breakfast fires.

The only one in the whole place who paid her any attention was a whiskey jack who sailed in and parked on the log beside her. Cocking an admiring eye, the little scavenger murmured sweet seductive nothings at the damsel, while his ever-present partner kept a lookout from a nearby tree.

Reflecting on the various unsavoury characters who lived in that campground, I again wondered how such truly beautiful girls could be attracted to such a grungy bunch of guys. However, a dead or dying deer awaited my ministrations. I drove on down the bypass and turned left at the intersection east of town.

The deer was already quite dead when I found it. It had become im-paled on the spikes of an ornamental iron grill fence, sometime during the night. A nice little female, she presented an obscene and gruesome sight. Her head and shoulders hung down one side of the fence, nearly on the ground, big eyes glazed milk-white in death. On the other side, her hind quarters were in the air. In her fatal struggle two of the spikes had torn into the abdominal cavity, and bowels and blood had spilled down the fence and were stiffening in the sun.

I looked around at the house and the neighbouring yards. There was no one to be seen, and although I sensed the eyes behind drawn window shades, no kind person came forth to help or even offer sympathy for the poor dead thing. After all, what was one more dead deer? Just nuisances anyway!

Putting on my gloves, I took a deep breath and grasped the animal around the hind legs. A swarm of blue bottles rose in my face. During the struggle to free the deer from the spikes, the smell of blood and bowels assailed my nostrils. In the end, as I lifted the deer, I was fighting not to throw up. Finally the body came up and as I dropped it to the ground, I turned quickly and tried very hard not to be sick. After awhile I put the rope around the dainty hind feet and pulled the poor remains into the back of the truck. As usual, once upside down, the body regurgitated a mess of half-digested grass and browse—over the tailgate.

I drew off my gloves and threw them in the back of the pick-up. Then I removed my Stetson hat and wiped the sweat from the band. Settling the hat firmly on my head, I slowly turned and looked hard at the house and at the house on either side. All the bitterness I felt towards the people who put up iron fences in deer country was to be seen upon my face, all the contempt for other people who let their dogs run loose in park towns to chase the deer into the picket fences. Then I climbed into the green truck, slammed the door and drove away. In my diary and under the heading of Wildlife Observation for that day, I would later write: "One nude hippie, female, enjoying the morning sun. One mule deer, female, died on picket fence."

Part Three

*Strange, remarkable and
sometimes haunting stories
of search and rescue.*

Snow Angel

He came to Banff by bus on a Saturday morning, a young man with a pair of cross-country skis and a rucksack, and an ill-defined plan to explore the west side of Sulphur Mountain. An attempt to get a companion to come with him had been unsuccessful and he left no travel plan with anyone and did not register out for the trip. When he disappeared into the timber some time before noon he went alone and unnoticed.

The first few hours of the trip went fairly well, although he was somewhat dismayed that his narrow skis did not perform as well as he had hoped in the deep, unbroken snow. When he stopped for a sandwich, the sun gave an illusion of warmth and a couple of Canada Jays, that had been covertly trailing him all morning, settled in a pine tree over his head and chattered away in a friendly fashion. Their presence lent a feeling of companionship, even though he suspected that they were more interested in his lunch than his welfare.

Towards mid-afternoon, however, the aspect of the day began to change. Hazy clouds obscured the sun and the cold grew more noticeable. The travelling remained heavy and, to make matters worse, his feet were slipping sideways in the ski bindings. When it became obvious that there was no hope of any sort of a nice run and all that remained was hard work, he decided to turn back. Even so, he might have been all right had not an overstrained harness chosen that moment to break, throwing him down and twisting an ankle.

An experienced mountaineer carries a repair kit for such emergencies in his pack, but this skier was not in this category. Nevertheless he spent valuable minutes trying in vain to fix the binding before starting off on foot, carrying the skis. He had lost track of time while trying to make repairs and now was alarmed at how quickly darkness was setting in. Taking a spare bootlace, he tried to tie the damaged ski to his boot but all he succeeded in doing was again sprawling in the snow. Furthermore, it was now so dark that he was having trouble staying on his own backtrail and the ankle was throbbing painfully. Unable to travel further, he crawled into the hollow space beneath a large old spruce and broke off a few dry limbs to make a fire, but he was shivering uncontrollably with cold and fright and his paper matches were useless, and soon squandered. After trying to coax a drink out of a bottle of frozen fruit juice from his pack, he managed to strip a few green boughs of the same tree to keep himself off the frozen ground and prepared to sit out the dark hours.

That merciless night beneath the distant stars must have seemed endless to the stranded skier. At first he forced himself to get up and exercise vigorously, but around midnight he fell into an exhausted sleep. With no blankets and no bivouac bag, the deadly cold crept into his body.

The skier, at dawn on the Sunday morning, his hands, feet and face badly frozen, had staggered off. His tracks now veered east, bringing him to a trail which follows the foot of the mountain and of which he seemed previously unaware. He was in fact backtracking, parallel to his own previous route. Still alternating between trying to ski and walking, he made little progress and was soon exhausted. Sitting on a log during one of many rest stops, he was gripped by despair when he realized that his last stopping place was still in sight.

By afternoon he was crawling through the snow on hands and knees; towards sunset he twice fell into a small stream. This seems to have pretty well finished him. In the last hour that he was capable of movement he crawled into a small group of trees. Here, he managed to get to his feet and break off a number of dry under-branches from the spruce, either to make a shelter or a bed. The branches were simply scattered around, however, and in the end he went on through the trees and lay down on the far side, on his back on top of the snow.

On Monday morning, a concerned employer phoned the park office and soon the Warden Service received word of a presumed missing person.

Someone remembered that the man had mentioned going to Banff on the weekend to do some skiing and that was pretty well the extent of available information. Nevertheless, the rescue warden on duty decided to do a reconnaissance, by helicopter, of the townsite vicinity.

The first indication that he might be onto something occurred while searching the area along the foot on the west side of Sulphur Mountain. Here, in a chain of small open spaces, the warden and his pilot began to see marks in the snow, which they at first attributed to the movement of animals. A little further on, however, they were able to identify the marks as ski tracks, odd, disconnected, wandering tracks, which for some reason failed to appear in another opening about a mile away. It was now nearly four in the afternoon. The rescue warden asked to be set down in this meadow, and on foot walked back toward the last seen tracks.

Before very long he picked up a ski trail which led to a bed of boughs near the foot of a spruce tree. It had the appearance of having been an overnight camp but a very poor one and obviously unplanned. There was no evidence of a campfire or shelter of any kind. Lying in the hollow was a plastic juice bottle. He was in fact looking at the place where the unfortunate skier spent Saturday night, out in -35 to -40°F. weather. Not very far away, possibly four to five miles, other skiers had been relaxing in their favourite bars or tucked in beside cheery fireplaces in Banff's many fine hotels.

Airborne again, the warden was now following the tracks made by the skier on the second day of his ordeal, when he was trying to return to the trailhead. With the light fading rapidly, the warden flew back to town. He radioed ahead for help, with the result that four more rescuers were soon geared up and ready to be lifted to the site. These searchers were dropped off at strategic intervals along the area in question.

Now a new and unexpected player threatened to complicate what was already a difficult task. On their return flight, the rescue warden and pilot were astounded to see fresh ski tracks across the last open meadow, where previously there had been none. After nearly four days, in critical weather, was this man still moving? Back on the ground, the warden hurried along this new track, and soon caught up with what turned out to be a different skier. Although it was nearly dark, and they were three to four miles from the road, this one seemed unconcerned. After explaining that a search was underway, the warden took the second pilgrim firmly in tow and picked up tracking where he had previously left off.

It was obvious, as he pursued the missing skier in 12 to 16 inches of cold sugar snow, that the man who made this track had been having difficulties with his skis. The track alternated between walking and skiing. It seemed likely that the skier had lost or broken some part of the bindings on the first day, maybe after dark, making control of the skis difficult. At any rate, he seemed to have had difficulty deciding which means of locomotion was easier.

The warden and his companion now came upon the place where the skier had spent some time sitting on a log and not long after that they found his rucksack containing a frozen sandwich and a sweater, lying on the trail. The warden recognized the signs. First the tracks begin to wander and the rest stops grow more frequent. Then came the indications of confusion and loss of reason; the discarded gear and clothing meant that not much time remained if they were to make a live recovery. It was the story of the last days of a person's life—written in the snow.

Soon the trail veered again, back towards the track made on Saturday. Now the warden and his companion found the man's skis, discarded in the snow and from there on the poor fellow had been literally crawling. This then explained the odd drag marks in the snow, first seen from the helicopter.

By this time, the park wardens on the ground were converging on the skier's final location, the senior man working down the valley and the others up. In touch by radio, they were aware that the space between them was shrinking and all were hoping for the smell of campfire or some other sign that the ending might prove to be a happy one. It was a faint hope.

The plight of the skier had obviously gone from very bad on Sunday morning to disastrous by that evening. The final touch occurred sometime late in the day when he twice fell into a small stream while in his crawling phase. About 7:30 pm, in pitch dark, one of the wardens at the north end of the search area spoke quietly into his radio, "We've got him."

The wardens' faces and parka hoods were rimed with frost, their breaths formed misty clouds in the icy cold, the light of their headlamps showed a sad, strange sight—a young man lying on his back—arms out at the side. His spectacles, covered by a fine powder of frost, gave the face an eerie, sightless look. In what may have been one last attempt to stay alive or motivated perhaps by a childhood memory, the skier had moved his arms and legs in his final moments. Someone in the group observed softly, "Look, he made a snow angel!"

It can hardly have escaped the other lone skier that, but for the grace of God and a chance encounter, there lay he.

The Obsession

As the full moon rose over the east gate of Jasper National Park, its light first touched the mountain peaks, then slid to timberline where it glinted in the red eye of a pika, blinking sleepily in its burrow. Moving lower the moonbeams filtered through sweet-scented pines throwing dappled shadows on the already dappled back of the fawn sleeping at its mother's side.

Spring had come early to the Athabasca Valley that year and by Easter many of the lower slopes were bare of snow. Now the moonlight gleamed on the breast of the mighty river, already swelling with meltwater, sparkling and dancing as it pushed back the burden of winter ice. And yet, in all this valley of mystery and magic, one mountain rose dark and sinister—sullen in its visage.

Roche-a-Perdrix is not an attractive mountain. It stands to the south of the Jasper Park entrance gatehouse, with a steep face to the east and cliff bands to the west. It is not particularly high, about 7000 feet, nor is it very hard to climb, although at one point you are on a ledge which hangs outward and the feeling of exposure is considerable. Under most conditions, the mountain looks uninviting and inhospitable.

A few miles away, in a small town, the same moon made weird shadows in the room where a man lay sleeping, but the shadows at play in his mind were stranger by far. I'll call him John Doe. His father had died in a plane crash somewhere in South America the previous year, the same year John F. Kennedy was slain and for some reason the ghosts of both their departed souls came to haunt John. His nights, in particular, grew increasingly troubled and he began having mysterious dreams in which he saw his father and President Kennedy on top of the mountain.

Each morning when he awoke, he knew he had to climb the mountain and he would phone the warden for a permit. The warden would stall and ask him difficult questions. John would spend the day brooding and frustrated. But this morning was different. In the hour before dawn, when the image of his father was still clear and sharp in his mind, a plan had come to him and he knew how he was going to fool this official who thwarted him. For the first time in many days, he met his co-workers at the pulp mill with a smile and a pleasant word of greeting.

For the district warden, the phone calls started the week before Easter. The caller was a male person from Hinton who wanted to register out for a climb on Roche-a-Perdrix, but admitted to having neither the necessary equipment, nor any experience. Although park regulations did not allow a warden to refuse such a request, he was uneasy with it, and did his best to stall the John, hoping he would change his mind. Rather than give up, however, the calls kept on coming and the warden was puzzled by what seemed to him a persistence bordering on paranoia.

Finally, on the evening before Good Friday, it appeared that John had obtained the services of a reputable guide to outfit him and take him up Roche-a-Perdrix. Knowing that he could not in any case continue to refuse, the warden agreed to sign a registration for them. As they were leaving very early in the morning, the warden agreed to leave the book at the front door so they need not awaken him.

Good Friday dawned clear and bright, a beautiful spring day. The lifts swung into action at the Marmot Basin ski hill and what promised to be a great Easter weekend got underway. I was on patrol between the town and the ski hill, and a number of other park wardens were in the area.

By midmorning, however, an ominous change began to take place in the weather. The wind began to blow from the north and cold dark clouds moved into the east end of the park. By eleven, when the warden climbed into his green pick-up and drove to the east gateway, the sun was gone and snow was falling heavily. He noted the little red car parked a mile east of the gatehouse and looked at Roche-a-Perdrix disappearing in the gloom. With a sense of impending trouble, he called me on the radio to be prepared.

For the gatehouse attendants, the drama began at a few minutes before noon, that same day, when they heard faint scratching at the rear entrance. Looking out, they were unable to see anyone. When they cautiously opened the door, suspecting perhaps a small animal, they were shocked to see a young woman lying in the snow. Only lightly clothed to begin with, her garments were ripped and torn and her flesh bore multiple lacerations and bruises. With her bleeding frozen hands pressed to her face, all she could say, as they carried her inside, was "He's gone. He's on the mountain. He's gone."

Already alerted to the fact that a search party might be required, we were quickly organized. Within 20 minutes of being notified, an advance group was on their way from town. The normal route up Roche-a-Perdrix is to follow a long ridge running up the north approach to the mountain. After about an hour, you are above timberline and just getting into the chimney. After awhile this brings you out on the exposed rock. One group of park wardens went up this route, where they eventually found indications that two people appeared to have reached a point just below the approach to the chimney.

Meanwhile, Warden Alf Burstrom and I were retracing the trail of the injured girl. On her track, which was simply a drag mark of her body in the snow, we found small fragments of flesh where she had pulled herself over rocks and deadfall. There were round bedding indents in the snow, where she had curled up to rest along the way like a wounded little animal. The trail took us eventually to a point below and slightly north of the base of the chimney. Above were a couple of cliff bands lying below the bottom of the chimney. The snow was now nearly a foot deep, visibility was poor, and terrain, which normally would have presented no problem, was becoming decidedly tricky. Alf and I actually passed within 100 yards of where the body lay, below one of the cliffs and covered in snow, but we were unaware.

Suddenly the Mounties were on the radio. They had been down to Hinton doing some research on the missing man and their findings were unsettling to say the least. It seemed he was a manic paranoid, had a record of increasingly violent behaviour including the use of firearms and he hated anyone in uniform. The sergeant sounded quite excited; the missing climber could conceivably be watching through the sights of his rifle as the searchers approached! This added a new twist to what was already a bizarre case. Needless to say we soon divested ourselves of our bright-orange, Gore-Tex parkas, preferring to brave the cold rather than present an easily seen target!

Alf and I joined the other search party at the lower portion of the chimney at about four o'clock. It was eerily dark and for the little group of wardens, who were now gathered peering up that outward sloping chimney, it was like looking into Hades. The mountain was completely socked in and heavy snow fell on a driving northeast wind. There was a strange moaning sound that sent shivers up our backs as we contemplated conditions on the open wall, high above. The larger group had already been some way up the chimney. They came back with the news that to try to ascend further would be suicidal. Mercifully, the chief warden sent word that we were to come down and call off the search for that day.

Next morning the park lay covered under nearly two feet of drifted snow. The travelling was brutal and dangerous at higher elevations. Not a sign of the previous day's activities was visible. By now it was obvious that the story about a professional guide was a hoax. John had fooled us, picked the climbing permit up before anyone was up and taken his wife up the mountain instead. They appeared to have reached the approach to the chimney around the time the storm hit and here for some reason they parted. Scraps of information gleaned from the battered and frightened girl indicated that she sensed at this time that her husband was leading both of them to their death and that in some manner she had eluded or broken away from him, subsequently falling over a ledge on the west side of the cliff.

As for the obsessed climber, there was no clue as to where he had gotten to. He did not appear to be on any of the lower reaches of the mountain, unless he was hiding. He was not in the lower portion of the chimney. That he might have actually scaled the chimney, in the storm, alone without experience or equipment, seemed extremely unlikely, but not absolutely impossible for someone driven as he was. For the next 30 days the searchers were to inch their way over nearly all the north, northeast, and northwest aspects of the mountain—without finding an answer. The top was even reached by helicopter and nothing was found. President Kennedy and Mr. Doe Sr. had, it seems, tired of waiting.

Three days after John's disappearance, another warden and I were back in the area at the base of the chimney, looking for clues. In a short stretch of gully, in deep snow, we uncovered a lunch box and some orange peel. Had the young people paused here, before tackling the chimney? Was this where the wife broke away, started down the ridge, and in haste? Was it possible that while he was violently pursuing her he had slipped over the ledge? If so, how much further did the madman go and where was he? Was he even on the mountain or had he watched his wife disappear over the ledge? Then in fear and remorse and confusion, did he run down the east side of the ridge and catch a ride out of the country?

During the first week of the search, another bizarre incident occurred. A car full of the missing man's relatives arrived, pushed into the room where the wife was still recuperating in the hospital and accused her of murdering him on the mountain! So violent and threatening was their manner that the authorities felt she was in danger, so she was secretly transferred to a different hospital to complete her convalescence.

On another day, with the snow slowly receding, two wardens and a policeman were searching a high basin east of the chimney, when a rock the size of a large teakettle came ricocheting down upon them. The instinct at such a time is to get as close to the cliff as possible, close your eyes tightly, and pray a lot. Your chances of survival are, however, a great deal better if you stand straight up and keep your eyes on the rock. The fact is that if it hits you, disaster is almost assured. The hard hat won't help much with a rock of that size and its weight and velocity will knock you from your perch, unless you are tied in. Falling into the end of the rope, perhaps unconscious, you will pull the next man off the mountain and the combined shock of both falling bodies will almost surely dislodge the man on belay. Away go all three of you! With only a few inches each way to manoeuvre, each man in turn kept his eye on the juggernaut and managed to dodge it as it thundered by. Again, close calls on high walls.

One month after the search began, the mountain was once more dry. We were finally able to move around on it with freedom. On the first of May, the Annual Regional Spring Training School for Park Wardens was convened at the park's Palisade Training Centre, and it was decided to give the entire group a day of climbing and searching experience on Mount Roche-a-Perdrix. Failure to find the missing man on this day would mean the official end to the search. No further clues had been discovered; no birds were seen circling at any time.

The assistant chief warden was in charge of the operation. Three groups of wardens accompanied by a sergeant from the Royal Canadian Mounted Police set out to comb the various aspects of the mountain for the last time. Between two and three in the afternoon, the wardens, working in the cliff bands below the chimney on the west side, spotted the dead climber. He was dressed as a labourer might dress for a stroll downtown. One leather workboot was missing, as was the back of his head. The demented brain, splattered on the ledge above, had long since dried in the spring sun. Various bones were broken, and in spite of a very dark tan, he was a most unappealing sight. On this hot spring day, after a month under the snow, the smell was horrendous. No bird or animal had touched him.

The consensus was that, in the gathering storm, after his wife's escape, he had gone part way into the chimney and then, for some reason, worked his way around to the exposed west side. There, he soon lost his footing on the snow-covered scree and tumbled over several cliff bands. He probably died within an hour of the time that his wife left him.

Last Seen Point

There is an expression in search and rescue terminology that refers to the point at which a missing person was observed for the last time. It is "last seen point." Most commonly used to describe the place at which a set of ski tracks enter the upper portion of an avalanche path, the term can also refer to such places as a rocky outcrop overlooking wild water or the campsite from which a child has strayed. Strictly speaking, the missing person is not always seen at this point, but it represents the last tangible evidence of the existence of a live person at a certain place on earth. From this point on, the missing one may have entered a shadowy world beneath the snow, secret caverns in dark canyons or simply moon-dappled pine forests with no beginning and no end.

When park visitors enter this netherworld they may be found alive, dead, or never found at all. When the warden search master arrives at the last seen point, his task is to try to see into the shadows that have swallowed the missing person. The accuracy with which he is able to do this and the speed of his response can save a life.

When the last trace of an avalanche victim is the entry of a ski track at some point of the avalanche path, obviously the person will be somewhere below that point. The surface is quickly searched for visible signs, such as mitts or ski poles. The snow buildups around obstructions in the slide path are quickly probed. As additional help arrives, a formal probe line is formed at the bottom of the avalanche and methodically works its way up. Speed of discovery is essential. Although avalanche victims have been known to survive under the snow for as long (on the average) as four or five hours. However, the chances of a live recovery diminish rapidly after the first 30 minutes.

In the case of a wild river, often in a canyon, the odds against saving a life are even greater, but it is still possible. Searchers are immediately deployed downstream from the last seen point and nets or some other means of retrieval are put in place at a point far enough away to intercept a body, depending on the current and time of the accident. The longer it takes to find a body in a river, the larger the search area becomes, although the person may be trapped in a pool quite close to the last seen point.

Searches for little children are the most rewarding when successful, and the most traumatic for everyone concerned when not. For parents, the worst ones must be those where careless neglect or perhaps harsh discipline causes a youngster to creep away into the woods. Feeling rebellious or unwanted, the child wanders around and soon loses his or her bearings. Often such a one will actually hide from searchers, making discovery even more difficult.

For the searchers it is a time during which every skill is single-mindedly applied to finding the victim. It is intense, exacting, often dangerous work; while there is still hope of finding a live person, rest stops are rare. Sleep must wait. Each new incident is a challenge; the searchers draw on all their training and past experiences in this life-and-death detective work. The very best are those who apply a certain uncanny intuition with dogged determination. "If you haven't found him yet, it's because you haven't looked where he is."

For those who wait at their campsite or by the telephone, it is a time of terrible anxiety. All their hopes rest on the Warden Service. When they bring them back alive, it's great. When they don't, the searchers cannot help but be marked by the grief of those who waited in vain.

For the missing person, the journey from last seen point to point of discovery may be a short and tumultuous trip—a trip that ends with the person (or body) crumpled at the foot of a cliff or tossed wildly to the surface of the river or avalanche. For others it may be a matter of waiting and enduring in some secret place, for hours or days, praying for discovery.

For Faris Evans, his last seen point would have been the edge of a huge crevasse on the Crowfoot Glacier, on a sunny Sunday morning in August 1989, just before the snow bridge collapsed beneath him. But there was no one there to see him; by noon the sun had erased the faint marks of his passing from the ice. His journey into limbo began with a terrible fall that broke his right arm and cracked a number of ribs. Bruised and battered, his time of waiting began.

By evening of that day, he crouched in eerie, semi-darkness in the depth of the crevasse. Craning his head to one side, he could see the tiny hole in the snow bridge, about 30 feet up, through which he had fallen. Another 30 feet or so below the ledge that had arrested his fall, he knew there was water; how much, he wasn't sure.

The protuberance that supported him was in fact less a ledge than a bulge of semi-porous ice formed on the side of the crevasse by meltwater. The lump stuck out about 16 inches and was about 24 inches long. When using this as a seat, another smaller lump somewhat below served as a footrest. It was probably the existence of other similar ice formations, plus the fact that the crevasse descended at an angle, which slowed his fall until he finally hung up in his present resting place.

The man wore summer-weight underwear bottoms and corduroy trousers, underneath nylon-covered rain pants. Above the waist, he had on the underwear top, a T-shirt, a long-sleeved shirt, a fleece jacket and finally a Gore-Tex jacket. He also wore a toque, and had used the plastic bread bags that had housed his camera and first aid kit to try to keep his boots dry. Most of this clothing had been hurriedly donned in the first few minutes after recovering from his fall, standing on one foot on his perch that was pink with blood and his body under a cascade of icy water. Relatively well protected now, he was still cold. In fact cold was to be his constant nemesis in the time to come.

On the pro side, he had in his pack one cold pork chop, one peanut butter and jam sandwich and a chocolate bar. Most wonderful of all, he firmly believed that he would be rescued. Crouched on his tiny ledge, his good arm wrapped around his knees, Faris Evans faced his first night in the netherworld.

Contrary to his expectations, he soon found out that the glacier was not a quiet place. The continuous splat-splat-splat of water drops hitting him or the ice beside him, and the drip-drip-drip of water into water below, echoed from the icy walls. Occasionally, something would hit one of the delicate crystal structures within the crevasse, making a tinkling sound which rapidly built to a crescendo as the structure cascaded down to the water. Periodically, the glacier would crack with a sound like a rifle being fired near his ear, an occurrence which never failed to startle him. Once or twice a day, the entire glacier would move with a great shudder and a very loud "grunk–like" sound. The actual movement was probably minute, but when 50 million tons of ice moved and the whole place quivered for a second or so, it was an awesome feeling.

By Monday morning an intensive search was underway involving two helicopters, ten wardens and a friend of Faris', while in a quiet home in Calgary, an anxious wife waited by the phone.

In the depth of the glacier, hidden beneath the snow bridge, the trapped hiker broke his fast with half the pork chop and half the sandwich. He had rigged his water bottle to catch drinking water from the constant drip in the crevasse. Although not particularly thirsty, he was determined on this second day to make himself drink frequently. After the scant meal he felt somewhat better. He had with him a small whistle, which he now hung around his neck. Throughout the day at regular intervals, Faris would blow three blasts on his whistle.

The search Monday produced no results. Conditions on the glacier were such that Faris' track was hard to follow, a problem made worse by a snowfall that day. And, to further confuse the searchers, several sections of the snow bridge collapsed, with the result that the spot where the unfortunate hiker fell through was not distinguishable as being a man-made hole. Meanwhile, he remained thoroughly hidden, unable to move into a visible area. In fact, one exploratory attempt on Monday afternoon resulted in a thorough soaking, and loss of valuable energy. As Faris faced his second night, he was colder, wetter and less hopeful. And in Calgary, his wife waited.

Tuesday morning arrived after what had been for Faris another sleepless night and for others a very short one. It had also been a very uncomfortable night for the man in the crevasse. Much of his clothing was wet, and he was sitting in ice water. Although not consciously aware of the changes going on within him, it is very likely that loss of sleep was taking its toll as well. On the one occasion, when he did doze off, he snapped awake barely in time to regain his balance before falling into the void below.

Faris ate the remaining pieces of pork chop and sandwich and resumed his routine of trying to stay warm, stay awake, and blow his whistle every few minutes. Even this was becoming increasingly torturous. The cracked ribs on his right side pained terribly with the effort of blowing, particularly on the third blast.

Up above, the search got underway again. Any search and rescue operation, no matter how well organized, is subject to the idiosyncrasies of fate—manifested in many forms—and the weather. The search on Crowfoot Glacier, Tuesday, August 15, held in store a number of ironical twists and one near miracle.

The search area for Tuesday was determined on the strength of a note, which the missing man left at home and that named a peak near the southwest corner of Bow Lake as his destination. It was decided to search the northerly approach to this rock so the wardens were deployed accordingly. As the foot of the glacier appeared also to be an area which Faris might have traversed to reach his goal, two wardens decided to cover it in their search pattern. Their proposed route would in fact have led them to the crevasse in which the victim was trapped, had it not been for unforeseen incidents.

As they proceeded across the ice in a north-northwest direction, another member of the party reported what might have been a set of footprints to their right. It was shortly after they veered off to investigate this report that they heard a very faint whistle. So indistinct was the sound, that the wardens could not be sure of its origin or location. It even occurred to them that it might have been a marmot. In attempting to locate the source, other searchers were located by radio and it was eventually decided that the sound could have originated with Faris' friend who was across the valley. At this time, the wardens were not aware that Faris carried a whistle as well, but the incident was to return forcefully to them later that day.

The second diversion that occurred was just shortly before noon. It arrived in the form of a sinister black cloud that came boiling over the mountains to the west. Beginning with a crack of lightning, the storm soon turned onto a baby blizzard, complete with sleet, blowing snow and whiteout conditions. For Faris, the sudden drop in temperature meant a welcome cessation from the perpetual melt water. But for the search party, the freak snowstorm made for hazardous conditions which disrupted the search pattern. The search leader, mindful for the danger to his group, gathered everyone together until they could be safely re-deployed. The net result of these various incidents was a less conclusive search of the glacier that the wardens might have wished.

Down in the crevasse, Faris whistled and waited but, if this sounds somewhat frivolous, his mood was far from light. He realized that the brief snowstorm would have obliterated any possible indication of his presence. As the day wore on, his thoughts were very much of his family and how they were to manage in the event of his demise. He fretted over whether Judy would locate a share certificate that they owned and wondered if his life insurance would be paid without a body.

Television viewers in southern Alberta, watching the early evening news, could see the leading edge of a new storm moving into Bow Pass. The mountains were darkening visibly and snow was beginning to fall. As the wardens gathered at Bow Summit, preparatory to calling operations off for the day, Faris grimly settled in for the third night in what promised to be his tomb.

Above ground, the search leader gazed at the mountain in frustration, unwilling to admit defeat. Through his mind ran the thought, "If you haven't found the person, it's because you haven't looked yet where he is." He was aware that the events of the day had precluded a thorough and professional examination of the glacier and particularly the crevasses. He decided they should make one more attempt to find the elusive hiker. As a result a tired rescuer climbed into one of the helicopters and instructed the pilot to go once more over the glacier where they proceeded to fly a search pattern of the crevasses.

Suddenly around 6:30 pm, Faris became aware that a helicopter was approaching at a low altitude along the west side of the crevasse. As it came nearer, the down draft from the rotor whipped up the surface debris. Standing up and craning as far as he dared, he saw a blue and white helicopter drift by his line of vision and disappear. It seemed the last hope was gone. It was, in fact, the moment of his salvation.

Thinking he had glimpsed a shadowy figure in the depth of the crevasse, the warden instructed the pilot to return for a second look. Hovering over the ice, he grasped his safety strap and climbed part way out. With one foot on the strut, he leaned out, as far as he was able in order to look into the hidden area beneath the snow bridge, and knew they had their man. In the last few minutes of the last flight, on what might well have been the last day of serious searching, in approaching darkness and blizzard conditions, Faris Evans was found.

With the location of the victim confirmed, plus the obvious fact that he was very much alive, the helicopter raced back to Base Camp to pick up more help and crevasse-rescue gear. Moments later the man in the ice once more witnessed the incomparable sight of the blue and white helicopter hovering in the sky light. Seizing his camera, he took what was to be a remarkable snapshot. The picture shows a dark-green wall of ice on each side and above the place where Evans perched. At the upper centre of the photo is a narrow strip of sky with the nose and front portion of the chopper, just feet above the ice.

Although normally fairly straightforward from here on, the rescue was performed under pressure due to the worsening conditions. In less than five minutes from the time of landing, the rescue team had the anchor in place and a man on his way into the crevasse. Faris, making up his pack, looked up to see the warden in safety harness peering down at him. "Are you Faris?" he was asked, and gripped by the irrational fear that a negative response might leave him stranded, he urgently shouted "Yes!"

On this day of minor miracles, there was still a revelation in store for the rescuer. The warden did a double take when, fitting Faris into the rescue harness, he noticed the whistle suspended around the man's neck!

Meanwhile, a second helicopter had delivered more wardens to the scene, so that when Faris was hauled over the edge he was to face four or five people, all staring at him with big grins on their faces. The next thing he knew, he was in the helicopter, flying back to the land of the living.

The two senior wardens came within a hairsbreadth of being left on the glacier. The last to be airlifted back, they owed their safe return to an intrepid chopper pilot from Jasper, Tod McCready, who returned for them in what was now a total white-out, and made it back.

As for Faris Evans, he owed his life to his friend, pilot Peter Koster, who flew the spotting helicopter, and to the thoroughness, tenacity, and sixth sense which is the trademark of Canada's finest Search and Rescue Wardens. Although apparently able to maintain a remarkable self-discipline throughout his ordeal, the moment of discovery was for him a time of deep emotion, as it still was, many years later, at the time of this telling.

The Grizzly and the Pontiac

It is very still beneath the pines, where the battered old blue Pontiac hangs upside down in a welter of skinned and broken trees, still and gloomy in the half-light of an early winter morning. On the lower side of the wreck, the driver's door hangs open nearly touching the ground; shattered glass and debris litter the snow. Cigarette butts, an empty Coke bottle, a potato chip bag and a dirty sock, a greasy rag and a deodorizer in the form of a naked girl lie scattered about. Standing there quietly, wondering where the body is, I hear the sound of something dripping.

When I was at Poboktan Creek, it was always my habit to patrol the highway during or right after a snowstorm. This was when you found the people—worried and scared—in the ditches, stuck or with their cars frozen up. Assisting these unfortunates was one of the more worthwhile aspects of the job. It was also after a storm that fresh game tracks were to be found and studying tracks was one of my abiding interests. On this particular morning, noting that it had snowed nearly eight inches overnight, I went out early and travelled north from the station.

Just before reaching the Sunwapta Teahouse, the tracks of a south-bound vehicle could be seen leaving the road on the downhill side. There were no skid marks. It seemed the driver might have dozed off or else missed the road in the storm. I stepped out of the Parks' green 4 x 4 truck, walked to the edge of the embankment and peered carefully over the side. You never knew what to expect. Every incident produced a new surprise, seldom pleasant. Directly below me was a steep slope and beyond that a thick stand of lodgepole pine. Early morning gloom still pervaded the forest, so that I had to peer into the shadows. It was very quiet: the nearby river muted by early ice, no wind, no traffic, the bungalow camp deserted. The pines were silent, in pristine white and there, making that ominous dripping sound, hung the Pontiac.

Sometimes it is gasoline, sometimes blood; this time it was antifreeze from the crumpled radiator. I am very tense; so far I have not found a body. Very few people walk away from an accident like this. But there is no body, no corpse with disarranged limbs stiffening in the cold. Now, watching the green stain spreading in the snow, I realize there is blood there, too. Blood and scuff marks, like a body falling and struggling below the car. The light is still very poor and the fact that I can't see any tracks leading away makes it even spookier. I half expect something to rise up out of the snow all of a sudden, or flop down out of a tree. I decide to go through the glove compartment.

There is a registration, a bill of sale and an insurance policy for the Pontiac, also a termination cheque stub from a local construction company. There is a dunner from a store in Edson, about the matter of a stereo set for which payments were overdue, and a lipstick with a cap missing. Finally there's a grimy package of Vogue cigarette papers. Under the picture of the blonde lady with swept-back hair was a thumb print, and on the front inside cover were the words in ball point pen: "Rosanne, Calgary, 238-4756."

So it appears that I am looking for a lone male person—construction worker: a person of untidy habits, judging by the interior of the car, a smoker, but not necessarily a drinker. The man was travelling south when he left the road and crashed into the trees. I have his name and a contact person in Calgary. But where has he gone in the middle of a stormy night—with injuries?

I'm on my second trip around the car when I discover the grizzly's tracks. The light is improving and the deep claw marks are unmistakable. The bear appears to have arrived after the accident and, upon circling the wreck, may have come upon the victim where he stood dazed and bleeding in the snow. From here, the bear's tracks go around the front of the car and disappear downhill, going toward the river. Has the bear carried the man off? There are no drag marks but the strength of a grizzly is such that it could have picked up its victim bodily. This is a very scary idea. It crosses my mind that I should give the chief warden a call on the radio, but I can already hear his response and the idea of my tracking, alone, a man-toting grizzly in heavy timber, does not appeal to me at all.

And then I see it—some distance behind the car, in an area which was deep in shadow when I first arrived but now lit by a ray of sunshine, there is a man's track angling up towards the road. Going back to the highway and walking north, I find where he crawled up the bank and stood for awhile, waited for a ride. The bear must have arrived after he had already left the Pontiac. It could have been a worse ending—for both of us.

Part Four

*Moving east; Pukaskwa
and tales from the haunted
North Shore of Lake Superior;
aerial adventure.*

A Cowboy on Lake Superior

By the spring of 1971, we had three boys in school and a newly adopted baby daughter. The black Labrador dog that had been Glennys' companion on the Rocky River was gone, the victim of an encounter with a porcupine which resulted in the dog having to be destroyed. In its place we now had a marvellous little terrier, Sharlow, that could think of more entertaining things to do in one day than any other six dogs or people. Slip, the old grey horse, was in semi-retirement, in care of the park warden at Athabasca Falls. The boys were all becoming expert skiers and competing in junior events, Glennys was much taken up with the baby, but I was becoming restive. There were beautiful and exciting national parks all across the country and I longed to see more of them. I also had a natural and understandable desire for advancement, but deep down, and most compelling of all, was a hunger for adventure.

After a number of unsuccessful attempts at chief park warden positions in other parks, I applied for such a position in Georgian Bay Islands National Park. This time at least, I was invited for an interview at the Ontario Regional Office in Cornwall. Two weeks later the letter came, in the usual sinister brown envelope, and as per usual it started off, "Dear Mr. Schintz, we regret to inform you…" I said a succinct expletive and threw the letter in the waste paper can.

Had I taken the time to read on, I would have found that I had placed second in the competition and thus stood at the head of an eligible list for Ontario for the remainder of the year. And so it was quite out of the blue when, on a sunny October morning three months later, the telephone rang and the Assistant Director of Operations, Ontario Region, asked me if I would like to be the first Chief Park Warden of Pukaskwa National Park.

I stammered that I would love to be the Chief Park Warden of Pukaskwa, but where was it and why was I being asked? The location of the park and my own eligibility having been explained to me, I went home for lunch, where Glennys was bringing in the last of the garden vegetables for the year. That afternoon, our decision to accept was relayed to Ontario.

There were the usual arrangements to make for removal to another province and region, all of which was new to us for our biggest move up to that point had been from the Rocky River to Poboktan Creek. There were also many good-byes to be said within and without Jasper National Park. I had been working closely with St. John Ambulance and Alberta Disaster Services, both of which had offices in Edmonton, and had good friends in both places. Ross Henry, the big, jovial man who headed up St. John at the time, actually took us all to the Edmonton Airport and saw us off on our journey—in a most cordial and reassuring fashion. Meanwhile, there was the big going-away party to get through. The original plan had been for a skating party on one of the lakes around Jasper, with hot wine to counteract the November chill. At the last moment, however, after all the wine was ordered, the venue was moved to the Palisades Training Centre. Neither Glennys nor I cared very much for wine, hot or cold, so I drank in moderation during the early part of the evening. Even so, between the wine, the heat of the building, and the nervousness associated with being the central figure of the evening, my head was buzzing and my stomach was churning by the time I was called onto the floor for the formal part of the proceedings.

This was the time I had been dreading. In an agony of self-consciousness, I had to stand before the assemblage while jokes and stories and kind speeches were made about me. Glennys, once we received our farewell gifts together, was able to relax in the audience and enjoy herself. After mumbling some inanities in response, I recovered my wits sufficiently to see that I was being presented with the standard, RCMP pewter drinking mug, normally reserved for departing members of that force. To my knowledge, it was the first time that such an honour had been bestowed on other than a Mountie. I was deeply touched.

While I was stammering my thanks, however, I recalled the little ceremony that goes along with the mug. At policeman parties, it is filled with a deadly mixture of undiluted whiskey, gin, rum, and vodka. After a night of good fellowship and hearty drinking, during which the departing member may be excused for perhaps indulging somewhat heavily, he suddenly has to stand before his colleagues and chug-a-lug this lethal dose. Failure meant that the remains in the mug were poured over his head. I had been to enough Mountie parties to know how devastating the effect could be. I had witnessed more than one big hefty constable head for the bathroom, pale and sweaty after the ordeal.

With dread I peered into the proffered mug. Somewhat to my relief it appeared to contain nothing more powerful than wine, but even so, I was not quite up to the task. About two-thirds of the way through the mug's contents, although I was struggling manfully, my stomach threatened to rebel and I had to stand, defeated, while the remainder was poured over me—warm wine joined the cold sweat trickling off my forehead.

The next day was cold and grey, and everyone was pretty much absorbed in their own affairs. Once the going away party is over, it behooves those departing to leave as expeditiously as possible. They are officially gone as far as everyone is concerned and it is disconcerting to have former friends and colleagues look up and, finding you still there, gaze at you with a slightly puzzled look, as if already having difficulty remembering the name.

So, move expeditiously we did, and in no time found ourselves at the Edmonton Airport, checking in our luggage. A wire cage had been rented for the little dog Sharlow and he was placed on the conveyor belt amongst all the other bundles heading for the baggage area. As we all watched him heading for the curtain, we were tickled to see the terrier standing stoutly upright, nose straight ahead and ears alert. Although his heart was going pitty-pat and his eyes were as big as saucers, the little fellow had his tail sticking bravely up between the bars like a flagpole. Whatever fate held in store, he was obviously determined to take it like a trooper! Any second thoughts or qualms about leaving at this point were quietened, our spirits bolstered by our pet's example.

Very few Canadian landscapes are terribly attractive in late November, and the North Shore of Lake Superior is no exception. It is Canadian

Shield country, an ancient and rocky landscape, awesome and forbidding. Stripped by autumn winds of birch leaf and blueberry, the cold granite hills surround bays and inlets stilled by winter ice. In between the hills, connected by meandering waterways, are hundreds of small lakes, their frozen surfaces ringed by stark, black spruce. Even the dark rivers that tumble impetuously into the great lake in the summer are muffled and subdued; there is a forlorn sense of solitude, and dread of winter, in a land where temperatures are alleged to have reached minus 70°F. Although used to the unforgiving Rockies, we felt here the presence of a much more implacable and harsh environment. It was a relief to make the odd pit stop in a tiny village along the way, hold a warm cup of coffee and see a few cheerful faces around about, before starting off again on the lonely, winding, snowy road.

An early winter dusk was already creeping up from the east when we turned off Highway 17 and drove into Marathon, on that dark November afternoon. We saw that the town sat on the east side of a harbour which had ice forming around the shores. At the left-hand side of the harbour mouth, beyond which lay a glimpse of the great lake, stood a hill, higher than most in that part of the country. On the top of the hill could be seen various structures which might have been radio antennae or weather recording devices. At the foot of this hill, dominating the entire scene was a pulp mill, its huge smokestack pouring out a thick column of whitish grey gaseous effluent which drifted east across the village.

In the days and months to come, we would grow used to the sour, throat-catching smell, and the fine-grey ash which, mixed with frost and frozen rain, covered our vehicles like a coat of armour every winter morning. Also very prominent, on the shore below the town, were two huge stacks of pulp logs like inverted cones. And overall—the rocky hills mostly denuded of trees, the big hill behind the plant, the village itself, with little rows of company houses and small garden patches—lay a blanket of snow, grey, sooty and depressing.

Peninsula, or Peninsula Harbour as it was first known, may have been visited by a white man as early as 1618, when one of Champlain's men, an intrepid explorer named Etienne Brulé, was believed to have visited the Grand Lac. By 1670, the harbour was clearly shown on a Jesuit map based on the circumnavigation of Lake Superior by Father Claude Allouez, three years earlier. The first actual settlement of any size did not occur until 1884, when Peninsula became an important link in the building of the Canadian Pacific Railroad.

If we could peel back all the mists which have rolled in from Lake Superior since that time, one hundred years of shrouding fog, driving rains and drifting snows, then reach down to part and push aside the final layer, we might see illuminated, as in a ray of sunshine, a lusty, bustling town of sorts sprawled along the bay shore. It was a town of shacks, tents, and clapboard houses inhabited by railroad labourers, teamsters and whiskey traders. It is said that at one time 12,000 men and 5,000 horses worked out of Peninsula. Then, with the driving of the last spike, as suddenly as they had come, they were gone. Before our astonished eyes the mist rolls in again, the light fades, and the town vanishes. The clang of hammer and pick and shovel die away; silence returns to the North Shore. The only difference is, that now in addition to the howl of the wolf, the eerie whistle of a locomotive can be heard occasionally among the empty lakes and granite balds.

For the next 50 years or so, not much changed at Peninsula. Only a station house, section houses, a few outbuildings and a small store were needed to accommodate the little community, which in 1935 amounted to 28 souls. A few prospectors and fishermen roamed the area; Indians trapped and harvested blueberries to be shipped out on the railway. Some artists, among them Canada's Group of Seven, tried to capture on canvas the rugged grandeur of the North Shore. The green summers came and went; the big lake smiled or growled as her moods dictated; the great blue irises nodded and dreamed by the sloughs, deep within the silent forests.

Then came the loggers, the end of the country as it had been and the beginnings of the town as it is today. In 1936, the Marathon Paper Mills Company of Wisconsin, through its subsidiary the General Timber Company, acquired the cutting rights in the area and, in 1937, these rights were extended on the condition that a pulp mill be constructed on site. Work began in April of 1944 and, by the end of 1946, the mill was finished. Logging camps had been established along the White, Otter and Pic Rivers. The company also built a town, complete with bunkhouses, private homes, a swimming pool and golf courses. Pulp was king in those days and the people who made their living in the shadow of the smokestacks like the serfs of old toiling outside the castle wall looked to the king for sustenance and protection as well as for instructions on how to conduct their daily lives. Marathon, once Peninsula, also briefly named Everest, after D.C. Everest, President of Marathon Paper Mills, was a company town in the truest sense.

By the time of which I write, the feudal grip was somewhat loosened. A highway had been built along the North Shore, various trades people were established and most essential services were available. A large arena and sports complex could be seen near the upper end of the main street and there was a hospital, a fire hall, municipal building and a school. A square, three-storey hotel overlooked the harbour and there were several side streets lined with private homes, not all of which were owned by the company. The little old station sat by the side of the track, quiet and forgotten, a relic of pioneer days, like so many others across this land.

Our first experience of Marathon was the Everest Hotel, named in honour of the town's founder when the Province of Ontario would not allow the town to be named after him. It is also referred to as the Neverest Hotel, because of the incredible racket in the pipes and radiators when the steam from the plant circulated through the building. The rooms, furnished in ancient red plush, were on the stuffy side and smelled strongly of generations of cigarette smoke. But there was a fine dining room with a great and, to us, fascinating view of the harbour. The staff went out of their way to make newcomers welcome.

After everyone was settled in and our troops had been fed, I decided to step outside for a few minutes and have a look around. I was startled to find that the world seemed to be vanishing. Darkness had fallen while we were in the hotel and the hills surrounding the harbour were lost in the gloom. But much more than the onset of night was taking place. The great hill behind the plant was no longer visible, and even the town was rapidly disappearing. All the streets and buildings more than a block from the hotel were lost in heavy mist and even the powerful lights in the mill yard were reduced to an eerie spectral glow. The mist came from the south, driven by the night wind, smelling of the lake. Besides limiting sight, the fog reduced sounds as well. Nothing could be heard from beyond the range of visibility, so that there was a real sense of everything beyond having somehow ceased to be. I had never experienced anything quite like it. I stood with my back to the hotel, making sure it didn't vanish as well, watching the grey shrouds drift past the upper storey and feeling the clammy touch of it on my cheek.

With very little imagination I could put myself in the boots of a railroad navvy in 1884, 500 miles from home, lonely and tired, standing before a soggy, filthy tent. Or, even before that, one of those doughty explorers, camped with the Ojibway guides on that strange and alien shore. The melancholy cry of a wolf somewhere in the darkness was all that would have been needed to complete the illusion. It was a relief to back into the warm, convivial atmosphere of the old hotel, leaving the dark night outside. We went to bed thinking of all we had seen that day; it had certainly been different from anything we were used to. As for myself, I went to sleep wondering just exactly where the new national park was.

The park's superintendent had been at the hotel to greet us when we arrived, and had instructed me to report to the office first thing next morning. As it turned out, the park office was simply another room in the hotel. The arrangements were rudimentary, to say the least. In addition to the usual stuffy room, filled with nicotine-smelling, red-plush chesterfields and chairs, a table had been set up to serve as a desk. On the table were two telephones, one black and one red. The black one was for local calls and the red one was a hot line to the regional office in Cornwall, Ontario, after the fashion of the crisis line connecting Washington to Moscow during the Cold War.

To the right of the table was a large cardboard box, two-thirds full of papers and documents. This was the filing system. Without being told in so many words, I gained the impression that I was free to use the black phone and to explore the filing system, but the red phone was reserved for the commander-in-chief. It was also apparent that the commander-in-chief did not spend any more time than was strictly necessary in the office.

The older man was a restless, garrulous wheeler-dealer. He roamed the country meeting with Provincial Ministry of Natural Resources officials to talk about law enforcement and fire control in the new national park. On other days he visited neighbouring towns and tradesmen to locate lumber, rental vehicles, and all the other goods and services which would eventually be needed to begin park operations.

When he did stalk into the temporary office, it was usually as a result of some emergency requiring special instructions from Cornwall. At such times he would plunk himself down behind the desk, yank his tie off to one side, light up a cigarette and haul out the big cardboard box. Then he would dive in with both arms, searching frantically for some half-remembered letter or policy directive. This very seldom produced any results because as soon as he tried to look into the box his spectacles would slide off the end of his nose and he would become totally frustrated. These sessions usually ended in him grabbing the red phone and dialling Cornwall.

When I was satisfied that I had pretty well mastered the office routine, I drove thoughtfully out of town and east on Highway 17. If one looks at the map of Lake Superior, it will be noted that along the North Shore, midway between Thunder Bay and Sault Ste. Marie, a large peninsula-like piece of land protrudes into the lake. This is Pukaskwa National Park. After driving a few miles, I stopped the car and climbed a tall hill, north of the road. Here I spread out a map of the area and looked to the southeast, in the direction I believed the park to be.

For the second time in two days, I made a strange and somewhat ominous discovery. The fog of the evening before had drifted away as mysteriously as it had moved in. The morning was wonderfully clear and bright, except over the proposed park area. There could be seen a large, dark mass hovering over the promontory which was Pukaskwa. The very fact that it is a sort of peninsula, and therefore subject to fogs which often hang over the lake, explains the phenomenon which I observed that morning. At the time, however, it seemed to convey a deeper significance, something sinister and brooding. The fact that Pukaskwa appeared as number 13, in the then-current list of national parks in the country, only added to my sense of foreboding. The premonition was validated by some of the events to come.

In writing about my experiences at Pukaskwa, I wish to give the reader a sense of the North Shore and the people who inhabit it. But primarily, I want to tell those stories which will portray the park, its mystery, its moody beauty and what it was like to be a park warden or patrolman in the early years of the park's history.

The park administration, based in Marathon, was first in the Everest Hotel and later in the old hospital building. The fledgling staff was quartered in town and their children went to school there; the wives, to whatever degree their natures inclined them, became Marathon wives.

It was a close-knit community, quite isolated in spite of the proximity of Highway 17; the people, many of French descent, were kind-hearted and cheerful. Even though some may have had only a vague understanding of what the national parks were all about, and others probably had mixed feelings as to the desirability of having one next door, they welcomed us and made us feel at home. Glennys gained at least one life-long friend. The boys would return in later years to marry high school sweethearts, work for the mill and raise their families on the North Shore—a telling recommendation for a warm little town in a cold, hard land.

As for myself, in late November, I went to the annual general meeting of the North Shore Minor Hockey League to enrol my youngest son in the local team. In a moment of uncharacteristic weakness I allowed myself to become elected president. And so, a man who had no interest in hockey except to the extent that my boy was involved, a man who never even learned to stand up on skates, found himself embroiled in hockey that first winter. I set up game schedules, drove the team around, filled in for absent coaches, referees and time-keepers, and opened the rink for early practices at 5:00 am on bitter winter mornings. Perhaps worst of all, I settled the incredibly vociferous disputes which continually arose between opposing teams and their volatile managers. I also joined the local fire brigade, as befitted my role as a park warden, but the fires that I attended were mild compared to the heated conflagrations that took place on the ice in that Marathon Arena!

In fairness to the place, it wasn't always storm-whipped, fog-shrouded and depressing. In the spring, the wild rivers broke free of their icy bonds and leapt tumultuously down to the lake. The birch trees came into glorious leaf and, on a special day, the garden truck would arrive on Stevens Avenue. Soon pathways and window boxes glowed with the bright colours of summer. There were picnics and beach parties—of the nice kind, at Penn Lake, and swimming in the big lake for those hardy enough to brave its icy waters. Then in August—the blueberries, for which the region is famous, ripened in the meadows and slashed-over areas. Pleasant, dreamy times were spent filling baskets with those wonderful berries.

The berries provided a sweet memory of summer to be savoured the next winter, when the snows were so deep that motorists in Marathon placed bright orange balls on the tips of their car's antennas, the better to see each other coming at the town's intersections! And of course, the winter brought curling. I played the game for the first time in my life, winning an award for rank beginner. There was also the hockey which became a total-immersion thing for everybody: I firmly believed that all the family should share the work as well as the joy. Then in February, half the town, including our boys, went smelt fishing at night. Those who didn't go out in the dark and the cold to sit on the ice drinking wine got to snip heads and tails until they truly believed they couldn't look another fish in the face. So, it was a good town, not a bad place to find oneself in after the first big move away from home country.

I soon found a house and, as luck would have it, it was on Stevens Avenue directly opposite the sports arena. In one way it was handy for once I got involved with the hockey, I was able to simply step across the street, but it also made me a sitting duck for every contingency that occurred at the rink, and there were plenty.

Although located in Marathon, the administration office at least related directly to the park. Here the superintendent and his tiny staff planned the operations, kept the records, maintained contact with the outer world, and performed the tasks necessary to support the patrolmen in their work of exploring and mapping the resources of Pukaskwa.

After some months, during which neither the "Super" nor myself spent any more time than was required in the stuffy hotel room, we were able to lease the old hospital as park headquarters. There were four of us by this time: a superintendent, a chief park warden, a secretary, and a clerk. As there was as yet no general works manager, I was given that job as well, and was soon heavily involved in procuring equipment, setting up a work compound, setting up mobile homes for future staff housing, and a host of other tasks in addition to my own. It is difficult, however, to write anything entertaining about administrative routines without getting into detailed accounts of individual personalities, it being the quirks and idiosyncrasies of people, and the intrigues and interactions between them, which lend colour to the world of 9:00 to 5:00. It has been observed that one office is much like another, however, it is also true that telling tales out of office is much like telling tales out of school.

It is enough to say that they all had some good traits and a sense of humour which helped greatly. Although from totally different backgrounds, they all became infected with the vision of a beautiful new national park and, like good park people everywhere, pulled together to make it happen. In doing so, they became a little family. As for operations in the field, weather and particularly fog, became a constant factor to be contended with. Boat travel was very dangerous with no visibility; flying was often impossible. I eventually designed a special, three-tiered basket for my desk: inbound, outbound, and fogbound. Most of my paper work at any given time ended up in fogbound.

Employment of Indians and Inuit in Canada's national parks is not a particularly new idea, although it is probably only in the last two decades that a serious effort has been made to get them involved. As early as 1922, the records for Wood Buffalo National Park mention a Cree Indian, Pierre Gladue, employed as a Buffalo Ranger at the park. But Pukaskwa National Park is probably the first in which the entire Warden Service, with the exception of myself, started out with native people. Later, it would also become the first national park to have a native chief park warden, although he would not be a local Ojibway Indian.

Travelling by canoe and living in tents, the Indian patrolmen did much of the exploring and mapping of Pukaskwa park. They rediscovered old forgotten trails, made note of potential future campsites, took water samples for chemical analysis and conducted wildlife and vegetation surveys. They also spent a goodly amount of time, often at considerable personal risk, determining the viability of Lake Superior as a major access route to the park. Some of their experiences were, at least in retrospect, quite funny, while other adventures on the big lake came uncomfortably close to being disasters.

An early traveller, writing in 1821, observed, "The coast is subject to sudden transitions of temperature and to fogs and mists which are often so dense as to obscure objects at a short distance and prove disastrous to canoe travellers."

The patrolmen soon experienced this firsthand. During a short exploratory canoe trip during their first summer, a strong offshore wind and dense fog suddenly overtook two of them. With the headlands rapidly disappearing from sight and the wind pushing them out to sea, what had begun as a small excursion soon became a desperate situation. Setting their Sylva compass due north, the men paddled furiously, while the wind increased and the fog thickened. Alternately checking the compass and exhorting each other to greater effort, the two were nearing exhaustion when a great grey slab of rock suddenly materialized off the bow. Momentarily free from the pull of the wind and water, the canoe shot halfway up the rock, leaving streaks of green fibreglass on the granite, while the patrolmen and their gear were thrown from their seats and scattered on the shore. Bigger boats, forced to seek the shore in times of danger, had no recourse but to throttle back to minimum speed in hopes of avoiding a similar fate.

Another close call, which only seemed humorous in retrospect, occurred the day the crew took the new Titan 18-foot aluminum boat for a test run. The Titan was an open craft consisting of nothing more than a shell and a couple of seats. It had a deep hull and handled well and, for some time, was the favourite workboat for the park. It had a drain plug, perhaps an inch and a half in diameter, low in the stern. I was a conscientious chief warden, trained to be safety-minded, so I was careful to see that the patrolmen had a spare motor, paddles, bailing cans, and flotation jackets on when they embarked at the mouth of the Pic River. I stood on shore watching them as they headed out to sea. They waved jauntily and gave me the thumbs-up sign as they roared off around the headland and out of sight.

Imagine my total horror upon walking into the equipment shed half an hour later, to see the Titan's drain plug resting in the middle of the workbench! With a shaking hand and barely-controlled voice I picked up a radio and called the boat. What I would have done had they failed to answer is a matter of conjecture, but it seemed likely that shooting myself would have been a distinct possibility. To my indescribable relief, however, the calm voice of the lead hand came on and assured me that they were safe. The boat had actually not taken on water while at speed, and it was not until they had throttled back that the leak was discovered. Then in true resourceful warden fashion, one of the men had seized an axe, whittled a plug from the handle and stopped the hole.

When I arrived at Pukaskwa and asked for the other members of the park's Warden Service, I learned that they were at Riding Mountain National Park in Manitoba. As they were all new to the Service, it had been arranged for them to take six weeks of orientation and training in an operational park before beginning their duties at Pukaskwa. Whoever picked the candidates for the nucleus of the first Warden Service of Pukaskwa had done a commendable job. Either by good luck or good management, with only one or two exceptions, they had chosen men who possessed the calm, unflappable, can-do attitude which characterizes the best wardens in Canada's National Parks.

They also had a marvellous sense of humour, which began to manifest itself once they became used to me and realized that I was prepared to share their risks and hardships on an equal footing. One who had a great sense of fun was "Big Ben," or "Gentle Ben," as he was sometimes called. Most of the patrolmen were big men, broad and deep-chested, but Ben was notable even in a crew, most of whom weighed almost twice as much as I did. With Ben well over six feet and probably close to 300 pounds, my station wagon would settle within an inch of the street when Ben lowered himself carefully into the passenger seat. Fortunately for the rest of us he was also brave and kind—a genial and considerate partner on the trail.

Ben did have one habit, however, which used to puzzle me. Ben liked to sing when he was in the bush. Not that there is anything wrong with singing, for many men, wardens included, have belted out a ballad or two when alone on the trail. But Ben seemed to do his singing only when I was with them. To add to the incongruity, he sang Christmas carols on hot summer days. The crew would be slogging along through steaming, black spruce swamp, the air humming with black flies and sweat pouring down their ravaged, bug-bitten faces, when all of a sudden Ben's booming voice would break out with "Ho-o-ly Night," or "...and the snow lay all around, deep and white and even."

I would smile along with the rest of the crew when this happened, but it was some time before I really understood what the others were chuckling about. One day I asked Ben why he sang Christmas carols in the middle of the summer. The big man regarded me carefully. Perhaps he was wondering just how well he knew this official with the gold stars on his uniform. Then slowly his eyes crinkled, and a smile crept across his broad face. Very softly he said, "I sing, Chief, because if I didn't, you would be lost every time we went out in the bush!"

It was true. Raised in mountain country, where every little stream runs into a bigger one, and every pass affords a view for miles around, I was hopelessly at sea in the broken, patternless terrain of the Canadian Shield. Once away from the sound of the lake, with the sun obscured, surrounded by black spruce, I had no idea where I was. At those times I relied on Ben's Christmas carols to bring me home!

Working with the Ojibway patrolmen was perhaps the second most rewarding aspect of the Pukaskwa experience, second only to the thrill of travelling and exploring the beautiful North Shore. There was a warmth and earthiness and honesty about the people of the Pic and Mobert Reserves. I became acutely aware of my feelings in this regard on the day that I attended the funeral service for a young child tragically killed in a house fire at the Pic. There was an emotionalism about the service, quite unlike the carefully orchestrated grief common to white funerals; the hymns, sung in what seemed to be a blend of French and Ojibway, were heart-rendingly beautiful.

At least one other occasion touched me deeply. It was the going-away party for Glennys and myself, when we left the national park three years later, to take up new duties in Nova Scotia. The affair was arranged in our honour by the patrolmen and their wives, and took place in a house on Sund Crescent. Actually, the house itself was part of the story. There had been a change of park superintendents towards the end of my tenure in the park and during the interim, between the departure of the old wheeler-dealer and the arrival of the new boss, I acted as the park's superintendent for about six months. It happened that during that period a problem developed with the furnace in one of the mobile homes being used to house park staff. This particular trailer was occupied by the storesman—a native, and his family.

When the complaint was brought to me, I went to check it out and agreed that there was a definite safety problem. Also, as it turned out, it would be some time before the problem could be rectified. There happened to be a house leased by the park, temporarily vacant on Sund Crescent, and I used my prerogative as acting superintendent to move the family into this house. To my surprise, the decision caused a number of raised eyebrows around town. Although I could scarcely credit the idea, there actually seemed to be a feeling abroad in some quarters that native staff should not be allowed into town housing. The very idea that such a prejudice might exist made me so irate that I was determined to stick with my decision at all costs. The family was moved into their new quarters forthwith and seemed very pleased, for it was a nice home. The patrolmen watched the whole affair with interest, and this probably gave some significance to the fact that our going-away party was staged at Sund Crescent.

Meanwhile, the neighbours also watched what was going on, although, in all likelihood, with less enthusiasm. After awhile their concerns may have abated, because the family with their young children lived quietly and were exemplary residents in every way. The night of the party probably awakened their fears all over again. One could imagine the "I told you so" comments going on, behind drawn window curtains, as large boxes of beer were being lugged into the home and the noise level of boisterous comings and goings grew louder and louder. The patrolmen were deliberately hamming it up for the neighbours.

Upon arriving, I even got a bit of a start when I saw "Big Ben" out in the back yard uprooting a large rock with the intention, loudly voiced, of hurling it through the bathroom window. It appeared someone had locked the bathroom door from the inside, and the solution arrived at was to knock out the window and climb through. The problem was quietly resolved by other means, but one would have had to be close enough to see the twinkle in Ben's eye to realize that the whole thing was a show put on for the benefit of those snooty people next door!

The party which ensued was pretty much like most parties, although smaller and more intimate than the one held for us in Jasper. Glennys and I both relaxed and thoroughly enjoyed ourselves, in the way that one can do only when truly in the company of friends. And that they were real friends, there could be no doubt for it was readily evinced as we progressed into the more formal part of the proceedings. At this point, a space was cleared in the centre of the floor and I was instructed to take a stand there. Then, one after another, each patrolman rose and stood beside me and recounted some incident in the park that we had shared together. Some of the stories were funny and others, like their travels on the lake, scary. But each happening was related with the honesty and sincerity so typical of that little group and every story was told in such a way as to reflect credit on me, the guest of honour. Nor was Glennys left out. The tea and cakes and coffee that she had dispensed so freely in her kitchen on cold winter days, were fondly recalled as well. It was with large lumps in the throat that we both went home that night.

As for the park itself, to describe it adequately is an even more exacting task. It is as challenging as a canoe trip down the rugged Lake Superior coast or a forced march through the steamy, fly-infested hinterland—both of which do justice to its moods and personality.

The Pukaskwa landscape is an ancient and massive formation of rocks cast together in volcanic cauldrons over two billion years ago. The rocks cooled, split and warped to form fissures, ridges and cliffs. Major ruptures or fault valleys dissected the terrain and were themselves dissected by smaller rifts. Eons of weathering and the advance of massive glaciers reshaped the topography of the rockscapes. Post-glacial lakes flooded the land; abandoned boulder beaches, hundreds of feet above the present level of Lake Superior, attest to the dramatic rise and fall of the Great Lakes during those awesome eras.

The coastline, including numerous picturesque bays, inlets and islands, forms the entire southern boundary of the park, a distance of 50 or 60 miles. From the shore, the land rises northward in a series of hills lying parallel to the coast. Most of the hills are solid rock, known as balds, usually with birch and willow in the crevices and lower areas, but devoid of vegetation on the tops. There are frequent small swampy areas and sloughs between the balds; strange plants are to be found in these dim and secret places. Encrusted saxifrage, normally found in the Hudson Bay and James Bay areas, grows here, as does the carnivorous butterwort, whose sticky glands trap insects and bugs. Bladderwort, sundew and the pitcher plant have all developed a palate for the insects of the northern waters and woods—although the impact on the black fly seems negligible.

There are a number of wild rivers which enter from the north and empty into the big lake. They include the White, the Willow, the Swallow and the Pukaskwa Rivers. Both the rivers and the lakes become quite warm in the summer and the waters have a blackish look. In the hinterland, the country tends to level off; birch, spruce, and the occasional stand of red pine cover the landscape. Here, in the many small lakes and meandering streams, the beaver builds his lodges and works his engineering marvels.

Dam building, rebuilding and modification goes on at such a rate as to astound the visitor and confound the human would-be road builder. Very often, streams that run in one direction one week will be found to have reversed their courses and flow in the opposite direction a week later!

Black bears are found throughout the park, although they are possibly the smallest of any in Canada. There are a few caribou, which winter on Otter Island and other coastal areas, and can best be seen in January and February. There are also wolves, which migrate in and out of the western end of the park, and a significant moose population. A number of fur-bearers can be found, the most visible being the mink due to their habit of sliding down snow chutes along the shore of Lake Superior. On sunny days, their icy runways are clearly seen from the air.

But, by far, the most prolific creature in Pukaskwa in the summer time and unfortunately the one with which the visitor makes intimate and bloody contact, is the black fly. The hazards of lake travel and the dangers of getting lost are minor perils in comparison to running into these bloodthirsty insects. A northern Ontario black fly is one of the most ferocious critters on this earth. If a grizzly bear from the Rockies were to visit Ontario and run into a black fly, he would wish he had never left home. In a matter of moments, he would be reduced to a pitiful, blubber-ing wreck; if he ran into a bunch of flies, he would be nothing but a spot of bear grease in no time at all. In a word, they are a fright. No one in this country knows anything about biting insects until they have encountered those denizens of black spruce country.

The following story illustrates the trauma which an encounter with these little monsters can create. As the story takes place in the winter, when the black flies are in their dens sleeping, a bit of imagination is required here on the part of the reader. Perhaps these particular flies made a mis-take on the calendar, and believed it was springtime. At any rate, one cold winter day I went to the Pic Reserve to help the crew get packed up for a skidoo trek in to the Louie Lake country. The gang had finally pulled away from the general store, which was the rallying point for most important events on the reserve, to the accompaniment of an enthusiastic send-off from all the dogs and bystanders gathered to see them off. About an hour later my business wrapped up, I was about to head back for Marathon, when out of the distance came a faint sputter of a skidoo returning.

I shook my head. Aborted trips were nothing new at Pukaskwa but this venture seemed particularly short lived. I leaned on the back of my truck and waited to see what had gone awry this time. The sputter quickly turned into a roar, as the first patrolman came back into camp under full power, left hand on the throttle, and in the right hand a short stick with which he was pounding the side of the machine like a jockey in the home stretch. This dramatic re-entry had caused most of the dogs and people, who had been straggling home, to re-gather at the store. There he was received with all the yelps, yowls, barking and general enthusiasm that had recently heralded his departure. As he cut the engine and stepped from his mount, it was obvious that something terrible had transpired out there in the snowy woods. The man who staggered toward the store was visibly shaken. I felt a sudden twinge of apprehension.

"My God, Frank," I said, "What on earth happened?"

"Chief," replied the patrolman, jaw clenched and lower lip trembling, "I just ran into three Pukaskwa black flies flying abreast!"

Wading around in the swamps, our eyes swollen shut from dozens of bites, and ears deafened by the whir of their ravening hordes, the patrolmen and I consoled ourselves with the thought that Pukaskwa must one day be a great park. "After all," we told each other, "a million black flies couldn't all be wrong!"

These comments may serve to give the reader a picture of the country and its denizens, but we have yet to get a feeling for the character of Pukaskwa. Every piece of wilderness has its own distinct personality, made up not only of those features we can see, but also much of what we sense.

Pukaskwa takes so much of its character from Lake Superior that it is essential to have a feeling for the lake in order to begin to know the park. To start with, the word "lake" is misleading. As the Reverend George Grant observed in 1872, "It is a sea. It breeds rain and fog like a sea. It is cold, wild, masterful, and dreaded."

This is one side of the face of Pukaskwa. But, there is a subtler, more mysterious side as well. In order to try to discover this aspect, let us wait for a sunny day in July, a day when the water is sparkling blue, gentle wavelets lap the shores of emerald-green islands, where the sweet smell of heath and ripening blueberries fills the air. Then we take a small boat and, watching out for hidden shoals and drifting pulp logs, work our way down the coast until we come to one of the seductive, secluded inlets. As we cut the motor and gaze about us, the first impression is one of peace, and unspoiled beauty. As our boat drifts to a stop, the wavelets caused by our arrival gently subside and we float on still, clear water of shimmering green. On all three sides, the birch forest comes to the water's edge, utterly calm beneath the summer sun.

As we trail a hand over the side, surprised, as always, at how cold the water is, we recall the words of an earlier traveller, Louis Agassiz. He must have stopped in a place like this, when he wrote in 1848, "Our little point was as silent as a piece of primeval earth. It was as if no noise had been heard since the woods grew, and all nature seemed sunk in a deep and dreamless sleep." We sit for some minutes, not moving, receptive to whatever sensations await us.

Oddly, we begin to experience a faint unease. We look carefully about, not sure what we expect to see. The water is the same incredible green, the sun still shines in a cloudless sky, the leaves of the birch still hang motionless in the warm air. But for the first time we realize how dark are the shadows behind those leaves. Next comes an unmistakable sense of being watched, though nothing stirs. Once suspected, it is impossible to shake this feeling.

Old legends come to mind, of what has more than once been referred to as the Haunted Shore. Suddenly we feel like intruders. We are aliens here, in this silent inlet, where a malign presence is making itself felt. It is a strange phenomenon, one which we cannot explain. Perhaps we are no longer comfortable in a land born two million years ago. Or, what is more likely, the ancient spirits who lurk here are not comfortable with us. Very quietly we pick up our paddles and creep towards the mouth of the inlet, suddenly anxious for the benevolence of the open lake. To start the motor here would be a travesty that might well disturb those who watch from behind the trees.

Hell and High Water

Picture a rocky inlet on the North Shore of Lake Superior. A narrow pebble beach runs up the right side and behind that stands the birch forest, drooping darkly. At the head of the inlet and along the left side are gray granite walls. Outside, beyond the mouth, the lake is running wild—a waste of wind-whipped waves and flying spray. Great waves explode upon the headlands, then surge hissing up the inlet until the beach is covered and the black water rises high upon the walls. As each rush subsides, there is a tremendous grinding sound, as hundreds of rounded rocks tumble down the beach, only to roll back up again a moment later. Paint above: a stormy sky; ragged mist; sheets of rain.

Enter this Pukaskwa Park Warden. As usual, I'm wet and cold and desperately focused on staying alive. I am alone, in a long, wooden canoe of peculiar design. This craft is deeper than most canoes, and has a square stern to accommodate an outboard motor. The most striking feature, however, is the very high prow. It is a boat superbly designed for conditions along the North Shore, but it must be handled with panache, a quality which I find myself sadly lacking.

As I motor cautiously up the right-hand side of the inlet, I peer intently at something on the opposite side. Travelling along the base of the wall across from me and running back out towards the lake, is a similar canoe. Slouched in the rear end is an old man, right arm relaxed upon the gunwale, left arm just as casually reaching astern to grip the throttle. In contrast to me, his posture is nonchalant; his boat handling sure and steady as he glides along like a shadow in the mist. He pays no attention to me nor does he look back.

Just ahead of the old man is a rocky headland. Huge breakers smash against the outcrop, sending geysers of icy spray high into the air, while at the foot of the rocks the waters churn and foam and surge this way and that, in a scene of incredible confusion. It does not seem that an ordinary craft, no matter how sturdy, could enter such a maelstrom and survive. Yet, the old man, sprawled in his canoe, drives onward, as relaxed as if he were at home on his living room couch. I am at the head of the inlet now, striving to copy every move the other man makes, when a sudden surge in the channel catches me broadside and nearly smashes me against the wall. Fighting to keep from capsizing, I glance up just in time to get one more look at the lead canoe before it reaches the point.

For one startling moment the mist clears and a ray of watery sunlight hits the mouth of the inlet. The lead canoe and its lone occupant are starkly outlined against a backdrop of wet, black granite. Then the skipper, his cap pulled low and collar up, cranks the throttle wide and the stern dips suddenly. The bow lifts high to meet the storm-whipped spray then, like an eel slides into the walls of water, is gone. Watching this and knowing that I must follow, I feel as though my heart is in my throat. Perhaps it is lucky there is no choice and no time to procrastinate. I steel myself to make the run.

It had started out as a typical Monday morning. The patrolmen were scheduled to move down the coast and set up camp at the mouth of the Willow River, for a week of exploring and natural resource inventory. I had contracted with K.T. MacQuage, at Heron Bay, for the use of two of his freighter canoes, complete with operators to transport the men and their equipment. I planned to go with them, see them safely located and return in one of the canoes. As invariably happened on a planned travel day, the mood of the lake was foul. A heavy storm had moved through the area overnight, leaving dark fog and turbulent water in its wake. Sitting at breakfast with the back door of the house partially open, I could hear the boulders growling on Pebble Beach, half a mile away. It was an ominous sound that would ruin many a Monday breakfast in the next four years.

My uneasiness increased when, upon arrival at Heron Bay, I found K.T. grimly bailing rainwater out of the longboats. The hired help had apparently had second thoughts about today's trip and were nowhere to be found. K.T. would run one boat but a driver would be needed for the second. My experience in the mountain parks had done little to prepare me

Perils of the North Shore

for boat handling—a fact of which I was painfully aware. Fortunately the lead patrolman volunteered and the trip down the coast, although rough and uncomfortable, was managed without serious incident. The waves were high enough to hide the boats from each other much of the way and there was concern at one point that the second canoe had lost its way. As it turned out, the motor was acting-up, causing them to fall behind.

Hunched up, drenched and cold, in the bow of the second canoe, I knew that I was going to have to bring one of the boats back. The prospect gave me a sick feeling in the pit of my stomach. The only alternative would be to have one of the patrolmen accompany me back to town and I did not believe that I could afford the loss of face that this would entail—both in the eyes of my fledgling Warden Service and also the office staff. Nor would the superintendent think much of having one of the bush crew back around the compound for a week. The "Old Man," for all his eccentricities, was actually quite an intrepid boatman and conducted himself competently out on the big lake.

Having made up my mind that I was committed, I turned to practical considerations. First of all, K.T. should lead on the way home. The man knew the coast like the back of his hand. However, if the old trapper had the better of the two motors, I strongly suspected that I would be left behind to fend for myself. In my dealings with K.T. so far, I had gained the impression of a tough individual and one not likely to have much pity for some cowboy from Alberta.

We reached the mouth of the Willow River shortly before noon and pulled the canoes onto the little beach west of the river. One of the patrolmen brewed tea on a Coleman stove while the rest unloaded supplies and prepared to set up camp. I did what I could to help but kept a watchful eye on the two canoes down at the water's edge. I wanted to be sure and remember which was which. When everyone gathered for lunch, I sat off a little way by myself. I nibbled on a sandwich, sipped hot tea and plotted. It was understood that I would drive one of the boats back, but no one had said which one.

When the time came for departure I anticipated K.T. and headed down to the lakeshore ahead of him. There, seemingly absent minded, I wandered over to the #1 canoe, the one with the good motor. Moving quickly now, for I did not want to get into any arguments, I shoved off, jumped in and yanked the starter cord. To my relief, the motor caught. Seeing K.T. climbing into the second canoe, I waved to the crew, and motored out into the bay. I deliberately took it slow, relying on the old man to take the lead due to his impatience and hopefully, a sense of duty. At any rate, it worked. Before I was halfway out the other canoe came snarling up, overtook me and steamed off without so much as a backward glance. I hunkered down and opened the throttle. I was determined to hang in there come hell or high water. I was convinced that the only way I would survive the next two hours was to keep the old man in sight.

Now the old man was gone, vanished into that violent turmoil of seething water and flying spray that obscured the point of land. My frightened-scale was at an all time high. It was above when the grizzly bear had chased me at Saskatchewan River Crossing and above when I made my first rappel off the dreaded Weeping Wall. The time the helicopter fell 600 feet into the box canyon of the Restless River in Jasper had not scared me as much as the wild, black waters that now threatened to swallow me and my canoe. What do you do when you never learnt to pray, and you don't have a God to pray to anyway? Now from far out in the lake a monster wave arrived and as the green, foaming crest towered over me I knew that to hesitate would be fatal.

Mustering every ounce of courage, I squinted my eyes against the spray, aimed for the last seen point of K.T. MacQuage and cranked up the throttle. A moment later, soaked and shaken but still in one piece, I was around the headland in open water. Better yet, the lead canoe was not far away, motoring along just off shore. I took a deep breath and exhaled slowly. Within me stirred the first tiny flicker of hope that I might actually be capable of making it home. I continued to copy the old man's every move.

Two hours later, we were drinking a whiskey together in K.T.'s mobile home at Heron Bay. The stormy skies were clearing and the late afternoon sun coming through the doorway lit the old man's rugged features as he told me tales of his early days as a fur trapper on the North Shore. For the first time since I had known him, the tough cockiness began to soften and I sensed that because of what we had come through that day I might have gone up a peg or two in K.T.'s eyes. Perhaps the old trapper was just as glad as I was to have the voyage behind. No doubt he had seen worse but it had been rough enough. Many months before, I had convinced an interview board in Cornwall that I was qualified to be a Chief Warden at Pukaskwa National Park, but when I went home this day, I knew I had just passed the real test.

More Perils at Pukaskwa

The land was white with no beginning and no end. The immediate foreground was a thing of vague forms and shadows, shapes that may have been real or imagined beneath the drifting snow. In the middle distance, in the rare moments when the storm abated, could be seen the gray ghost of a scrubby spruce tree. It would be visible for a few seconds, and then like a ghost was gone as the snow moved in again. There was no horizon, nor an indication as to where it might be. No ground, no horizon, no sky— because there were no reference points, there was no direction and no sense of movement. One could be travelling north or south, east or west, up or down and the only reality would be the traveller's own tracks, visible for a few yards and then they too would vanish.

With better visibility, the land did have form but to the uninitiated it would have appeared almost as baffling as the white-out just described. The terrain in the backcountry of Pukaskwa National Park is a series of balds—great granite humps, hollows, tiny lakes and meandering water-ways. There was no discernible pattern to this land. Every rounded hill was like another and the small streams ran in all directions, their flow being influenced more by the activity of beaver than by any aspect of the terrain.

A man, or rather a man and a machine, were in the bottom of one of these featureless hollows, one of possibly a hundred hidden by fog and snow. He wore an olive-green park warden parka over a dark-blue skidoo suit and a polished badge gleamed softly in the dark fur on the front of his hat. The machine, a big yellow double-track Skidoo was buried deeply in the snow at the bottom of the hollow and the man was having a difficult time. Although he had not been hurt, when his over-snow vehicle plunged unexpectedly into this hole, he was becoming very tired. This was possibly the tenth time in the last two hours that he had had to push and pull and wrestle the heavy machine back onto firm ground; the effort was beginning to tell.

Attached to the Skidoo was a sled, on which were lashed: cans of spare gasoline, an Arctic bedroll, a Coleman stove, snowshoes and groceries. All of these were caked with ice and snow. Each time the Skidoo had to be extricated from some difficulty, the sled had to be unhitched and manhandled back into place as well. I knew the routine well, for this time, I was the man. Now, I climbed stiffly from the seat, strapped the snowshoes on and began cautiously looking for the most feasible route back to higher ground.

As luck would have it, there was a narrow little gorge at one end of the hollow containing a few small birch trees and a sort of path which twisted its way back up to the ridge on which I had been travelling. After tramping a trail up this gully, I paused at the top to catch my breath and get my bearings. Off in the direction that I believed to be south, a line of stunted spruces showed vaguely through the storm. Pushing back the hood of my parka, and turning up the earflaps on the fur hat, I turned my head this way and that to listen. I was hoping for the sound of an axe or chainsaw or perhaps a skidoo, but all that greeted me was silence. Actually, there was an underlying sound out there, but it was nothing a man could use for direction—just a hollow, unearthly moaning that seemed to come from everywhere, yet nowhere. The only reality was the patter of hundreds of graupels, tiny pellets of frozen snow, hitting my parka as I stood there. Cold comfort in that sound; I turned and snowshoed back to my machine.

Covered with snow and ice, I was wandering around in a blizzard in the backcountry of Pukaskwa National Park, with only the vaguest idea of where I was, because I had taken it into my head to pay a surprise visit on the troops. For several days, the patrolmen had been camped at Ouiseau Bay taking weather, game and snow observations, as well as just generally checking out their ability to move around the area on their over-snow vehicles and survive in comfort.

As I had sat in my office in Marathon, looking out the window and thinking about them, I decided that I ought to go out and see how they were doing. It would look good on me and besides I hadn't had a winter wilderness experience for some time. Old memories of days on the trail were stirring.

As a result, I loaded an over-snow machine into the back of one of the park's big blue Dodge Power Wagons, packed my gear and despite a rather ominous weather forecast, motored east to Mobert Reserve. The forecasts were always ominous at Pukaskwa. If one were going to be intimidated, one would never leave home. Just east of the village I found the mate to the blue 4x4, parked near the railroad track, indicating where the patrolmen had begun their over-snow journey. The distance from there to the coast was about 35 to 40 miles.

The snow arrived while I was lashing my gear onto the sled. It came suddenly, driven by a north wind, whispering of cold and empty lands. The Skidoo trail made by the patrolmen's machines was still visible, so I decided to press on. It was about 10 am when I left the railroad tracks and headed south into the interior of the park. The first two hours went fairly well, even though the storm was intensifying. After looking at the map and deciding that I had probably covered about half the distance, I stopped for lunch in a stand of red pine. There were indications that the patrolmen had stopped at the same spot. As I sat thoughtfully munching a PREM sandwich and sipping tea, it began to storm in earnest.

It gave me a bit of a start to discover that I could barely make out the tops of the trees and the country to the south was disappearing behind a white curtain. I could not recall ever having seen a snowstorm quite like what was happening here. Odd as it may seem to some, it never entered my head to turn back. The fact is, I was beginning to enjoy myself hugely. I loved the complete aloneness and feel of the wilderness all around. It was a challenge, like the old days on the Brazeau River. Except, I'd never seen it snow like this in the mountains. Sometimes it came damply on one cheek and I felt it must be coming in from the lake; next it would blow cold on the other cheek, as if the storm had come straight from Hudsons Bay. And all the time it swirled and drifted and fell more thickly.

I thought, "If I'm going on, I'd better get at it." So after checking the sled and fueling the machine, I left the shelter of the pines and headed off into what proved to be a major storm. Half an hour later I could no longer find the trial, and after an hour I could barely find my own arse even using both hands. Soon after, I plunged into the hollow.

The patrolmen at Pukaskwa used to have a saying with which they were wont to caution each other, in times of imminent danger or right after a near disaster. "We've got to start acting more sensible," they would say. After extricating myself and machine from the most recent dilemma, I decided it was definitely time to start acting more sensible! The question was—how? As nearly as I could judge, I had covered about two-thirds of the distance, which meant there were eight to 10 miles still between me and Oiseau Bay. Perhaps 20 miles to the east, I knew the Pukaskwa River wound its way down to the lake.

I remembered the few lonely little graves at the mouth of the Pukaskwa and tales of old logging camps in that area in early times. Men would be recruited for the camps in the fall and moved in at the onset of winter. Mail and supplies were sledded in from the town of White River, about 60 miles away. Work and living conditions at the logging camps were primitive, not to say downright brutal. Legend has it that at night, the men's snowshoes were kept under lock and key to prevent anyone from trying to leave under the cover of darkness—a hard way to make a living.

Meanwhile, I had problems of my own. I was still in total whiteout and knew that I could not afford getting stuck. Taking a ski pole, which I always used when snowshoeing, I dug in my pack for a piece of orange survey tape and tied it to the handle. Then, moving carefully along the ridge, until I could just barely see the Skidoo, I planted the pole, snowshoed back and drove up to it. Using this method and referring often to my Sylva compass to confirm that I was still going south, I was able to proceed, slowly but surely. Going ahead on foot not only made it possible to avoid places which would trap the machine but also helped the treads to get a grip.

By 3:30 in the afternoon, I was encouraged to find the terrain beginning to drop toward the lake and soon after picked up the beginning of the creek which runs to the northwest corner of Oiseau Bay. I was back in the shelter of the trees by this time and was even able to pick up the patrolmen's Skidoo trail leading to their camp. Comfortable in the knowledge that I had survived the journey and was home safe, I stopped to check the load, put everything ship-shape and set my fur hat at a jaunty angle. Then I clattered around the last bend in the trail and idled nonchalantly into camp, for all the world as if I was just dropping in on an afternoon stroll. The patrolmen, for their part, exhibited a gratifying degree of surprise and even amazement at my dramatic and unheralded appearance.

The Elephants are Marching

There were five of us in an 18-foot open aluminum boat. Four native patrolmen and I were in a frightening situation. In the few hours that had elapsed since we left the mouth of the Pic River, Lake Superior had gone berserk. Having started under relatively calm conditions, we were now surrounded by towering waves, drenched in freezing spray and in imminent danger of being swamped and drowned. Although trying hard not to show our feelings, our pale set faces gave lie to the small jokes and casual comments with which we tried to bolster each other's spirits.

We were surrounded by water, cold grey water that hissed and seethed under and around us with incredible power. One moment our little craft would be lifted to such a height that the legions of breakers were plainly visible, smashing on the mist-shrouded headlands. Next moment, we would be buried in a trough so deep that nothing could be seen but the unspeakable blackness below. And always, there was the fearful spectre of the next wave towering over us until it seemed there could be no possible escape.

To his credit, our chosen boatman that day was doing as well as anyone could hope under the circumstances. With a calm eye and a steady hand upon the throttle, Lester was three-quartering the waves, reducing the chance of foundering and ensuring that the propeller had purchase at all times. However, when one storm overrides another, as was happening this day, cross-waves can occur without warning. These are swells running at a different angle to the pack. A boat set on course for the regular waves may be totally in the wrong position to deal with the rogue wave. The rest of the crew and I had watched with awe as our friend, by some miraculous slight-of-hand, managed to wriggle through this contingency each time it occurred. The question in everyone's mind, and possibly on Lester's as well, was how long could his luck last?

Although it did not strike me that I was living moments that made legends, it did occur to me that it would be worthwhile having some pictures of the scene to show if, on the remote chance, we ever got back to shore. Accordingly, I dragged the camera out of my pack and proceeded to capture the intrepid boatman plying his magic at the stern, as well as a few shots of the wilderness around us. It was while I was thus engaged that I realized that the waves appeared smaller when seen through the camera than when viewed with the naked eye. Consequently, I spent a considerable time, from then on, apparently taking pictures, although a keen observer would have noted that my finger seldom pressed the shutter.

The North Shore locals—sensible souls—take their boats out of the water in September. They leave the great lake to her autumn rages so the huge swells rolling in from the watery vastness find no fishing boats or weekenders to trample underfoot and grind upon the granite shores. On stormy days in October locals walk or drive to the lookout points and watch the freighters carrying steel or prairie wheat—the silhouettes rising and falling on the horizon. When conditions are truly awesome, even large ships remain hidden for moments at a time in the troughs. More than one 600-footer lies rusting at the bottom of Lake Superior, as Gordon Lightfoot attests in his dirge to the *Wreck of the Edmund Fitzgerald*. On days like this, when the awesome waves come thundering up the beaches, the Ojibway say, 'The Elephants are marching."

To the fledgling Park Warden Service, which was growing more confident in boating ability perhaps to the point of overconfidence, it seemed a shame to quit using the lake so early in the fall. After all, if legend were to be believed, the early trappers in the area canoed, with a load of furs, the North Shore well into December, working their way home in time for Christmas.

There has always been an adventurous side to the Warden Service, a tendency to push limits in some of the activities in which we are engaged, an urge to see if it goes and, if so, how high and how far. So it was that on a quiet morning around the tenth of November, my little crew and I took the 18-footer and decided to extend the boating season on Lake Superior. Nowadays, thanks in large measure to the National Parks Service, there is an excellent marine weather channel available to the residents of the

North Shore. In those days, there was not and we had no idea that we were sailing into a terrible trap.

In addition to checking out the lake, our main objective that day was to build a tent cabin at the mouth of the Willow River, about 20 miles down the coast. It was one of the places we hoped to be able to visit in the winter, so the presence of a roomy, plywood and canvas shelter would reduce considerably the amount of gear to be hauled later on. That morning on the lake, there was a fairly heavy chop running up the coast from the east, but the Titan took it in stride and by 10 o'clock we were at Willow Bay. Once in the bay, the water was dead calm and under a grey sky the air was very still.

We unloaded the wood and our tools and began to build on the west side of the river mouth. The work went well and by noon we had the canvas draped over the frame. We lit the Coleman stove, made tea and ate our lunch while sitting on a couple of driftwood logs in front of the cabin. After lunch some of us rolled cigarettes. We talked quietly about the work still to be done on the shelter and then for a few moments just sat, each with his thoughts, gazing at the woods and the brown river. Meanwhile, something very ominous was approaching the mouth of the bay.

The wave started at Duluth, at the southwest corner of the great lake. Just a ripple at first, running northeast before the wind, followed by another and another. Soon the wind strengthened and as they travelled, the little waves grew bigger and new ones came from behind and pushed them on. By the time the ripple was halfway across the lake it was a large wave and it was the forerunner of an army. Lake Superior is notorious for the way in which a sea will build in a matter of a few hours; the water can change from calm to a two or three-foot chop in a matter of a couple of hours. Within four hours the waves can be of such size as to put a small craft in danger. Although not as large as ocean swells, the waves on Superior are steep and travel closely together, making operation of a boat very difficult. Some of the strongest winds to cross the lake come from the southwest, and the fetch from Duluth, to the northeast, is the longest on the lake, allowing the biggest build-up. We were in for a rude surprise.

There was a sudden disturbance at the entrance to the bay when the ripple from Duluth made its surprise arrival. Spray shot skywards from the rocks, there was a rustle and churning of water, then the invader rolled across the harbour and slapped the beach with a resounding smack. I stopped with a cigarette halfway to my lips. I glanced at my companions and saw the same reaction. Each one sat listening intently, as one might at the sound of an intruder in the house, late at night. At that moment a second wave, bigger than the first, hit the beach with a sound like a pistol shot.

Getting slowly to our feet and facing towards the lake, we were conscious of a change in the air and an escalating roar like that of an angry mob still some distance away but approaching fast. A premonition, cold and queasy, crawled up the back of my neck. The relaxed atmosphere was replaced by anxious activity. Quickly securing the canvas on our tent cabin, we threw in the airtight heater and stove pipes we had brought, hid an axe beneath the floor, and loaded the rest of the tools into the boat.

We hurriedly pushed off and motored cautiously out to the mouth of the bay. As we feared, there was a rising sea running in from the southwest. It looked bad. I conferred with the boatman. We all knew that there was no such thing as just going out a little way. Under those conditions, the most dangerous place to be is close to shore. If one is going to travel, the trick is to get well out onto the lake and then cope with conditions as you find them. Lester made his decision and drove her out. We were committed.

The hours that followed were some of the worst that we ever put in on the lake. For awhile the three-quartering technique served us well but as we approached the headland at Hattie Cove, it became necessary to face the waves straight on. Watching Lester coping with this, I was reminded of a prospective employee that we had interviewed a few weeks earlier. The man professed to have navigated 40-foot waves in a 20-foot boat. I wondered how the fellow would have performed that day. In the meantime, it was plain that we had one of the best hands in the business taking care of us. Whatever his inner thoughts, Lester remained calm while performing miracles. Even when we finally had to run for the mouth of the Pic River, leaving ourselves at the mercy of a horrendous following sea, no flicker of emotion crossed his imperturbable features. He delivered us all, safe and sound, to the beach.

At the mouth of the Pic River, there is a small piece of ground which although not sacred, might well lay claim to be so. It is the spot where men, having tumbled out of their boats and taken three shaky steps inland, fall full-length upon the sand and kiss "Old Terra Firma." If we failed to perform the rite that day, it was because we doubted our wobbly legs would have the strength to stand up again.

A Skipper Goes Missing

It was a good night to stay off Lake Superior. The heat had been building in northern Ontario all week, and in the pre-dawn hours a massive thunderstorm swept down from the timbered hills around Manitouwadge, and treated the denizens of the North Shore to an awesome display of sheet and forked lightning, strong winds and pounding rain. It set fire to the Wardens' Camp at Oiseau Bay in Pukaskwa National Park, and then moved offshore where it grumbled and growled most of the day. The sun shone briefly in late afternoon, heating the moist air again, while the wind shifted to the southwest. Towards evening the storm moved inland with renewed vigour. The few stars that had been visible to the townspeople of Marathon disappeared and gale force winds pounded the shore with rain and spume from 20-foot high waves.

★   ★   ★

My three sons and I, as well as a number of the park patrolmen, were asleep in the camp that had been struck by lightning early that morning. We had been out for 10 days rediscovering old, forgotten trails, locating possible future campsites, and collecting water samples for later analysis. The best part of each day was the evening, when we returned to the blessed coolness of the beach and a swim in the clear water of the bay—away at last from the cursed black flies. Then the Coleman stoves under the fly tarp would be fired up and supper would be underway. In the evening we would write up our day's observations and compare notes. Finally as evening shadows turned the bay a deep, dark-green, we would prepare a late snack of coffee and toast, peanut butter and strawberry jam, before turning in.

The patrolmen were a merry crew and very good to the three boys. It would have been an idyllic 10 days if, on the eighth day, I had not succumbed to temptation and taken a drink of water from a warm, inland lake. A few hours later I had my first encounter with what in the Rockies is now known as Beaver Fever. For the next 48 hours I was wracked by nausea, fever and diarrhea.

Then, on top of that, came the thunderstorm and the lightning strike which started a ground fire in the middle of our camp and led to some frantic fire fighting in the middle of the night. This night was just before the day that our rented tugboat was due to take us back to Marathon.

As a result, it was an exhausted chief park warden who crawled from his tent the next morning to take stock of the situation. I noted that the hills were shrouded with ragged mist and there was an ominous roaring sound beyond the harbour mouth. This was interspersed with distant thunder. A light rain was still falling, and the sky over the lake was black. I saw the three boys were gathered at the cook shelter with the patrolmen. Set near the edge of the open beach, the shelter was designed to allow the cool air from the lake to keep the black flies away. On this particular morning the green Coleman camp stoves were hissing and sputtering in the wet gusts from the lake and the cooks were having some problem even getting coffee underway.

After awhile, I was able to manage breakfast and we conferred as to what should be done. It was decided to pack some gear but leave the tents up, pending arrival of the tug or its no-show, whatever the case may be.

At approximately 10:30 am, we were surprised to hear the throb of a diesel and to see the tug rounding the island in the harbour mouth. Tents were quickly struck and gear loaded. By 11:00 am, we were on our way to Marathon—despite the conditions. The little camp boat, a 14-foot aluminum outboard, was towed behind.

It had been apparent from the beginning that Lake Superior was the key to Pukaskwa National Park. Not only was the coastline a thing of rugged grandeur and rare beauty, the shore was really the only area of the park that could be enjoyed in comfort during black fly season. It was also clearly a transportation corridor, though the best way to utilize it for public access was the subject of much conjecture that resulted in some rather far-fetched ideas. Aware as well that we would soon have to develop a marine search and rescue capability, the superintendent and I spent much of our time trying to decide what type of vessel would make the best patrol boat.

In the meantime, a few trips with the famous long canoes were sufficient to convince us that a more stable and secure craft was necessary for moving work crews and equipment up and down the coast. One option readily available was a type of tug in common use on the North Shore. These boats, used for pulpwood salvage along the coast, ran to 50 feet in length and were built with heavy steel hulls and had thick, iron-mesh propeller guards. They would bash their way with impunity through heavy logs or even run aground, bow first, with no ill effects.

The first tug that the park rented, was owned and operated by Bob Collins Sr., a man of 60 or so at the time. Bob was also the officer-in-charge of the lighthouse at Otter Cove, one of the most enchanting places on that spectacular coastline. His assistant was a wizened, one-eyed old native known locally as "Napoleon" or "Old Nappy." He employed a Metis, whom we shall call Charlie, to operate the tug.

The rate for this boat was $200 per day. Authority while on the water was shared by the operator and whoever was the leader of the park personnel on board. The park officer was the leader of the expedition in overall terms but the operator had the last word on the movement of the vessel. The intricacies of this arrangement were brought home to me on my first trip with Charlie.

It was another one of those nasty weather, Monday mornings. Through the kitchen window on Stevens Avenue, I could hear the boulders growling on Pebble Beach. On the hillside behind the town, a small birch tree—another of my weather indicators—was bent nearly double in the wind. "It's blowing fit to twist the head right off a moose," I thought nervously, quoting an Ojibway expression. Then I consoled myself with the thought that at least we were going out in a pretty sizable boat this time.

Two hours later, having loaded crew and gear, the tug's engine rumbled to life. Slowly and carefully, with Charlie at the wheel, we headed south out of Marathon Harbour. And I, a cowboy from Alberta, whose total previous sailing experience before going to Pukaskwa consisted of a boat tour on Maligne Lake in Jasper National Park, stood in the wheelhouse as co-commander.

There was a heavy sea running from the southeast that morning, so the first wave hit the tug just as she began her turn around the headland. It was huge. The boat was inundated. Finally, the bow rose and she shook herself free. As the water streamed off the wheelhouse, Charlie slit his eyes over at me to see how I was taking it. Before I could comment, another wall of water crashed into and over the tug, sending men and gear tumbling across the enclosed deck. I was shaken. "Whaddya think?" enquired Charlie, whiskey-voiced.

I allowed that it might be prudent to turn back and was amazed at the speed with which Charlie contrived this manoeuvre. Only when I got back to the office did I become aware that I had just blown $200. I had barely settled down at my desk when the "Old Man" came stamping down the hall and slapped the tug's contract down in front of me. With a tobacco-stained forefinger, the superintendent indicated the fine print, which spelled out that if the park officer requested a return to harbour for whatever reason, the tug still collected a day's pay. On the other hand, if the operator decided to abort a day's journey, he forfeited the $200. Thinking the whole thing over, I felt convinced that the lake really was too rough that day and, if left on his own, Charlie would have turned back anyway. Realizing I had been out-pokered, I made up my mind then and there that I would never again order a retreat, no matter how damn rough it got!

A few months later on another stormy morning, we sailed out of Oiseau Bay. Bob Sr. was on board and Charlie was at the helm. There was also another crew on board that had been out in the park doing fisheries survey work and had been picked up farther down the coast. One member of this group, a camera and other equipment hanging from his neck, wandered into the wheelhouse and spent some time talking with Charlie. Charlie by this time was steering entirely by the big box compass at his right hand, as navigation, on this sort of day, consisted of following a series of known bearings at a set speed, for so many hours and minutes.

Unbeknownst to anyone, something in the passenger's equipment began to pull the compass needle away from its true bearing. Charlie, not realizing what was happening, kept adjusting the tug's course, with the result that we were soon sailing south into the middle of the lake. By the time we realized we were lost, the boat was wallowing in heavy seas, it was raining hard and visibility in the spume and fog was limited to a few yards.

It was the skipper who first deduced that something had gone wrong with the navigation and almost at the same instant, while everyone ran to the nearest lookout position, the 14-footer broke loose. In the hectic moments that followed, while Charlie circled in search of the missing boat, our position became even further ambiguous.

At the portside, rear of the tug, was a huge steel sliding door and we had opened this a few feet during the attempt to find the errant 14-footer. When we did locate it a few minutes later, Charlie managed to get so close to it that Byron, the lead patrolman, was able to lean out and catch it by hand. I, wedged behind an angle of the door, was hanging on to Byron. The small boat was nearly a third full of water, making it very heavy and when the two vessels began to move apart, both of us nearly ended up in the lake. It was only by a very determined effort that we managed to hold and secure it.

Meanwhile the conditions were, if anything, worsening. The search had been tricky business, forcing the tug into unfavourable positions with regard to the run of the waves, and as a result the crew had received quite a shaking-up. The heavy odour of fish and diesel fuel in the dim confines of the hold, where men and gear were being tossed around, added to the discomfort. More than one man had been thrown heavily against the steel floor or the walls and most were green around the gills.

With the navigational problem discovered and the camp boat once more in tow, the tug's master set the course due north, ordered dead-slow ahead and cleared all passengers out of the wheelhouse. We had no way of knowing exactly how far we were from shore and there was every chance of running smack into a granite wall when we did reach it. Straining our eyes, we crept slowly through the fog while the tug rolled sickeningly. As luck would have it, a ray of sun broke through the murk just in time to help us safely into Peninsula Bay. Our first glimpse of land showed us the huge oil-storage tanks that stand at the foot of the big hill on the south side of Marathon. From there we made our way around into the mouth of the harbour and chugged gratefully up to the dock beside the mill.

While the gear was being unloaded, I questioned the captain as to his intentions regarding the trip back to Otter Cove. Bob stated that he intended to remain at the dock for the night, in the hope for better conditions in the morning. Then, because everyone had had a very rough day, I invited Bob and Charlie to my house on Stevens Avenue, for a much-needed drink of Scotch whiskey. After that, I drove them to the grocery store where they purchased a very modest little bag of groceries and then to the headache store from which they emerged with a much larger sack—full of liquid refreshment. It was about six in the late afternoon when I left Bob and Charlie at the dock, with the understanding that the tug would remain there overnight.

However, down at the docks below at the American Can plant, two men, who should have known better, downed the last of a 40-ounce bottle of whiskey. They then removed the moorings of the tugboat, *Dorelin II*. Five minutes later, the tug rounded the headland and disappeared in the storm and darkness. Her destination was Otter Cove, 50 miles to the east

When I arrived at the office next morning, the first thing I learned was that the pair had left the previous evening. Miraculously, it seems they nearly made it. According to the testimony by "Old Nappy," he received a message from the tug at nine at night. He heard them say, "We're okay now, we can see your light." Then, for five hours on that dark and storm-tossed lake, there was no sight or sound from the tug. When it finally docked below the lighthouse at two in the morning, Charlie was the only one on board.

One can only surmise as to what transpired out there. Demon rum certainly played a hand, as it has in so many sinister events at sea. Charlie was in a very drunken state when he arrived and the tale he told that night did not jibe with the one he related the next day, nor with any of the other versions that he came up with in the next ten days.

The evidence showed that between them, in addition to what was consumed in town, the two men put away a 40-ounce bottle of rye and various amounts of beer and wine. This wasn't an extraordinary feat for sailors. With heavy drinking and rough seas, accidents can easily happen. The old man may have slid the big steel door aside at the stern and held onto the side while he relieved himself, then the tug rolled unexpectedly and he is gone. His partner, stupid with drink, wouldn't even miss him until long after the drowned man was on his way to the bottom, never to come back.

Bob Sr. was never found and it is typical of Lake Superior that she does not give up her dead. The lake is like a giant deepfreeze. Even on a sizzling summer day, when black flies are teeming inland in the hot forest, you can lean over the side of your canoe a quarter-mile offshore and see your breath across the water. Bodies consigned to that icy hold do not decay as they would in warm water and, as a result, remain at the bottom. So the Ontario Provincial Police dragged for the old man's body with no success and questioned Charlie until they were blue in the face. They finally let him go. The evidence was inconclusive.

In the normal course of events the story would end there, except for a strange thing that happened the following winter, shortly before Christmas. My lead-hand and I had business in Sault Ste. Marie and stayed over night in a motel. After supper, for something to do, we went out for a few beers. Who should we find in a waterfront bar, but Charlie. He was sitting alone at a small, round-topped table near the door, a single beer in front of him with his chin on his chest—half-asleep.

He roused up at the appearance of company and cheered momentarily at the sight of a fresh round of beer. Soon he sank back into melancholy. He had a sad tale to tell. It seems he was blacklisted on the Great Lakes, and had not been able to land a job since the incident at Otter Cove. As Charlie grew more and more maudlin, Byron and I exchanged looks that said it was time to leave. We had always harboured mixed feelings about the man, even before the disappearance of the tug's captain, and were not of a mind to listen to a lot of self-pitying beer talk.

As to what happened next, the exact details may have become confused by time which has a tendency to dim some recollections and harden others. Byron had already risen from his chair and was heading for the door and I was getting ready to leave, when I turned back briefly to say goodbye. What I saw gave me quite a start. Charlie was looking up at me with undisguised malevolence and, as I stood dumbfounded, I heard him say, "That's two of you bastards now!"

There were allegations that this was, indeed, the second time that this Metis had been involved in the disappearance of a white man on the Great Lakes. It does not appear that charges were ever laid in either case.

The 30-Second Window

To begin this account of aerial adventures we return briefly to Jasper on a sunny, summer morning, many years ago and to a box canyon somewhere between the Medicine Tent and Restless Rivers. There, in the shadow of an enormous rock wall nearly 2000 feet high, a little red helicopter—looking like a tiny, brightly-coloured insect—struggled to ascend. Swinging violently from side to side, shaking with exertion, the machine was about two-thirds of the way up the cliff when it hit a powerful downdraft. Seconds later we were plummeting into the canyon, the rotor flapping helplessly.

There were two of us inside the bubble of the Bell 47-G2: Bob the pilot, the plastic tip of a Colt cigarillo clenched in his teeth, and myself. He was an experienced flier, but new to mountain terrain; as for me, it was only my second time in a helicopter. It was 1968, and helicopters were beginning to play a significant role in park operations. The smaller machines were ideal for search and rescue work, forest-fire suppression, law enforcement and wildlife counts. Some terrific pilots would come to be associated with the Warden Service in various parks. They were brave, skilful, unflappable men, in whose capable hands, the wardens placed their lives. The careers of many of these pilots would in each case make a book that deserves to be written. But like the wardens, who rode with them or hung beneath their machines, the majority were quiet, self-effacing men reluctant to tell their own adventures.

As for me, I simply loved to fly. I didn't care if it was in a helicopter, a small airplane or a jumbo jet, once in the air, I put complete trust in the pilot and concentrated on my own work, whether spotting fires or searching for missing people. And I never got sick.

On the morning that we ended up in the box canyon, we had started out to see how the Bell 47-G2 would work for spotting game. While flying up the Medicine Tent, we remembered having heard of a good bighorn sheep, grazing area over on the Restless. A spur-of-the-moment decision to cross over had brought us to the wall. I wondered aloud, "Can this machine fly over it?"

Forgetting the old airman's dictum that a 180° turn is often the safest manoeuvre in the business, Bob decided to try. We were about 300 feet below the summit when the downdraft hit us. I tried to figure out what was going on. The motor was still running, and the rotary wing was still going around, but the familiar pop-pop-pop sound was missing. It was as if the blade was operating in a vacuum, with nothing to support it. Meanwhile, we continued to drop.

The rock face, which shot past us like the shaft of a high-speed elevator, was so close we could see the lichens in the crevices. I cut my eyes to the left and looked at the pilot. Bob sat immobile, no expression on his face; his knuckles, as he clutched the cyclic, were white and he appeared about to bite through the plastic tip of his Cigarillo. Just as it seemed certain that we would crash in the scree at the foot of the cliff, the pop-pop-pop sound began to come back—hesitantly at first, then with a steady and reassuring thunder. I began to breathe again. With control of the machine back in his hands, the pilot swung away from the cliff. He glanced casually at me. "I guess that answers your question," he said.

Although at first, helicopters were used mainly for game counts and anti-poaching patrols, it wasn't long before their usefulness for forest-fire detection and suppression was recognized. One of the first big parks to use helicopters for fire fighting was Wood Buffalo (WBNP), on the border between Alberta and the Northwest Territories.

I was one of a number of wardens who got my first "fire flying" at WBNP. It was a summer in the late sixties and the park was having a horrendous fire season. The million or so dollars normally reserved for suppression had been spent twice over and there was no relief in sight. In late July, a few other wardens and I from the mountain parks were seconded to assist our colleagues in the north. The airstrip at Fort Smith, where we landed, was hidden beneath a heavy pall of grey. Later, sitting in a room in the old Pinecrest Hotel, waiting to be contacted by the chief warden, we gazed curiously through the dingy window. The outlines of the town were blurred by smoke and the hot July sun shining through the haze turned everything a glaring yellowish-white. We sat conversing in low tones, wondering what we had got ourselves into.

I ended up on Fire #66, north of Fort Smith. It was an ill-fated fire. One man had already been killed. He was a native person, who was sent into town for supplies. Returning late in the evening, possibly under the influence of alcohol, he rolled the pickup truck. Another firefighter, later on, would also die, as a result of walking into the tail rotor of a helicopter.

One of my duties was to fly the fire each day, in late afternoon, and chart the progress of the various fire fighting crews, also noting potential trouble spots. I would then return to camp and prepare a map as part of my situation report for the fire boss. Late in the evening, this map would be carefully studied by the planning team and strategy devised for the next day. There were a half-dozen helicopters coming and going on this fire and eventually I ended up in one piloted by a man whom I immediately classed as "The Kid."

Not only was this fellow very young to be a pilot, he also gave the impression of having a lot of rough edges, both culturally and as a flyer. Much of the time, the boy did his own maintenance which, upon careful observance, I decided was pretty sketchy. His take-offs and landings were rough and his handling of the machine was clumsy. "The Kid," in both mannerisms and capability, gave the impression of a backwoods farm boy who had somehow managed to step directly from his tractor into an airplane, without any upgrading of skills. I was never very comfortable in his machine.

After three weeks of concentrated effort by 70 men, nine bulldozers, seven helicopters, and a fleet of water bombers, Forest Fire #66 was deemed under control. The park wardens from Jasper National Park were told they could go home. On the morning of departure we were standing, with our duffel bags, in front of the camp and waiting for the car to take us to Fort Smith. "The Kid" was tinkering around with his machine. Most of the other helicopters had been released. After a few moments, he walked over to our group and in his eager and impulsive way offered to take me for a last flight over the fire. As our ride wasn't in sight yet, I said, "Hey let's do it!"

"The Kid" went to warm up his helicopter, only to find that it refused to start. Several minutes went by while he tried to coax it into life and the park wardens watched. Standing there, looking at that sorry machine coughing and hiccupping in the morning sun, I began to get a very strange feeling—a premonition of something bad. I thought of the dead truck driver and the man who walked into the tail rotor, and I thought of the Law of Three. Just as the helicopter fired, the car arrived. While "The Kid" beckoned excitedly, I waved and gratefully climbed into car's back seat. It was the only time I ever turned down a chopper ride.

While there were many exciting days on Lake Superior, not all the wild rides at Pukaskwa were on the water. Patrols by air also provided some hair-raising experiences, including being shot at by disgruntled hunters who resented the creation of a national park. At Pukaskwa, light aircraft were used frequently to explore and monitor activities in the new proposed National Park. There were flights with park planners to explore access routes, with biologists to observe wildlife, trips in the winter to monitor ice conditions and snow depths—to mention but a few activities. Much of this work was done using Cessna 180 float planes owned and operated by a local air service.

It was fortunate that I loved flying, because there were days when anyone not totally committed to that mode of travel might have experienced second thoughts. On my first flight with this particular company, I climbed into the cockpit, only to discover that the passenger seat was nonexistent. Upon drawing that small oversight to the attention of the pilot, I was hurriedly instructed to drag an empty fish-packing crate forward from the rear of the plane and perch on it as best I could.

Having solved the seating problem, I directed my attention to the instrument panel. I was intrigued to see three large open spaces where various aids to flying, normally considered essential, were obviously missing. When I enquired as to these instruments, I was informed, "The radio's in Thunder Bay for repairs; the altimeter, which normally fits here, is in the shop; as for the compass, well—. Anyway," the pilot continued, looking at me cheerily, "not to worry. All set? Here we go!" And he roared off across the lake, while I hung onto my fish crate.

There were some jobs, such as finding a suitable location for a hilltop repeater station for the Park's first VHF radio system, that required a helicopter rather than a fixed-wing aircraft. The process called for many landings in remote areas of Pukaskwa, and along the coast. A small helicopter company from the Lakehead was engaged for this and other work. Tim, the head pilot, did much of the flying himself. I grew to like and respect this man. He was an affable person—cool, sensible and efficient.

Then came the bad forest-fire summer and I became aware of a change in my friend. He often seemed tired and inclined to take risks that he would normally not have done. After awhile I learned that Tim and his partner were putting in nearly all their time on forest fires in the northern part of the province. Fire season is prime time for helicopter companies and Tim was determined to get in as many hours as possible. Perhaps he was trying to get out of debt or get money ahead. Whatever the reason, he was pushing the outside of the envelope in terms of his own endurance—something a pilot can ill afford to do. Finally, at the urging of his family, he agreed to accompany them on a short vacation. Halfway to their destination, he turned the car around and drove back to Thunder Bay. It was a sign someone should have picked up on but, in any case, who can stop a pilot from flying his own machine?

Tim's last flight for the park took place in early fall. There had been rumours floating around that persons, believed to be American hunters, were anchoring in various bays along the coast and coming ashore to hunt moose. I decided to check it out, and called for the helicopter. Starting off on a calm, sunny day, we had flown for some 45 minutes without results when we happened to spot what appeared to be an American vessel, handily tucked in behind a small island.

There did not seem to be anyone about. As it happened, a small river, which might bear looking at, emptied into the lake close by. The banks of this stream were lined with dead spruce trees, victims of beaver activity in years past. As the root systems eroded in the water-logged soil, these dead snags tended to lean out across the river like crossed swords at a military wedding, sometimes forming a tunnel of considerable length. We were approaching one of these places when a green canoe became visible. It contained three men and what appeared to be guns and fishing gear and was in the middle of the channel below a series of leaning snags.

The helicopter was hovering at the entrance to the tunnel when Tim asked if we should check these guys out. I was about to nod in the affirmative when it suddenly occurred to me that the pilot was poised to fly under the trees. This idea startled me to such an extent that I hastily shook my head and emphatically motioned upward!

We were able to land in a small green, open space a few minutes later, although so close to the canoe that the prop wash nearly blew the occupants into the water. The men were U.S. citizens, who appeared to have arrived without the benefit of Canadian Customs knowing about them. Although there were a number of charges which could be laid, the complexities of trying to bring American citizens to court for actions committed in a proposed national park with unmarked boundaries were more than I was prepared to get into at the time. We therefore gathered what information we could, warned them in strongest terms against any further transgressions on Canadian soil, and watched them motor back towards their yacht. I hoped the unexpected and dramatic checkstop would impress them sufficiently that they'd heed the warning.

Soon after, Tim met his demise when he flew into a steel cable at the Lakehead. The tragedy weighed on everyone who had known him. I took the helicopter cap that Tim had given me and hung it on a nail in my room. At least once a day I would stop and regard the hat in a private moment of silence. But flying had to go on, and the park found another company.

Another fine day, I was back in one of the Cessna 180 floatplanes. It was in the fall and I was taking a count of active beaver lodges in the park. Lodges can be seen and counted at any time of year, but in preparation for winter the beaver build food caches below the surface of the water to sustain them during the time when the lakes are frozen. Seen from above these food rafts show up as a light-green patch, just adjacent to the animals' lodges and thus mark it as an active residence rather than one which may have been abandoned.

Working together, the pilot and I had devised a grid pattern for the flight; time and fuel had been calculated accordingly. About halfway through, however, we encountered a troublesome north wind. That, and an unforeseen need to fly some extra lines, had the effect of depleting the margin of fuel that all aircraft are required to maintain as a safety measure.

Our base, a little lake, was only about 60 miles to the northeast, so we decided to finish the job before turning back.

A northern front was forecast to cross the district later on that day but, as sometimes happens, the timing was off by a few hours. Flying low along the shore of Lake Superior, we were not aware that the system was about to overtake us until wisps of cold, grey cloud began drifting overhead. Concentrating on the ground, I was not conscious of the change until an urgent tap on the shoulder from the pilot made me look up. When our eyes met, the decision to leave was unanimous. The Cessna was already banking steeply to the north as I hurriedly completed the charts and gathered up the maps. As the little airplane gained altitude, we were surprised and uneasy to find the tops of the coastal hills obscured in low clouds. Dark, wet-looking tendrils of vapour infiltrated the valleys and behind us the lake was almost hidden. Climbing rapidly to avoid the ridge tops, we were soon enveloped in the mist. The light dimmed and streaks of moisture tracked across the windows.

When we finally emerged in brilliant sunshine, there was a solid deck of cloud below us for as far as we could see, in every direction. Little rumples extended all the way to the horizon with, here and there, a swollen hump that probably indicated a hilltop. There was no sign of a break. The pilot studied his fuel gauge again and consulted his charts for alternate landing places. Outwardly calm he set his bearing for White River. As we floated on, a tiny silver speck high above a sea of cotton wool, I though how quickly things can go wrong in the air. A faulty instrument, an error in the weather forecast, a slight bending of the rules to get a job done and, all of a sudden, you were in trouble. The landing lake at White River was quite small and we did not know if it would be visible when we reached it. For the next twenty minutes, there was nothing to do but settle down and fly, hoping for a break.

When the pilot's calculations indicated that the town of White River should be directly below, we renewed our efforts to find an opening in the clouds. Luck was not with us. Nowhere could we find even a dark shadow to indicate that "Mother Earth" was close beneath. The pilot flew slow circles while he grappled with our problem. He knew that he had only enough fuel to stay in the air about five more minutes. If he climbed higher, giving himself a wider range of vision, we might spot an opening somewhere, but that was still no guarantee that there would be hospitable terrain below. Furthermore, the climb would exhaust his last reserve of fuel. On the other hand, to descend blindly into cloud in the desperate hope of hitting the lake, was far more likely to bring us up against a power line or spruce tree.

There were no certainties this day, except one and that was that very soon we would cease flying. He decided to risk everything in one short climb, grasp whatever clues he could find and drift down while he still had power. Just as the pilot banked to the left for the ascent I looked over my right shoulder and glimpsed a sparkle of blue water. "There's a hole back there," I shouted. Moments later we had dropped through it and were on the lake. It even turned out to be the right one. I thought it must be the most beautiful bit of water I had ever seen.

We taxied up to the wharf and the engine slowed as we drifted alongside. I was about to step out and secure the ropes, when the pilot turned his impassive countenance toward me and said, "Now that we're down, want to know how much flying time we had left?"

"Yes, I would."

"About half a minute," he said softly, "30 seconds."

Part Five

On the move again;
stories from Newfoundland
and the Atlantic Region.

The Wardens Called Me "Dearie"

I gazed out of the window at the rain streaming off the wing tips, and wondered just how far above the ground we really were. I was on a flight from Halifax, Nova Scotia to Deer Lake, Newfoundland in my new position as the first Warden Service Coordinator for the Atlantic Region of Parks Canada. The plane was one of those short-bodied jets used by Eastern Provincial Airways in the 1970s and the weather was horrible, as was usual around "The Rock." Floating high above the Cabot Strait, tiny whitecaps just visible through the ragged mist, I had been musing over my experiences so far in the Maritimes.

Not only did I have a whole new array of wonderful parks to work in, I was also getting exposure to a lot of Canada's history of which I had been only vaguely aware while growing up in the West. One very important aspect of this history was the juxtaposition of French and English. A great park in which to enjoy the two cultures is the senior maritime park—Cape Breton Highlands. A spectacular drive, the Cabot Trail, takes the visitor from the old Scottish-English village on the east side of the park; up across the north tip of the island high above the sea, down to the delightfully French-Canadian town of Cheticampe, with its old church, on the island's west side. In one day, it is possible to soak up Scottish pioneer culture at Ingonish, view the rugged highlands and the sea, then have lunch or dinner at a little Acadian restaurant on the west side.

There is wonderful oral history to be had at Cape Breton as well. Whenever I had an opportunity to visit with the locals, I would be treated to elaborate tales that illustrated the nature of man and the adversities of the land—all of these told with great panache.

Another place richly endowed with French and English history is the Fortress of Louisbourg, on Cape Breton's east coast. Now an outstanding national historic site, the original village was first established by French fishermen from Placentia, Newfoundland in 1717. Louisbourg did well, developing into a major fishing station and port of trade. In 1745, the town was captured by New Englanders aided by the British Navy, only to be returned to France in 1749. Finally in a six-week siege in 1758, British forces under General James Wolfe captured the fortress and the site changed hands for the last time. Because my new job included responsibility for public safety, law enforcement and fire prevention at historic sites as well as at national parks, I visited wonderful places, like Louisbourg, as part of my duties.

All the maritime parks were beautiful in their own way and I tried to take the family to see them whenever circumstances permitted. There was Kejimkujik, a two-hour drive south of Halifax, with its beautiful lakes, wonderful mixed forest, and the biggest, most bloodthirsty ticks in North America. When we stopped for lunch beneath a big old tree just outside the park, we looked down in horror to see hordes of these frightening creatures literally swarming up our legs. Our daughter flew into a panic and our little dog had to be rescued and put back in the car. We were told that these ticks originated in the U.S. and were migrating further north each summer. I seldom wish any of God's creatures bad luck, but I hope that, by now, those ticks have reached the northern tip of Cape Breton and marched into the North Atlantic.

Kejimkujik Lake, lying in the centre of the park, is a destination for many visitors from Halifax. Jacques Landing, at the north end of the lake, is often the point of departure for eager canoeists from the city. One story, which deserves to become a legend, was about a man who arrived at the Landing one day with his canoe and made preparations to go out on the lake. The water was very rough that day and the canoeist was inexperienced. When he was loaded and ready to go, he had no weight in the front, with the result that the wind caught the upraised bow and twirled him around like a top about 200 yards from the landing. Not just a little rattled, he came back to shore, where one of the park wardens had been watching his dilemma.

As he was getting ready to try it again, the warden pointed to a large rock lying nearby and suggested the man place it in the front of his canoe.

As was to be expected, this added weight in the right place held the little craft steady and the visitor paddled happily off. Two days later, another warden described having met this person on one of the portages that occur along the canoe route in "Kedgie." The Warden was amazed to see that, although the day was hot and the canoeist sweating heavily under his load, he was determinedly packing along a 40-pound rock, on top of everything else!

Meanwhile, there were far more serious things going of at Kouchi–bouguac, the new national park in northern New Brunswick. Here, I became involved in the unbelievable saga of an Acadian squatter who for years defied the power of the court of New Brunswick, the Royal Canadian Mounted Police and indirectly the Supreme Court of Canada.

The root of the trouble lay in the fact that, beginning in 1969, a number of small farms and homesteads, in the St. Louis de Kent and Richibucto area of north-eastern New Brunswick, had to be expropriated in order to put together the land for Kouchibouguac National Park. Unfortunately, expropriation is a process that can lead to a great deal of ill will, which is the last thing in the world that a new park needs. In this case, the man simply refused to co-operate. Even though a sum of money was offered him that was more than equal to the value of his property, he refused to pick it up. A long and increasingly bitter struggle ensued and continued for years. As the pressure mounted for the family to leave, there were riot scenes at the park's administration office. Park buildings were set on fire and visitors harassed. Finally, when every reasonable avenue had been tried and failed, the clan was removed from the park by force and the house, which was little more than a shack, was bulldozed to the ground.

This should have been the end of it but it was only the beginning. Incredible as it sounds, they managed to move back in and set themselves up in another shack, this time with a sunken floor, sandbags, and rifles. It also became obvious as time went on, that they were getting support from an undisclosed, possibly foreign source at a fairly high level. They began driving a new, bright red Jeep, and did not seem to have any difficulty in paying for thousands of dollars worth of legal fees which accrued over the years. To the best of this writer's knowledge, the source of this support has never been made public. Neither has the reason, although the motive almost certainly must have been to embarrass Parks Canada and the federal government.

Old Ships Sail Out of the Fog

Harder yet to explain was the fact that officialdom suddenly adopted a hands-off approach to any incident involving the squatter clan—in spite of the very serious nature of many of these incidents. At various times shots were fired at park wardens and visitors were assaulted in the campgrounds. This inexplicable, hands-off behaviour on the part of all levels of government had all the indications of a political decision at a very high level, not a word of which ever leaked down to me, or to the wardens and police in the field.

After one particular court decision went against the protestors in Moncton, the office of the Parks Canada's lawyer was fire-bombed; as a final outrage, the park superintendent was assaulted in his own home on Christmas Eve. Through it all, park officials had to try to operate a national park and protect their staff and visitors, while cabinet ministers stood around wringing their hands, seemingly unable to make up their minds to put an end to the travesty occurring at Kouchibouguac.

Finally, on October 26, 1987, the then-outgoing premier of New Brunswick, as his last official act, placed his signature, beside that of the individual concerned, on an agreement which granted them a piece of land outside the park and a considerable sum of money if they would leave. Incredibly, the agreement did not specify a date for his departure and, when I last enquired, this family was still living in Kouchibouguac National Park.

It was into this mess, some of it past, some of it on-going, and much still in the future, that I, as Warden Operations Manager, tip-toed with even more than my customary caution. To my surprise, I found the wardens in good form. Although isolated and alone, dealing almost daily with difficult and dangerous situations, they were up-beat, outgoing and irreverent. During the years that I worked to encourage and support them, I often wondered at their ability to remain cheerful in the face of constant trouble and frustration. In spite of the troubles, I grew to look forward to my visits to the park, where business carried on in a delightful and high-spirited mixture of French and English.

Meanwhile, the abrupt lowering of the wing flaps brought me back to the present. The fog was still so thick you could cut it with a knife but, conditioned by many scary landings, a tightening of the sphincter told me that the tops of the spruce trees at Deer Lake were getting dangerously close. Seconds later they seemingly zoomed up out of the murk no more than 20 feet below, and then we were on the runway—braking at an incredible rate. Just as it seemed the stubby little plane was about to stand on its nose, it came to a stop with barely enough room to turn around.

I sank back in my seat and let out a long breath. I was still trying to get used to Eastern Provincial's pilots. They seemed able to find their way around in any kind of weather, as indeed they had to do if they were ever going to get off the ground. Ironically, the only time I experienced a late departure was on a bright, sunny morning at Stephenville on what they call a "civil day" in Newfoundland. That day I sat in the little terminal for two hours, looking at my plane waiting on the tarmac. There were no repairs going on, and in typical Newfoundland manner, no explanation was forthcoming as to why they weren't loading up. I stared at the airplane again and it stared back, sunlight glinting off the cockpit windows. Nothing moved, either in the plane, or around it.

Finally a big, grey cloud blotted out the sun and almost immediately the airport came to life. The captain and crew could be seen marching smartly out to their plane, the baggage checker appeared at his place, the ticket agent arrived at her desk. Ten minutes later we were lifting off into the usual fog and rain. All of which led me to wonder if Eastern Provincial's pilots became disoriented in the sunshine.

At Deer Lake, I rented an economy-class car at the tiny airport, picked up a road map, threw my suitcase in the back seat, and headed north. My first stop would be the new Gros Morne National Park. When I arrived in the park area it was already evening, so I got a room in the hamlet of Lomond. I had been warned that motels in Newfoundland tended to be rudimentary, and this proved to be true. It was also my misfortune to have a bunch of party-animals move in next door and I soon learned that "Newfies" take their partying seriously. The whole building was made of plywood and when they began to dance, the vigour of their stomping literally shook my bed. They danced until near dawn.

Finally, while trying to salvage an hour or two of sleep between daybreak and sun-up, I was awakened again, this time by what sounded like someone retching outside my window. Now thoroughly out of temper I rushed outside prepared to give whoever it was a piece of my mind. Imagine my surprise when, instead of a drunk, I came face to face with the amber stare of a very big, black Billy goat! The animal seemed just as astonished to see me. After sizing me up for a long minute, it shook its head, gave one more loud "Baa-aa-a," and ambled away. I gave up, packed my bags, and went in search of breakfast.

In the restaurant, I enquired about the ferry to Norris Point and was told it would arrive about 10 o'clock. It was nearly one in the afternoon before it came chugging in—with no explanation. The operator obviously felt that if he managed the trip across the inlet once a day, he was doing his job. I was learning that time here was often irrelevant.

So it was afternoon when I arrived in the little town of Rocky Harbour and rocky it certainly was. Newfoundland beaches tend more to stone than they do to sand but this place was exceptional. There were rocks in the town used for decoration, rocks all over the beach, rocks out into the water as far as one could see, and way off to the south-west, a number of great pillars of stone guarded the entrance to the harbour.

After securing a place for the night in the town's only hotel, I went in search of the Gros Morne Administration Office. This I found, in a quiet little hollow on the hillside east of town. After paying my respects to Mac Estabrooks, the Superintendent, I settled down in the chief warden's office for an introduction to their Warden Service. Chief Warden Freeman Timmins was a canny, craggy-faced Cape Bretoner with whom I soon established a good rapport, and before long he was telling me about his law-enforcement and public-safety problems in the new park, as easily as if we had known each other for years.

Gros Morne is a wilderness park of exceptional beauty, a fascinating combination of sea and mountains. The most spectacular section is Western Brook Pond, a deep-water fjord running inland between tremendous cliffs, nearly 2000 feet high. Above the cliffs to the south is high, open-alpine country and at the far end of the fjord the ground rises to become mountainous terrain. Caribou inhabited the country beyond those mountains and hopefully still do if the poachers haven't killed them all; if a proposed power dam hasn't flooded their habitat; if the wildlife biologists haven't studied them to death.

I learned that poaching of moose and rabbit was a problem in the new park, as it would continue to be for many years. Poaching of wildlife is an ongoing challenge for the wardens in most, if not all the national parks, but it is particularly difficult to control in the "Land of Fish 'n Fog." There are a number of reasons for this, one being the poverty and chronic joblessness prevalent on "The Rock," where game and birds are a valued supplement to a poor-man's larder, a supplement which may be denied by the creation of a national park. Another reason is the fact that, in Newfoundland, there is no social stigma attached to poaching. Something of a Robin Hood mystique remains where poaching the king's deer is akin to an honourable profession and getting anyone to inform on a poacher is nearly impossible.

Perhaps this is not surprising. To begin with, although it's the oldest settled province in the country, a frontier point of view still prevails in much of the island, but there may be another, more subtle reason as well. In order to fathom the attitude towards authority of many of the poorer segments of society, one needs to look at their roots and background. A large percentage of the early settlers were Irish, fleeing from lives of terrible poverty and hardship in their homeland.

In order to procure passage to St. John's, where many of them first landed, they had to enter into a bond with the master of a trading vessel. These agreements stipulated that the passage money would be paid immediately upon finding employment in Newfoundland. Property of friends and relatives in Ireland was put up as security, meaning that failure to honour the debt would imperil those at home. Once in St. John's, the new immigrant would go to work for one of the fish barons or merchants who usually was a member of the predominantly English ruling class. The employer would pay the passage money owing the ship and mark the amount against the worker's account.

At this point, the unfortunate workman became little more than an indentured vassal to his employer, subject to a shameful system of extortion which often enslaved him for life. He was compelled to purchase all his raiment and supplies at the company store—at outrageous prices. The system was geared in such a way that, in spite of faithful service, the debt was never paid off until death cleared the accounts. The despair and hatred thus engendered may have had more than a little to do with the fact that, during its first 200 years, St. John's was nearly burnt to the ground on several occasions. Much of the populace apparently stood by and watched or, worse yet, plundered the burning shops.

It was thus that the old feudal attitudes were perpetuated even in the

New World; the distinction between aristocracy—the haves, and the peasants—the have-nots, vestiges of which linger yet. I was surprised to be addressed as "Sir," or "Zur," by many of the wardens and other park staff, something which had never happened to me before. I couldn't figure out if it was because I was from the mainland or because I was considered a "Big Shot from the Regional Office." I found it quite disconcerting, and tried hard to convince my new co-workers that I would rather be an equal, than a Sir. I was apparently successful, because by the time I was getting ready to leave, they were addressing me by such terms as "Love," "Dear Man" and "Dearie"—a practice which also took a bit of getting used to.

As for public safety, a number of searches and rescues had already taken place in the short history of the park. Most of them had occurred on the alpine plateaus south of Western Brook Pond and involved hikers who had been caught by a sudden storm in the high country and lost their bearings. Some were suffering from acute hypothermia before being discovered. The park Warden Service was fortunate in that a helicopter was being used to develop radio communication for Gros Morne and could usually be called upon for rescues if necessary.

Another concern, pointed out by one of the western alpine specialists who had been asked to do a hazard evaluation for the park, was the 2000-foot cliffs over the pond itself. For rock climbers, these granite walls presented a challenge equal to those of Yosemite and other world-class sites. It was believed that it could only be a matter of time before the climbing world discovered Gros Morne, after which the wardens might expect problems far beyond their ability to cope. The only organization in the country with the expertise for rescues on 2000-foot walls were the park wardens in the mountain national parks. I decided to get some help from Western Region to train the Gros Morne Wardens, and made arrangements, in case of an emergency, to fly east a few western, rescue wardens.

I spent four days at the park, boating up fjords, flying the high country, and hiking some of the trails. During much of this time, I was accompanied by Curling Laing, a rugged old warden, who had been a Provincial Ranger in the area before the national park was established. He told me fascinating stories of patrols along the coastline; long, lonely trips of perhaps a month at a time. On the third evening of my visit, with a cold, dark fog rolling in off the Atlantic, we shared a bottle of rum in the hotel room.

As rain pattered on the window, and the headlands faded in the gathering gloom, the old man reminisced about earlier times, tales of terrible hardship and isolation. There were no doctors for the sick, nor teachers for the children, nor clergymen to administer to the dying; it was a hard life spent scratching out a living between the cold sea and the brooding rock.

Then as the shadows in the room grew darker, and the wind picked up, battering a loose shutter somewhere on the outside wall, the ex-ranger's voice grew quiet. Speaking almost in a whisper, he began to tell of strange happenings—of wagons rumbling down lonely roads in the dark of night, when morning would reveal no sign or track. Of ships and men, known to have disappeared or perished years ago, but still sailing out of the fog, almost running over the fishermen in their dories before vanishing as mysteriously as they had come.

I heard the story of how if you dream of a friend or loved one and that person is walking away from you, you may depend on it that you will see them again in waking life. But if they come toward you in a dream, alas, 'tis the last time you will see their face! And, of course, there were many instances recalled to prove this was true. Suddenly I realized that I was hearing folklore of Newfoundland, where ancient legend and superstition still dwell close beneath the surface and I listened enthralled, far into that stormy night.

There was a newly constructed section of trail, of which the park was particularly proud, and I determined to look at it the next morning, a grand day which had the harbour sparkling under a bright sun. Curling accompanied me as guide. The path took us through a coastal area on which grew wind-shaped stands of stunted balsam fir and spruce, known in Newfoundland as tuckamores. The crowns of these trees are so flattened and entangled by the wind, that they form a mat upon which a person can almost walk. Trying to travel through those trees is so hard on skin and clothing that it is tempting to see if you could walk on top.

After an hour or so the ground became wetter and we began to encounter patches of sphagnum bog in which grew strange plants that I had not seen before. There were insect catchers like the pitcher plant—the emblem of Newfoundland, and a large berry—the bog apple, favoured by the local people for making pies.

A boardwalk had been constructed to take the visitors across these boggy areas, and it was along one of these sections that we had a close encounter with another of the natural wonders of the island. We had just turned a corner and entered a small clearing when we were met by four young ladies hiking in the opposite direction. Now there are big, handsome girls in the West, and fine-looking girls of the prairies, but nowhere are they quite as buxom as on "The Rock." The healthy good-looks of Newfoundland girls are legendary. Early visitors, while describing the appalling poverty and hardship that they observed in their travels, would stop to comment on the flaxen hair, rosy cheeks and robust figures of the young women.

After meeting the group on the boardwalk, I had to agree. They appeared to be in the mid to late teens, and had curves in places where many girls don't even have places. They wore cut-off jeans and, three of them, believing they were alone on the trail, had taken off their shirts and had on only their bras. By the time the girls realized they had company, it was too late to cover up, but there was no coyness or feigned embarrassment there. With one accord they squared their hefty young shoulders, stuck out those wonderful chests and marched past us with much jiggling and giggling. The old ranger apparently felt obligated to provide some commentary on what we had just witnessed. With a sideways look at me he cleared his throat, "Tis all the codfish and potatoes they's raised on, me son," he explained, "that makes 'em grow that way!"

On my last day at Gros Morne, I sat down with the chief warden and reviewed my visit. The Pukaskwa experience enabled me to relate to the problems of a new national park, and there were a number of things that could be done, to make things easier during the transition years, both in the field and at the Regional Office in Halifax. As usual, several pages of my notebook were filled with things to do when I got home. After thanking my hosts for their hospitality, I placed my old briefcase in the back seat of the rental and took the road leading north up the peninsula.

It was late afternoon when I got to the picturesque little town of Port Aux Choix and another dark Atlantic fog was rolling in, making it seem somehow more urgent than usual to find a warm bed for the night. I decided to try a Bed and Breakfast for which I had an address. I finally found the house on a narrow road on the outskirts. Stopping the car a short distance away to size the place up, I almost changed my mind. It was an old, two-storey affair, standing on a rise facing out to sea.

Some distance away, brooding headlands loomed darkly through the mist; and tendrils of fog, which now filled the harbour, were creeping up the hill to surround the house. Overhead a solitary gull wheeled slowly, grey against a grey sky, while in the foreground a few tired clumps of dune grass bowed before the rising wind and completed the dismal picture. The arrival of the first raindrops on the windshield forced a decision. I drove up, climbed out of the car and, with some trepidation, knocked on the door.

I was met by the mistress of the house, a plump cheerful lady. Once inside, I immediately felt better. I found myself in a very cozy, old-fashioned parlour, spotless linen on the table and silverware gleaming softly in the light from an open fire. Leading me up the spiral staircase, the landlady showed me into a wonderfully clean room with a hardwood floor and a large four-poster bed. Exploring my surroundings, I was intrigued to find a candle and a box of matches in the top dresser drawer. It was something I would encounter often in the Maritimes and particularly in Newfoundland, testimony to the uncertainty of electricity when aging power lines were hit by violent winter gales coming in off the Atlantic.

With perhaps an hour of daylight left, I went for a walk along the pier. Boats fascinated me almost as much as did airplanes and I loved to smell the sea and the salt. I thought about the colourful names of the fishing vessels and what the stories might be behind those names. The heavy fog shrouded the rigging and I conjured up images of Alfred Noyes' "ghostly galleons tossed upon cloudy seas."

Leaving the harbour, I found a tiny waterfront bar where I had a drink of Scotch; soaking up the warmth, and enjoying the friendly atmosphere typical of small-town Newfoundland pubs. By ten o'clock I was back upstairs in the old house, snuggled deep beneath down-filled comforters, while the wind moaned around the eaves and rain tapped upon the windows.

I went to sleep marvelling at all the strange and wonderful places the National Parks Service had taken me. What a contrast between a room like this—with its spotless linen, and a pack rat-infested, log cabin—with smelly-horse blankets in the back country of Jasper National Park. I awoke after a great sleep, looking forward to the bacon and eggs I had requested for breakfast, then I noticed the unmistakable odour of fried crab wafting up the stairwell. Could there have been a mistake in my order? Descending somewhat apprehensively to the parlour, I was relieved to see that there was in fact bacon and eggs on the table, but there was no mistaking the fishy sea taste which pervaded everything. I decided that my host's old cast-iron frying pan had cooked so much codfish and crab over the years that the flavour was permanently embedded in the metal.

Accustomed to making my own meals on the road, I discovered that grocery stores were scarce in many areas and the shelves often quite bare. Fresh fruit was hard to find, as were milk, eggs, and even bread but beer was available everywhere. There were two favourite brands: Blue Star and Black Horse. The Blue Star suited me very well and was actually much like the old Calgary, Alberta beer, which used to come in the tall brown bottle featuring the horseshoe and buffalo head—a most refreshing brew. Black Horse, which by the way became Black "Arse" in the vernacular, was a heavy, dark beer, and not at all to my taste.

On a later trip, I was surprised, therefore, to find that my colleague, a young Englishman from the Engineering Section of the Atlantic Regional Office, seemed to prefer this brand above all else. Most evenings, after supper, found us happily ensconced in a cozy "Newfie" pub. Here I would sip on my favourite Blue Star, while Tom invariably roared for a Black "Arse." One night, when I queried him about his preference, the young fellow admitted that he could barely stomach the stuff, but he couldn't resist shouting, "I'll have a Black 'Arse'!"

Driving up the peninsula, on that first visit to the island, I was intrigued to see horses and cattle grazing freely along the side of the road, I learned that Newfoundland Range Law, contrary to the rest of Canada, did not require the owners of stock to fence in their animals. Rather, landowners erected fences to keep other people's animals out! I was also surprised, at first, to find potato patches and vegetable gardens planted in the roadside ditches, sometimes miles from anywhere. For some of the people, these ditches were the only arable land available. They apparently respected each other's gardens, for very seldom were they raided or damaged.

As I drove north towards St. Anthony, the weather grew very warm, and a relentless southwest wind blew diagonally across the peninsula. The road at the time was unpaved, and before long the dust began to permeate the car and all its contents. It got into the upholstery and the glove compartment and formed a thick coat over the dashboard. The road was an endless series of potholes, which shook the car mercilessly, bouncing the dust around. I was amazed to find dust even inside my closed suitcase when I unpacked it at night. Wilting in the heat, choking in the dust, I began to long for an ice cream cone.

Meanwhile the road went on, pothole after pothole, bump after bump. Heat and dust and wind and nothing wet in sight, but the salty sea. In late afternoon I came to a small service centre somewhere west of St. Anthony. At a Dairy Queen, ice cream and milk shakes were prominently advertised. Nearly beside myself with anticipation, I stepped inside. There were two husky girls in the place, one behind the counter and one sitting cross-legged on a stool. They were deep in conversation, and barely looked up as I approached, but I was dying for ice cream. With great anticipation, I placed my order but, to my astonishment and disappointment, I was bluntly told, "Ain't got none."

I turned back on the road toward St. Anthony. This turned out to be a small, picturesque town on the northeast tip of Newfoundland's Great Northern Peninsula. It had its beginnings as a seasonal fishing station for French and Basque fishermen in the early 1500s. This is how Jacques Cartier found it in 1534, when he named the protected harbour St. Anthony Haven. It was growing dark as I approached the historic old town. I had an impression of houses propped up on the rocky hills surrounding the harbour. Many seemed to be supported by stilts under the front porches.

Out to sea, an iceberg gleamed enticingly against the darkening sky. Meanwhile on land, it was still very warm and dusty. At the edge of town, someone had set up an outdoor ice-cream stand. About a dozen people stood in line in the gathering dusk, talking in low tones as they shuffled forward. I left my car and joined them. As I approached the little wooden stand I apprehensively noted that the cones being handed out appeared to be getting smaller. Finally, there remained only a little boy of eight or nine between me and the head of the line.

The vendor dug deep. He scratched and clawed around in the bin and barely scraped together enough to build a cone for the little boy. My heart sank as I watched. As the lad turned to go, his treasure in hand, he stumbled; the cone wobbled and, possibly, the last scoop of ice cream on the northern peninsula, plopped into the dust. The little boy and I looked down and watched as the lovely cold stuff turned into a dirty brown blob and the tears ran unashamedly down both our cheeks.

Giving up on ice cream, I started looking for supper. I found a small restaurant and went inside. There were only two other people in the whole place and they were not eating anything I could recognize. I found out why, when a plump and cheerful waitress came bustling up and presented a menu containing a half-dozen entrées. I started hopefully enough by asking for the roast beef but this, it seemed, had run out for the day. After all, it was almost nine in the evening. The story was the same for the veal cutlet and the filet. My stomach gave an angry twinge. I was on the verge of walking out, but decided to try once more. Moving to the bottom of the list I asked for the round steak and mashed potatoes. To my relief the waitress seemed to brighten at this suggestion and hurried off to the kitchen. Maybe it would be all right after all.

After a few moments, however, she was back, nervously chewing on her pencil. Due to the fact that they had had a very busy day and everything was running low, they wondered if I might like a nice slice of bologna in place of the round steak. And, oh yes, the mashed potato was really potato salad left over from lunchtime. I was beginning to feel almost as sorry for the embarrassed waitress as I was for myself. "Okay," I said weakly, "that will be fine."

The next morning, after an uneventful night in a nondescript motel, I walked into the town. At first it looked not unlike most of the other 1300 or so outports which dot the coastline of Newfoundland. There was the harbour, surrounded by the usual filigree of ramshackle wharves, stages, fish flakes (racks for drying fish), and cleaning and salting sheds known as fish stores. The holes in the floors of these sheds, through which fish guts and gurry found their way back to the sea, sometimes served double duty as outdoor privies, an expediency resulting from the fact that digging holes is a fruitless and discouraging business on "The Rock." The difficulty of digging is also the reason that many of the fronts of the houses were supported by stilts. This brought the front level with the backs which rested on solid stone. To build a basement and pour a proper footing are a major undertakings in most places on the island. Besides which, the spaces below the raised fronts of the houses, make a fine shelter for dogs, sheep and goats, and the occasional chicken! And over all, hangs the awesome stench of rotting fish guts and kelp.

In most aspects, St. Anthony was a typical, small Newfoundland town, but what did surprise me was its massive four-storey hospital. By far the most impressive building on all of the Great Northern Peninsula—the

Charles S. Curtiss Memorial Hospital, is the legacy of Dr. Wilfred Grenfell, the beloved healer who devoted his life to helping the poor and sick in Newfoundland and Labrador.

After a fascinating morning spent learning about the Grenfell Institute, I climbed back in my dusty little car, and took the narrow, bumpy gravel road to L'anse Aux Meadows, the 1000-year-old, Viking site at the very tip of the peninsula. Believed to be the place where the Norsemen first landed in North America, the site was discovered in 1960 by Norwegian explorer and writer, Helge Ingstad. When I visited the site in the 1970s, Parks Canada was in the process of restoring the long boats and sod houses used by the Vikings during their first winter in the New World. A harsh winter it must have seemed even for those intrepid travellers. As one draws near the tip of the peninsula, there is a sense of growing desolation and of moving back in time. The land flattens out as it reaches toward the sea. Scrub trees give way to gorse and dune grass. On many days the weather is grey, bleak, and cold.

The Vikings may have found a few berries and the odd hare. There would have been fish. No sizable timber grew anywhere near, although sticks and small railings were used to frame the sod houses; the presence of hearth pits and charcoal attests to the use of wood or brush fires. Soon the Vikings took their boats and sailed south in search of more hospitable surroundings.

Centuries later a new breed of men landed on the shores of Labrador and northern Newfoundland. They also came from far away, but these people were swarthy, and had names like Abraham, Jacob and Jeremiah. When I walked down to the edge of the sea at L'anse Aux Meadows and was introduced to four of the present residents—great, wild-looking fellows with bushy beards, I learned that many still bore the biblical names of old. I also found it difficult to understand their language, even when they were obviously trying to communicate openly with me. When they chose to exclude me from the conversation, I could not comprehend them at all.

Fortunately, they were, like most Newfoundlanders, a warm and friendly people. One of my most cherished memories of the island is, after much beer and barbequed fish, of sitting in a circle of men and women on a living room floor—all swaying together from side to side, and listening to the singing of old folk songs and sea chanteys.

The Odd "Divil" Likes It

As Warden Service Manager for the Atlantic Region, one of my responsibilities was to interview recruits for the Warden Services of the various national parks. It was the following August, during one of these competitions that I had occasion to return to "The Rock." This time I flew to Gander.

As I packed my battered Government of Canada briefcase, I reflected that the old leather satchel had been my constant travelling companion for much of my career. The bag wore insignia dating back to the time when national parks were a branch of the Department of Indian Affairs and Northern Development. The thing was already a veteran, in 1968, when it accompanied me on my first trip to Ottawa. Since then, we had travelled many miles together. It was probably true that I had spent more nights in hotel rooms with this old briefcase than I had spent nights at home with my good wife. Small wonder after all those miles that we were both coming apart a bit at the seams.

One of the trademarks of an old park warden is that he knows how to pack. My lessons began with horses and packboxes. Each set of boxes has to be carefully balanced, and every square inch of space used to advantage. Every thing was packed that was needed to survive in reasonable comfort, but not an ounce of unnecessary weight. When I traded in my saddle for a briefcase, I applied my packing skills to the case. I abhorred taking luggage, but so adroit had I become at putting my stuff together, I could manage for days on the contents of that satchel. Getting ready for a week away from home, I carefully packed the following items: one mickey of Scotch, two sets of spare underwear, one spare pair of slacks, two extra shirts, one spare tie, one light sweater, and spare socks, one large file of study material and homework; a compact book containing a Scottish romance by Walter Scott, three pepperoni sausages, four ounces of cheese, one crusty roll, a package of soda crackers and a pat of butter, a small jar of instant coffee, one soup, a plastic spoon, half a dozen tea bags, wallet and keys, spare pens and pencils, a small book with names, addresses and telephone numbers, one small shaving kit containing a razor and brush, toothpaste and toothbrush, blood pressure pills, two small first-aid dressings, shaving lotion, small scissors and a roll of adhesive tape. Then, to top it off—a light overcoat!

At the Halifax International Airport, I removed the bunch of keys before approaching the security gate. In the habit of passing through without a hitch, I was surprised to see my old bag arrested on its way down the conveyer belt by the heavy hand of one of the guards.

The shaving kit came out first, was opened and examined; then out came the cheese and crackers, next the spare underwear. The guard hesitated momentarily then dug in again and hauled out the shirts and tea bags. This time there was a definite pause while the man tried to gauge the number of layers remaining. He was obviously thinking about having to replace all this stuff before giving the briefcase back to its owner. When he got to the pepperoni sausages and socks, he gave up. After poking a finger hastily into the homework file, the guard stuffed all of my treasures back into the bag, snapped the latch shut and shoved it at me. It was plain, he wished us both well out of his sight. Miraculously, the Scotch still lay hidden beneath the sweater. Outwardly nonchalant, but inwardly gleeful, I slouched off to the departure lounge.

To my surprise, the sun was out and the weather was warm when I stepped onto the tarmac in Gander. There are two weeks in August every year when summer comes to Newfoundland, and for the second time in a row, I had arrived on "The Rock" during this period. These are the two weeks when many of the Islanders take their annual vacations and go camping in borrow pits, picking berries, drinking oodles of cold beer, and just generally relaxing and having a whale of a time. The interviews were to begin on the following morning, in a hotel in Gander, and it was at this hotel that I presented myself late on Sunday evening.

After loaning the desk clerk a pen in order to register me, I went to check out my room. Upon entering I noticed that I had a large picture window with a view of the back alley. At first I was impressed by the clarity of the window, but then discovered that there simply wasn't any glass. I could literally step right out into the alley. Another unique feature of the room was the coat-hanger aerial on the television set, which, after a fashion, surprisingly worked. The second of twin beds appeared to have been dismantled and hauled away.

I realized it would probably be useless to complain, but decided to go back to the desk and at least register the fact of these damages to the room before I might be held liable for them. The clerk cheerfully acknowledged the open window and the various other unique aspects of the accommodation and asked if there was anything else he could do for their guest. I wistfully admitted that I could sure use a cold beer, but didn't suppose there was much hope of finding one on a Sunday evening. To my astonishment, the clerk disappeared for a moment and returned with a half-dozen wonderfully cold Blue Stars. I went to my room, and unpacked. Then I sat on the window ledge, leaned against the frame, with one leg in the room and the other hanging outside. I enjoyed the warm night air and the ice-cold beer and reflected that Newfoundland really was a wonderful place.

Next morning, I joined the other board members in the room rented for the interviews. It had been a short night, and I had only a glass of water for breakfast. Our first candidate was due at 8:30 am. I soon learned that job interviewing in Newfoundland can be a depressing business, almost as much so for the interviewers as for the candidates. During the 1970s and 80s, competition for park warden positions right across Canada was fierce, but nowhere so desperate as on "The Rock." Wonderfully bright young men and women came before the board, their body language pleading for a job, while they struggled with the questions. It was heartbreaking to know that at best there were perhaps six positions to be filled and from 60 to 70 candidates wanting to fill them. Many told of having been to numerous job interviews in the past month and more than one spoke of walking off the nearest pier if they couldn't soon find work.

By 11:50 am, we had seen three candidates and were ready for a lunch break. I, in particular, was beginning to feel decidedly hollow and we had a long afternoon ahead of us. The next interview was set for one o'clock. Together we went to the spacious hotel dining room and settled at a corner table. While we waited for someone to take our order, I noted there were only three other people in the room. All they seemed to be having was coffee. For some reason, this made me faintly uneasy until I reminded myself that the hotel was one of a respectable international chain.

Moments later, a comely young lady came and poured us some coffee and took our orders. There followed a considerable length of time during which not much of anything happened. After twenty minutes, the waitress returned to refill our cups. She looked at us warily. "Bad news," she said, "Cook's not in," and hurried away before anyone could question her further.

Another fifteen or twenty minutes went by while I and my companions fidgeted, and took turns staring out the window while our empty stomachs growled under the overburden of thin coffee. Finally, the waitress hurried back to our table. After filling the cups for the third time, she leaned over the table and spoke "sotto voce" behind her hand, "Cook's in now," she confided, "but he's in a bad mood!"

All the hopeful diners gazed after her retreating figure in dismay. Our time was up; there was to be no lunch. As we were about to leave the hotel foyer, we looked back at the desk. The young manager waved cheerily, obviously relieved that our ordeal was over. "Sorry about lunch," he cried, "come back and see us for supper sometime!" For supper, we discovered a small café and patronized it for the rest of our stay.

It took most of the week to see all the candidates. On Saturday morning, my two companions embarked for their return trip to the mainland, while I rented a small car at the airport. I intended to spend the next few days visiting the wardens at Terra Nova National Park, after which I would go on to the historic sites at Castle Hill and Cape Spear.

Like much else that I experienced on "The Rock," my visit to Terra Nova National Park was different. It was protocol, when visiting a park, to first call at the superintendent's office to pay one's respects. Park "supers" are traditionally wary of unannounced, official visitors infiltrating their offices. This was never so true as in the feudal atmosphere of the maritime national parks where the appearance of a visitor of any kind constituted a noteworthy event. Accordingly, I made my way to the seat of power in the handsome stone administration building at Glovertown.

I was ushered into the presence of a long lanky individual and exchanged the usual pleasantries. I was about to get into some business, which my bosses at the Regional Office had instructed me to pass on, when I noticed the superintendent was shifting around uncomfortably. "The walls are paper thin, you know," the man whispered confidentially. "Come on, I'll take you for a drive through the park."

By the time the superintendent had finally completed his report on park and office conditions, we were nearly out of the park. After turning around he seemed to recall his obligations as a host and, as we worked our way back to the administration building, he pointed out various aspects of Terra Nova which might be of interest. Once inside, the "super" retreated to his office, carefully leaving the door open a crack. I glanced quickly through the notes I had made during our conversation, folded the paper into my shirt pocket, and went to visit the chief warden.

I found this individual, a heavy-set man with a military moustache, ensconced in a pleasant room looking to the south, as opposed to the Super's which was on the north side of the building. The insubstantial quality of the walls, however, appeared to be a problem throughout the building; for no sooner were we comfortably seated, than I found myself invited out for another tour of the park! These sort of let-me-show-you-my-kingdom trips were a frequent occurrence when visiting with chief park wardens, so I went along willingly enough. I had always been more comfortable talking things over on the move rather than sitting stiffly on opposite sides of a desk.

Finally arriving back at the park's office, after promising to try to alleviate at least the more obvious of the chief's problems, I was looking forward to bidding the place good-bye and going off somewhere quiet for a drink of Scotch. But such was not to be. Instead, to my amazement, I again ended up in the superintendent's car for private discourse.

By the time I had completed this third trip along the Trans-Canada and had undergone a further debriefing, I was tired, dusty and hot. I longed for a tall, cold drink, and wondered if I could find a reasonable spot to have a swim in the sea. I had to find a motel first. I could hardly believe my good fortune when I finally found a room in a place with a swimming pool—swimming pools being as common on "The Rock," as icebergs on Miami Beach! The unit was very warm, kind of stale smelling and dusty when I let myself in, but the thought of spending an hour or two in the pool, in the late afternoon sunshine, more than made up for any minor inconveniences. After rinsing out the smallest of three odd-sized glasses found in the cupboard over the sink, I poured a drink from the bottle of Scotch that had eluded the security guard.

Taking my drink in one hand and a towel in the other, I went out to check the pool. This pool did not contain clear clean water. It was about two-thirds full of tepid water of a deep, chocolate-brown colour. Never having seen anything like this before, it gave me a bit of a pause. After sticking a tentative toe into the soup, I gingerly sat down in a deck chair to think things over. It was obvious that the pool did not get its water from the same source as the rest of the motel, but exactly where it did come from was a mystery.

While I was contemplating whether to chance it or not, a father and son arrived at the scene. The pair appeared to be on a family vacation. The lad, about twelve years old, wore trunks; the dad was in Bermuda shorts, shoes and stockings. The advent of a swimming pool was obviously a new and unexpected challenge. An earnest discussion ensued, probably about how to enter the pool and who should go first. Father took the lead. Holding his nose between his thumb and forefinger, he gave a funny little hop and jumped in, shoes and all. Not being able to see through the murk, he may have misjudged the depth; at any rate he landed hard in about four feet of water and lost his false teeth. After groping futilely around on the bottom for some minutes, he clambered out. Now came a somewhat passionate discussion as he exhorted his son to dive into the soup and look for the missing teeth.

Meanwhile, sipping my Scotch, I was rapidly losing enthusiasm for a swim. The idea of shoes, socks and false teeth led me to wonder what other, even more unsavoury, items might lurk in the muddy waters or lie embedded in the effluvium at the bottom of the pool. When I rose and went back to my cabin, the boy was on his twelfth dive.

Fortunately, things at the park took a turn for the better the next day. A boat patrol of Clode Sound had been laid on for me, with a promise of some cod jigging—a brand new experience. The warden's boat was an old, wooden-hulled vessel named *Shawna'dith*, after Shawannadithet, a Beothuk native girl, who at one time worked as a maid at the Governor's Mansion. When she died, in 1928, she was the last recorded survivor of her race, the rest having been slain or fled from the island. How much more fun to stand on the bow of this stout little boat, breathing in the crisp salt spray, than sitting in a stuffy station wagon on the Trans-Canada Highway listening to park managers' woes!

The boatman, one of the park wardens and I, left the wharf shortly after 9:00 am. At mid-morning the diesel engine slowed and I glanced around looking for the cause. We appeared to be out in the middle of the Sound, with nothing of particular interest in sight. The boatman knew something I didn't. By some sixth sense, he had divined that we were directly over a school of codfish—although nothing was to be seen on the surface. With the engine stopped, the two old "Newfie" hands showed me how to drop over the side a large, weighted hook on a stout line. Then the line was drawn up slowly and at the first sign of resistance was given a sharp tug or jig. The resistance is the hook encountering the side of a cod and the jig is to set the steel firmly into the creature's flesh, after which it is rapidly hauled on board.

I was amazed to see a dozen or so fish flopping out on deck after a mere 20 minutes. When I pulled out a three-footer, the champion catch of the morning, my companions indicated that we had enough. Now I was initiated into the art of skinning and it is not an occupation for the squeamish. Taking a sharp knife from his belt, the boatman made a circular cut around the head of my codfish, just behind where the ears would have been, if it had had ears. Then I was instructed to take a firm hold on the fish's head, by wrapping my hands around its jaws and pushing both thumbs deep into the eye sockets! When this was done and no breakfast lost, I was told to brace myself and hang on, while the boatman seized a flap of skin on either side just behind the cut and, with a mighty pull, jerked the entire hide off in a single motion.

Then, while I tried to find a rag or something to wipe the slime off my hands, the boatman went into the little cabin and began to work culinary wonders with frying pan and kettle. Soon the odour of frying bacon, boiled onions and potatoes wafted out and soon blended with a marvellously salty, fishy smell. Going below, I found a large saucepan, filled with a delicious codfish chowder, bubbling on the stove. It was one of those rare meals, often encountered in the most out-of-the-way places, which live in memory as a very special event. While I tackled my bowl of chowder with a rare appetite, my companions told me more "Newfie" tales, including the reason the old sailors and fishermen were often referred to as "Bluenoses."

The old timers, I was told, were in the habit of wearing a lot of heavy wool to ward off the North-Atlantic cold. They wore woollen caps, sweaters, and mitts. These garments were knitted at home, often with wool grown, carded and dyed there, as well. The favourite dye was dark blue. When outdoors in cold weather, the nose tends to run a lot, and fishermen wipe away the drip in whichever manner is most expedient—usually on their sleeves. The home-dye job would run, too, so that by the end of the day the old sailors would come home with a distinctly blue smudge under and on the nose. Hence the name "Bluenoses!"

When we had finished our meal, there was still a substantial helping of chowder left in the pot and this was poured into a jar for me to take to my kitchenette. I was also presented with several codfish steaks, packed in ice, to take home. And finally, as we were having an after-work drink, I was given a bottle of Screech to commemorate my visit. All in all, combined with the good stories to carry home, I had "a pretty good scoff," as they say on the island!

My next stop, after leaving the Terra Nova National Park, was the national historic site at Cape Spear, where I was scheduled to do a public-safety inspection. Arriving in the parking lot on a rather civil afternoon, I turned off the ignition and sat for some time getting a sense of the place.

What I saw was a large, rocky hill, barren, as usual, except for a fringe of grass along the top. The ridge extended for some distance to the south, but to the northwest the hill descended to form a small promontory jutting out to sea. Various old pathways wandered down this promontory towards the water; at the bottom was rough, broken ground, and a number of surge channels. At the very top of the hill stood a historic lighthouse and below the lighthouse, as I would learn later, was a sheer cliff down to the sea.

Cape Spear is the most easterly point of land in North America and the light, which has been in operation since 1836, was the first landmark for trans-Atlantic ships approaching St. John's Harbour. In fact, what appears to the ships is not the light itself, but a series of timed-reflections off a mirror. These beams are sent out to sea and form a coded signal which is the signature of that particular lighthouse.

There are two gun emplacements on the cliff north of the old lighthouse for soldiers were placed on guard here during World War II. Two of these servicemen became the first recorded casualties by drowning at Cape Spear. They are commemorated by a black, iron cross driven into the rock partway down the slope on the north side of the hill. It is a grim, sullen-looking cross. No light reflects from its dark surface.

I noted that visitors, after leaving their vehicles in the parking lot, climbed the path to the lighthouse. Once there, they went in and spent some time taking in the history and workings of the place and admiring the view to seaward. Returning outdoors, they took photographs of the lighthouse, the sea and each other. Some stayed for a time on top of the cliff, sitting in sunny nooks among the rocks and windswept grass. Others started down the path to the parking lot. Most people, obviously Maritimers, were careful around the cliffs and respectful of the sea.

After awhile I left the car, and climbed slowly up to the lighthouse. There I found a sheer cliff on the seaward side, dropping at least 300 feet into the combers of the North Atlantic. It was a dizzying sight and I had a momentary vision of losing my footing, hurtling into space and drowning moments later in that cold and frightening sea. I drew back from the edge carefully. There was a bit of protective fencing on either side of the lighthouse but it did not extend very far. I took some photographs, then walked down one of the trails leading to the promontory.

Meanwhile, a small station wagon with Saskatchewan plates pulled into the parking lot and stopped near my car. The rear doors flew open and three young children burst excitedly from the confines of the warm and cluttered wagon. They had been cooped up for a number of hours and were dying for some exercise. The sea, sparkling in the sunshine caught their eye and, like children everywhere, they ran toward the water. The parents, grateful for the temporary respite, rolled down the windows, leaned back in their seats and closed their eyes. Although they had never seen the ocean, they were prepared to rest for a few minutes, knowing the view would still be there when they got around to going for a stroll. It never occurred to them that their children might not be.

In the meantime, I had arrived at a point about midway down the side of the largest surge channel. These channels are steep clefts in the rock, running inland from the sea. The ocean swells rush up these crevices with tremendous force, as can be seen by the logs and debris hurled far into the rocks at the upper end. Then, as the wave recedes, the water rushes back, sucking any loose object out to sea. Meanwhile, the rock walls of the surge channel are worn as smooth as glass from centuries of wave action, and are usually covered with green slime, offering little hold to a person. Even the best of swimmers has no hope, should they fall in.

Now, as I listened with one ear to the explosion of water which heralded the arrival of a new wave, I noted, further down on my left, a lone photographer had his tripod set up on a rock at the entrance to the channel. In this seemingly precarious position, the man behind the camera was able to catch the full effect of the exploding spray and the subsequent inrush and outrush of the sea. After noting that several consecutive waves failed seriously to threaten this person, I was about to go on with my walkabout when a movement on the other side of the channel caught my eye. The three children from the station wagon, two young boys and a girl, were standing on the rocks, on the far side of the channel midway between me and the photographer.

They had walked down the path to the point where they could see that it led nowhere and now obviously wanted to get back to the parking lot. They stood undecided as to which way to go. Even as I watched, the boy, in a red jacket, crouched, put his hand on the rocks and extended a tentative leg down to the ledge below. Offshore, about 200 yards away, a rolling swell approached, the crest glittering wickedly in the afternoon sun. In moments the surge channel would fill with water.

I shouted to the children but they didn't hear me. I was afraid they would be too far down the bank before they realized the danger. Still yelling and waving my arms I began to run down my side of the channel while, at the mouth, the big roller towered high and seemed to swell like a great green foam-flecked monster poised to pounce. With only seconds to spare, I was able to get the photographer's attention and he managed to catch the eye of one of the kids. As all three began to scramble up the bank, the little girl slipped and for a moment it looked as if she would fall, then one of her brothers seized her by the sleeve and pulled her up. They were safe.

I was badly shaken. There were few, if any, warning signs anywhere in the area. There was no rescue gear of any sort readily available. I had come within a hair's breadth of witnessing a tragedy which I would have been powerless to prevent and equally powerless to effect a rescue. After awhile, I picked up my camera and climbed to a point just below the black, iron cross. Lying in the rocks, with that sullen symbol of death starkly outlined against the grey evening sky, I took a picture. When I returned to my office, that cross would go on the front cover of my report, a mute reminder of the awful danger lurking at a family holiday destination point.

The day at Cape Spear marked the end of my trip to Newfoundland. It turned out to be my last visit to the island, for I was soon to return to the West. The position of Warden Operation Manager for Western Region—a post I had long coveted, had finally become available, and by dint of much manoeuvring, not to mention some downright grovelling, I was able to get a transfer back to my beloved mountains.

As the kind Eastern Provincial attendant packed my codfish steaks in ice for the trip back to Halifax, I reflected on the generosity of Newfoundlanders and the way that they had opened up to me, a cowboy from the West. I remembered the cozy old home at Port Aux Choix, the late night sing-song at L'anse Aux Meadows, and the jolly girls of Gros Morne. I realized this was my favourite province in Atlantic Canada. After all, as one writer has put it: "The complaints is many and various, but the odd 'divil' likes it!" Maybe I was just odd enough to be one of those "divils."

Part Six

*Back to the west; the Wardens go to
Expo '86; exploring the Queen Charlottes;
my last job for Parks buying horses for
the Ya-Ha-Tinda.*

The Wardens Go To Expo '86

It was midnight in Vancouver, British Columbia and raining cats and dogs. My Parks Canada van stood in the parking lot beneath the north approach to the Granville Street Bridge. I had just finished rolling all the windows up tight, pressing all the lock buttons, and slamming all the doors shut. Now, by pressing my nose hard against the streaming windowpane on the passenger side, I could just make out the keys dangling from the ignition. I sagged dispiritedly against the van while the rain ran down my neck and wondered what folly had brought me to the back entrance of Expo '86, on a Sunday night in May, when I should have been safe in bed in Black Diamond, Alberta, getting ready for another Monday morning in the Western Regional Office.

In fact, I pretty much had myself to blame although there was a little help from my friends and one alpine specialist in particular. The whole thing began, in the spring of 1985, when we were casting about for high-profile events in which to involve the Warden Service as part of Parks' centennial year celebrations. There was a lot of talk at this time about the upcoming World Exposition being planned for Vancouver in 1986. It seemed to offer a perfect venue to show off our search and rescue, and medivac skills, to an international audience. First of all two things had to happen: we had to decide on a suitable exhibit and/or demonstration, and Parks needed an invitation to Expo.

It was no surprise that our discussions centred around heli-rescue. Since its introduction in 1971, the technique had proven extremely successful in saving lives and reducing the trauma of evacuation for persons injured in the backcountry. The problem was to devise a rescue that could be viewed by significant numbers of people at the World's Fair. Obviously an event taking place somewhere on a mountaintop north of Vancouver would not meet the bill. It was while we were mulling this over that someone mentioned gondola rescue. In spite of the fact that a number of gondola lifts were operating in the mountain parks and the potential for lift failure was always there, Parks had so far not attempted to apply heli-rescue techniques. Many of the lifts ran at considerable height above ground, requiring slow and cumbersome rescues with ropes and ladders, often in sub-zero temperatures. It was a problem that had been on our minds for some time. It occurred to us that if, in time for Expo, we could perfect some form of gondola evacuation by helicopter not only would Parks be able to put on a spectacular demo, but valuable experience would be gained at the same time. The presence of an operating gondola lift on Grouse Mountain, within easy reach of the Expo grounds, offered an excellent site—providing the lift owners approved.

The first step was to approach the management of Sulphur Mountain Gondola, in Banff National Park, to see if they would allow Parks to practice heli-rescue techniques on their lifts. Aside from the Expo angle, the exercise could prove to be a valuable safety measure in the event of possible lift failure. When they agreed, a series of letters and phone calls commenced to Department of Transport, to Vancouver, to Grouse Mountain, to the managers of Expo '86, and to Parks Headquarters in Ottawa.

All responses were positive, although predictably the approval of DOT was hedged with various riders and conditions. DOT would remain nervous about the project throughout. There were a number of people in the Department who never had been comfortable with the idea of a non-releasable load beneath a helicopter and viewed this latest proposal as one more step in a direction that probably never should have been allowed in the first place. Besides which, when approval had been grudgingly granted for sling rescue, it was on the strict condition that the procedure was only allowable in cases of real emergency. Putting on a show at Expo hardly qualified. As it turned out there were enough critical factors at work during the eventual demo at Grouse Mountain to rate the exercise an emergency, but it may have been that DOT drew a distinction between responding to an emergency as opposed to creating one!

There was also concern at Park Headquarters, where doubts about the safety and validity of the proposed operation were mixed with questions as to how and where the initiative had come from in the first place. Oddly enough, the fact that Schintz and Fuhrmann were involved did little to put their minds at ease.

☆　☆　☆

Meanwhile, Peter Fuhrmann had been working on the invitation. Always well-connected, savvy and persuasive, he soon located the person or committee in charge of selecting participants to Expo and proceeded to tell them all about Parks Canada and the Warden Service. He no doubt expounded on our role in search and rescue, the evacuation of casualties and told them of our plan to practise a gondola rescue on Sulphur Mountain. This, if successful, could be re-played on Grouse Mountain near Vancouver. The theme for Expo '86 was to be Transportation and Communication and Peter argued successfully that our mountain rescue work would be a dramatic and valuable contribution. However Peter did it, a letter arrived in the office of the Director of the Western Region on May 28, 1985, inviting us to participate in a one-week, special event in search and rescue. A letter of acceptance went back on July 15.

It was obvious that the Parks Service would have to man an exhibit, or stage some form of activity, at the Expo grounds, in addition to the rescue demonstration at Grouse Mountain. An exhibit of cable and other rescue equipment in one of the large pavilions on site was decided upon. While I went to work on this project, the alpine specialists came up with a third idea. This one entailed a cable-rescue demonstration that would take place twice daily on a huge, artificial wall supplied and also used by a team from the University of Calgary.

By this time autumn was well advanced and it was imperative to have the first practice on Sulphur Mountain before their gondola closed down for the winter. As my group of experts and I began to hammer out the technical details of the operation, the pilot of the Banff SAR helicopter was brought into the discussion. The situation to which the rescuers would respond was envisioned. In the event of a lift failure, a number of gondolas would be left stranded at considerable distance from the ground. Evacuation of passengers by conventional means would be a time-consuming process with high potential for injuries and frostbite. The seriousness of this situation would be compounded by the fact that the harsh terrain below many of the towers would hamper ground approach by rescuers and make the evacuation of passengers difficult and possibly dangerous.

Most gondolas have a door on the roof and also on the side. In normal operations neither door can be opened from the inside—except with a special key. The rescue plan called for a helicopter to lower a man onto the roof of the gondola, from which he could gain access to the inside. Once with the passenger or passengers, the rescuer would explain the process and then proceed to place the first evacuee in a specially designed harness, appropriately named a "Screamer Suit."

This rig, which actually tied the rescuer and victim together in a sort of bag, could be linked directly to the end of the helicopter sling by means of a locking carabiner. When all was in readiness the helicopter would be recalled by radio. The rescuer would open the side door of the gondola with his key and would station himself in readiness to seize the end of the sling when it was lowered within reach. After making the connection, the rescuer was to eject himself backwards through the open door taking the passenger with him. The whole operation called for precision flying and expert coordination on the part of the rescuer. There was no room for last minute hang-ups, either on the part of the equipment or the evacuees. Once free of the gondola, the two people would be hoisted up until clear of the lift.

The first practice was to take place on an afternoon, in early December. The two alpine specialists, the rescue wardens and I met in the boardroom on the third floor of the old administration building in Banff. From where I sat at the north end of the room, I could see the lower half of Sulphur Mountain. The late autumn colours were fading, and a change of weather was brewing. The wind appeared to be picking up and wisps of grey, ominous-looking clouds were drifting across the slopes. For some reason, a number of petty and unnecessary disagreements broke out over the various details of the proposed operation, arguments which I had difficulty chairing. I began to despair of ever getting the show on the road.

Finally, we were assembled at the foot of the lift. I had volunteered to be a stranded passenger and so had a lady from Information Services in Regional Office. Her name was Elaine MacNeill; it was she who was preparing pre-Expo publicity for the Parks Service. Later she would cover our participation at Vancouver. The two "victims" were locked into a gondola, moved part way up the mountain and stopped at an impressive distance from the ground. Gusts of wind rocked our cupola while the helicopter hovered nearby, bouncing and flapping in the turbulence. I had a bad case of butterflies but outwardly I tried to remain calm. Elaine was excited and cheerful.

It was after the helicopter had successfully landed the first rescuer on the roof of the gondola that a serious problem arose. Once freed of the man's weight, the lower end of the sling showed a nasty tendency to wrap itself around the lift cables and power lines that traversed the towers above the gondola. It was a very dangerous situation. If the sling succeeded in flipping itself around a cable, the pilot would be unable to fly away and equally unable to land. He would have no option but to hover until he ran out of gas. After a few anxious moments, he was able to extricate the sling. The problem was temporarily solved by keeping a weight attached to the end of the line. When the wardens went to Expo the following May, the difficulty had been neatly resolved by threading the four knotted ropes of the sling through a 10-foot length of plastic water pipe. Not only did this eliminate the tendency to flip, it also made the lower end of the line straight and smooth and unlikely to catch on any protuberances in its path.

The Sulphur Mountain practice was successfully completed. Now there remained a great deal of paperwork and many long distance calls to make before the spring. One problem, which took some time to resolve, was the matter of finding personnel to serve as passengers in the gondola at Grouse Mountain. While the helicopter rescue technique was intended for the rescue of civilians in an emergency, it was not deemed advisable to subject people off the street to the potential hazards of such an operation. The same attitude applied to the employees at Grouse Mountain. Nor did the minimal budget for Parks' participation at Expo allow for the transportation of extra wardens to Vancouver for what might, at the longest, be a two-hour exercise.

In fact, while Peter and I were flapping around in helicopters, working the phone lines and generally having a ball, the actual burden of finding enough money to make it a success fell on the shoulders of our Resource Studies Co-ordinator, Pat Benson, who was acting chief of the section while much of this was going on. She must have wondered by what trick of fate she was always in the chair when Peter and I dreamed up another grand and glorious, un-budgeted scheme for which she had to scramble to find funding.

Pat had been acting chief also, in 1982, when Peter and I were largely instrumental in bringing the annual meeting for the International Commission of Alpine Rescue to Banff, a perfectly reasonable thing to do in light of the fact that member nations were expected to take turns hosting the event and Canada had been a member for a number of years. The proposed event had caused some ripples of unease in Ottawa. There seemed to be something about the way that Peter and I operated which often led to consternation among our counterparts at headquarters. Now, listening to me getting wound-up on the long-distance telephone, I think Pat tended to side with Ottawa. What had she, an innocent resource-studies co-ordinator, done to get mixed up in this?

Meanwhile, we still needed personnel to act as victims at Grouse Mountain. There seemed to be no ready solution until I learned that a group of American Rangers were planning to attend Expo. Here were government employees, albeit of another country, who were hired and trained to perform search and rescue just like the wardens. Working through Parks Canada's External Affairs Section, I was able to contact the officer who would be in charge of the rangers' visit to Canada. In what had all the appearances of being a great public relations move between the two countries, and a win-win deal all around, the Americans cheerfully agreed to act as trapped passengers to be rescued by their Canadian counterparts.

There was only one catch and it did not appear to be insurmountable. It seemed that the rangers would be subject to a regulation, or condition of employment, which did not allow U.S. personnel to fly beneath the aircraft of a foreign country. More phone calls ensued until the appropriate level of official in Ottawa spoke to his or her counterpart in Washington. The word was that sanction could be granted in this case. All that was required was for the chief ranger to write a special request to Washington.

Putting the rangers on the back burner, with a note on file to return to them later, I turned to the matter of accommodation for my crew when they got to Vancouver in May. Never having dealt with anything like Expo before, I was startled to discover that rooms in Vancouver were already booked solid by early December. I finally ended up on the telephone with the manager of the Johnny Canuck Motel on East Hastings. It says something for my powers of persuasion that I talked this individual into reserving six rooms for us for a week. What was even more amazing, was that it was managed without benefit of cash or even a credit card number. We could not access the very tiny Expo budget until after April 1—another bureaucratic hurdle, which I struggled with all winter.

The next big scramble was to find a helicopter that would do the demo for free. Incredibly there was no money for this either, the assumption being that any aviation company would fall all over itself to do it just for the publicity of participating in a rescue exercise at Expo with Parks Canada!

Not only did we have to find a helicopter company which was prepared to fly us for nothing, it followed that the machine should be based in the Vancouver area. While it would have been nice to take our favourite pilot and his machine from Banff, the long trip to the coast and back would have been time-consuming and costly. It would also have meant that the mountain-rescue helicopter was away on fun and games when it might be urgently needed at home. Obviously, that wouldn't do. After some shopping around, and many long distance calls, an agreement was reached with Quasar Helicopters Ltd. at Vancouver. In addition to the pure technicalities of the gondola evacuation itself, there were all the questions of liability to be resolved; there were various permits to be obtained, including permission for the helicopter to land and take off from the lift property on Grouse Mountain.

To add to the confusion, midway through March, several Expo officials were relieved of their positions and replaced by others, necessitating new contacts and rehashing of old information. At last, everything seemed in place. The rangers advised that they were momentarily expecting a green light from Washington, and Quasar confirmed that all the required permits were in hand. I cleared my desk, went home and packed my battered old travelling bag.

When we left for Vancouver on a snowy Saturday morning in the first week of May, we were travelling in a small, Parks' station wagon, and a large van borrowed from the government stores at Banff. Most of our personal and rescue gear was in the van. The trip was largely uneventful.

The first official function, which was to take place that evening, was a reception for us and the American Rangers, hosted by the Canadian Coast Guard. It was all very well intentioned and nicely done, but my spirits were immediately dampened to learn that the rangers had failed to get permission to partake in the rescue exercise on Grouse Mountain. Coming at this late date, without prior notice, the news was disconcerting and the telling—almost as an afterthought, irritated me more than a little.

After awhile I drifted down to the water's edge and sat down quietly on a pier to rearrange my plan for the gondola evacuation. It would mean that the wardens would have to play both the role of stranded passengers and rescuers. As I pondered, I became aware of a bedraggled-looking heron perched on a piling not far away. The bird was balanced on one leg and it contemplated the murky waters with a dark and brooding eye. "Life is the pits," it seemed to say. Peering into my own murky waters, I tended to agree.

I was still in a pessimistic mood when I pried open my tired eyeballs on Tuesday morning. The intervening time had done little to bolster my confidence. One of the bizarre rules of Expo was the stipulation that new exhibits had to be set up between midnight and morning, compelling my little company to wend our way on a Sunday night—through a strange city in pouring rain. Even so, when we finally found the north end of the Granville bridge and the service entrance to the exhibit area, we were still too early. After a brief discussion about what to do, someone noticed that a number of the pavilions were still open for visitors, so we decided to take a quick tour before setting up the show. My companions having already started off while I was closing up the van, I was by myself when I locked the keys in the ignition.

Now I stood trying desperately to figure some way of getting into the van. After awhile, I wandered into the grounds and eventually located the Expo Administration Office. After numerous phone calls, I was fortunate enough to find a locksmith, on duty after midnight, and 20 minutes later I was back in the driver's seat of the van—rattled, relieved and $45.00 out-of-pocket. The guys straggled back soon after and we proceeded to our assigned pavilion to assemble and set up the SAR exhibit—at one o'clock in the morning.

Here we soon ran into another snag for we learned that all exhibit areas had to be carpeted with a particular shade of blue commercial carpet. I thought it was incredible that no previous mention had been made of this requirement in all the correspondence with Expo over the last eight months, correspondence which now constituted a file almost two inches thick. There was no problem getting the stuff—it was on sale at the site.

The problem was the $700 needed to pay for it. Anyone who has worked for or encountered a federal bureaucracy ruled by nitpickers and bean counters can appreciate the dilemma this posed, at 1:00 am on a Sunday. Not only was there an ironclad law in the regional office that no goods or services would be paid for unless authorized before the fact, I was painfully aware that in the "Expo account" there wasn't going to be ten cents left to rub together when all the bills were paid.

We held a 2:00 am brainstorming session. Surely Parks Canada would not want us to abort the exhibit now for the sake of a lousy $700. So, we'd find the money now and try to collect it later. We scraped the money together, laid the precious carpet and assembled our display. The sun was almost up when we got back to the motel for a couple of hours of badly needed sleep. The climbing wall was already in place so, for the next day, we would man that exhibit and perform cable rescue. Tuesday was the day for the big gondola rescue on Grouse Mountain.

Tuesday morning dawned dark and cloudy. A pale ray of sunshine gleamed feebly, only to be extinguished a moment later. A system was obviously moving in from the Pacific. The mountaintops north of the city were already disappearing. First no rangers, and now this, added to my sense of foreboding. I found my crew at McDonald's discussing the day's plans with what seemed ridiculous optimism. As I watched them cheerfully munching McMuffins and slurping black coffee, I realized once again that, for these men, everything was doable. Backing down simply wasn't in their vocabulary.

Thinking back over the years, I realized that it had always been that way. On the high walls where the slightest mistake could mean your ass was in the grass, they didn't back down: not in the face of forest fire, or following seas, not to the killer in the car at night on a lonely highway. There was no task so daunting that it couldn't be managed. Because they were convinced of this, they usually did manage. I wondered why I could not be more like them. When, during my time in the Atlantic Region, an assistant director had praised me as having been "a pillar of strength for the Warden Services," I had glanced around, convinced the man must be speaking about somebody else. Feeling better at the recollection, I managed some bacon and eggs. By 9:00 am, we were in front of the lower terminal determined to go on with the show.

It was while we were deciding that the second set of lift towers would be the ideal spot for a rescue that the Department of Transport arrived, in the form of a very dour official with a demeanour as dark as the clouds over Grouse Mountain. He looked as if he wished he had never heard of helicopter sling rescue or park wardens. After listening to us for a few minutes, he took me aside.

"See that set of towers?" he said, pointing at number two and looking at me very hard. I nodded emphatically.

"When you can't see them any longer, you shut this operation down!" An ominous rumble from somewhere up on the mountain drove his words home, as he turned on his heel and slammed into his car.

We turned our attention back to the mountain. It was now 20 minutes to show time and spectators were beginning to arrive in the lower parking lots, but of the helicopter there was no sign. Had they forgotten what day it was? Or had they decided the weather was too uncertain for flying? Searching frantically through my notes, I found the number for Quasar. They assured me everything was going ahead as planned. The chopper should soon be within range and, because we had been supplied with a hand-held radio on the company frequency, we should be able to contact the pilot momentarily.

I had barely hung up when I was called back to the telephone. It seems that at the last minute Parks Canada had decided to send a VIP party out from Ottawa to witness the big event. Given the jaundiced attitude that Headquarters had displayed toward our project from the very beginning, this came as a total surprise. Wondering if they came to cheer us on or watch us go down in flames, I gave them directions to Grouse Mountain, and went back out to find the helicopter approaching.

This was good news, but once again an administrative oversight on the part of a partner to the enterprise, was to complicate matters. The permit to land at Grouse Mountain had not been obtained. The pilot could hover but he couldn't land and fifteen minutes was too long to hover. "I'll be back," he said, and promptly disappeared in the murk. Five minutes later, he was out of radio contact as well. Once again the second tower was hidden in mist and thunder rumbled—closer this time.

Exchanging glances that said, "Are we really going to do this?" we climbed into the gondola. Moments later the lift came to life, our cabin rocked for a moment and then we were gently wafted up to a spot just short of the second tower. The lift closed down and all was quiet—very quiet. The mist was halfway down the towers, hanging just over the roof of the gondola. We anxiously checked our watches and peered out at the weather, and looked at our watches again. I tried to reach the pilot by radio, but there was no response. It seemed to be getting darker. At five minutes to show time, with still no word from the pilot, I glanced down at the parking lot and was electrified to see the Parks Canada Western Regional Director, the Director General and the Assistant Deputy Minister for Parks Canada, all standing there, gazing around expectantly.

It was almost more than I could stand. I decided if the damn helicopter didn't show up in the next 10 minutes, I would open the door of the gondola and hurl myself down the mountain. These gentlemen had come all the way to Vancouver to see a show and they deserved a show. As they stood around surveying my poor broken body they would at least be able to tell themselves that they had not come for nothing. In fact there might even be some satisfaction in going back with knowledge that Michael Schintz, Warden Operations Manager of Western Region, was finished, wiped out along with all his goofy ideas.

Fortunately, before I could act on this desperate resolve, the radio crackled into life and the pop-pop of the helicopter could be heard approaching. Moments later the rotors were thundering overhead, at the same instant the storm broke. Lightning flashed and rain pounded on the gondola as the first rescuee and rescuer hooked their "Screamer Suit" to the sling and jumped into space. Not a breath was drawn, on the ground or in the air, as the pilot, fighting wind and weather, coaxed his passengers to the pavement, landing them almost at the feet of the awed spectators. Then it was time for the alpine specialist and the warden manager to make their debut. They leaped into pounding hail, illuminated by a single ray of sunshine and landed breathless—laughing with relief. It was over.

A few minutes later, when the operators attempted to start the lift, they were astonished to find it quite dead. At first there was great consternation over the possibility that the sling below the helicopter had shorted out the lift's power lines. In fact, a bolt of lightening had hit a tower high up on the mountain. The rescue operation, performed under dramatic conditions, had been flawless.

Flamingo Inlet

It was my great good fortune that, before I retired, Parks Canada decided to establish a new reserve in the south Queen Charlotte Islands. I was also lucky in that the Warden Service was now the first arm of the Department to be deployed to a new proposed park rather than the engineers—as was once the case. The reason for this was an increasing awareness of our role in public safety and was spurred by an interesting phenomenon that almost invariably occurs when visitors start coming to a new park.

Where once only the locals fished, skied or boated, the area is now inundated by hordes of wild-eyed tourists plunging off into the wilderness, determined to indulge their dreams of adventure but with little knowledge of the hazards they are facing. At the same time, whichever government agency or organization was previously responsible for search and rescue, steps back and washes its hands of the responsibility—glad to let someone else take over. As a result, the new park staff, many of whom have also come from a different environment, find themselves scrambling to adapt their rescue skills to the new terrain in the face of an escalating accident curve.

After going through this experience a number of times, the Parks Service devised a new approach—a Preliminary Hazard Assessment and Evaluation, and it works this way. As soon as a new park is designated, a team of public-safety wardens go and spend two or three weeks in the area, studying the terrain and, in this case, coastal waters. Data is compiled on potential visitor activities and associated hazards. Local guides and outfitters are interviewed, as are members of previous search and rescue agencies. This way the Warden Service becomes familiar with the park before the visitors arrive. Dangers, whether they be cliffs, crevasses, rip tides or grizzly bears, are identified, rescue techniques devised, suitable equipment purchased. It was an eminently sensible idea, and it provided me with an opportunity for an experience that I still consider one of the highlights of my career.

I chose Peter Fuhrmann, Banff Public Safety Specialist, for my partner. Without doubt, he was the most cheerful, capable and resourceful person one could have as a team mate in adventurous and dangerous work. Because the Canadian Coast Guard (CCG) and the Provincial Emergency Preparedness Organization of British Columbia were the erstwhile guardians of public safety in the South Moresby area, we started off by arranging a meeting, in Victoria, with officials from both agencies. The details of that meeting have faded now with time, but the outstanding fact is that we walked out of there with an agreement that we were to have full use of the CCG ship, the *George E. Darby*, with two Zodiac-Mark V inflatables and a crew of 16, for a two-week period, for exploration of South Moresby. The deal was sealed with nothing more binding than a handshake. Peter and I felt as if we had landed with people of our own kind.

While I attended to last-minute details, back in my office on the fifth floor of the Federal Building in Calgary, Peter set about outfitting us for two weeks on shipboard. I was subject to some good-natured ribbing from the other members of our section when I donned my grey-flannel sweat pants and pullover, bright-orange floater suit and deck shoes—the cowboy boots didn't go.

We joined the ship at Sandspit, Queen Charlotte Islands, on August 11, 1998, and that night we sailed south around the bottom of South Moresby and up the west coast to Tasu Sound. Although it was not an actual part of the proposed park, Captain Tom Hall had decided to start our two weeks of exploration by showing us the deserted townsite and works of the Falconridge Mine. Next morning, accompanied by Dave Kaegi, a CCG Special Projects Officer, we went ashore and walked into one of the strangest places one could ever hope to visit. Once a huge operation, the American owners had closed the mine down on a day in October 1976, and walked away leaving the entire town and hundreds of thousands of dollars worth of heavy equipment behind. The result was a real ghost town.

Very few of the buildings were locked. They stood open and empty, doors swinging in the wind—a strange, capricious wind that swooped down from the mountains and chased dry leaves along the deserted streets. It made wires hum as if they were still alive and it mimicked the sound of children's voices in the schoolyard, where no children were. Catching a loose apartment door, it flung it open, so that one could imagine hearing a shout, or perhaps a mother calling to her child. But of course, there was no one there. The wind even invaded the little schoolroom. Stealing through a partly open window, it fluttered pictures still clinging to the walls from some long-ago art class. And it stirred the pages of the children's scribblers, dated on the day they left, still lying open on their desks, some 12 years later.

On the hill behind the town, an access road led up to the mine. At some point a dragline had been brought in to salvage some of the equipment. Partway up the hill, it broke its drive shaft which caused it to freewheel back down the road, eventually toppling over and crashing into the back wall of a huge, three-storey shed. It was still there, its upper works resting on the shed roof.

Inside the shed were five enormous diesel engines. These engines, each the size of a locomotive, once generated the power for the mine and the town. They stood in a row, facing a raised platform. On the platform, behind heavy glass, were five desks; on each desk lay a large logbook, open to the day the mine shut down. The minute and the hour that the generators stopped were carefully recorded in each book.

What catastrophic event had taken place to cause the mine owners to order the great engines stopped and cause 450 people to pack their belongings and leave? Why was nothing salvaged? Was it simply cheaper to leave the trucks standing on the mountain, and the refrigerators in the apartments, than to ship them out?

The eeriness of the scenes was enhanced by the invasive vegetation of the Queen Charlottes. As we poked about, we were startled time and again to find a branch intruding through an open window or a tree root forcing its way up through the floor of a room—where the presence of the previous occupants was still a palpable aura. The last building we visited was the tiny, one-storey hospital. Here in the operating room, or perhaps it might have been the recovery or intensive care, life-sustaining equipment hung above the empty cots, pools of dried blood and other fluids still lay on the floor, where they had drained when the tubes were disconnected at the last minute. From a dim and shady corner, a dark-green creeper groped its way stealthily into this strange silent room.

The sun was gone and it was late in the day when we left the Falconridge dock and sailed out of the forbidding walls that guard the entrance to Tasu Sound. As the *George E. Darby* turned south, a heavy Pacific swell began to break on her starboard bow, while down below, snug in our bunks, my little crew and I were lulled to sleep by the steady rumble of the diesels and the gentle rolling of the ship.

The ship was our floating base. A young lady-sailor, Kathy, had been assigned to operate the Mark V and, each morning, the crane on board the *Darby* would swing our little craft over the side and lower us into the ocean. Some days we sailed into secluded inlets where we would cut the motor and glide quietly over still, dark waters, feeling as if we were the first people ever to enter these secret places. On other days, we found ourselves in sparkling sun-kissed bays, surrounded by mountains clothed in shimmering green, from which 1000-foot waterfalls tumbled silver into the sea.

Indeed the scenery and wildlife exceeded our wildest dreams. No sooner would we coast into a lagoon than the water around us would be filled with the friendly, whiskery faces of mink and otter as they swam curiously about the Zodiac. Big, fat black bears—some of the biggest in the world—rummaged on the beaches. High in the hills, wild goats and the tiny Sitka black-tailed deer left their delicate hoof prints on leafy, hidden trails. Each bay and inlet had its resident pair of bald eagles, nesting in a Douglas fir somewhere near the water, and out on the barrier reefs, seals and sea lions basked on the sunny side of the rocks while the Pacific swells burst into spray around them.

Sometimes we went ashore to find tiny grassy meadows and the rotting remains of old logging camps. There would be a wooden wharf, the moss-covered foundations of a few houses and perhaps an ancient truck, with vines and creepers climbing up through the floorboards. On other days, we would venture cautiously into deep woods, where trees up to

12 feet in diameter towered above us and even the first rings of branches were far above our heads. Here in places where the sunlight seldom reached, we stumbled on odd little beehive-shaped shelters and weird hippie shacks of tin and scraps of boards—remnants of the 1960s. Sometimes a child's toy, long forgotten, lay mouldering in the moss, beneath a giant tree.

Short of being stranded on a desert isle, our escape from civilization could hardly have been more complete. There were no cars, phones or fax machines, no buses to catch, or schedules to regulate our lives. There were just magic mornings when the ship's crane lowered us gently onto the swelling breast of the Pacific; days of discovery and exploration amidst breathtaking scenery; and at night, the *George E. Darby*, sailing to new wonders beneath the August stars. Only the muted chatter, on the ship's radio in the evening, reminded us that the busy world of 9 to 5 still throbbed somewhere out there, far beyond the islands.

Sometimes, if the weather grew stormy late in the day, we would have to make a run for it back to the ship. Some of these trips were brutal, with icy rain beating in our faces and numbing us from head to toe. Kathy had a seat behind the controls of the Mark V, a seat somewhat like that on an over-snow vehicle. Crouched on that, and with a firm grip on the controls, she hurled the rigid-hulled inflatable through the chop with a panache that left the rest of the crew hanging on for dear life. There was a rack that supported a winch at the stern of the boat, and some days we literally had to tie ourselves to it in order to avoid being tossed out.

Nor was the struggle over when we got back to the ship. If the swell was troublesome enough, the captain would position the *Darby* broadside to the waves, so that with each roller the Mark V was lifted high against the *Darby's* hull. Then we would have to scramble to our feet in our heavy, clumsy floater suits and, although tired and shaken from the ride, raise numbed fingers and leaden arms to grasp the rope ladder on her side. Once committed, we had to hang on and climb or drop into the sea.

But, oh, the satisfaction of sitting down to those excellent dinners at the captain's table after a day like that! Or, the enjoyment of sitting snugly in the cabin of an evening, making up the daily trip report and planning the next excursion. And then, as dusk approached, turning into one's bunk to the sound of the anchor being raised and the engines starting. And finally, drifting off to sleep as the throb of the diesels and the steady rocking of the ship meant we were underway to tomorrow's destination. I could have wished it to go on forever but, as it turned out, our trip was about to come to a sudden and surprising finish.

At 11:00 am on the seventh day we were about two-thirds of the way up Flamingo Inlet, at the southwest corner of South Moresby, when the radio crackled into life. It was Captain Hall and the urgency in his voice was unmistakable.

"This is the *George E Darby* to Mark V," he said tersely. "Return to ship at once. We are leaving the area."

We looked at each other in wonder. What on earth was going on? Dave Kaegi thumbed the mike, "Mark V to *Darby*, we're on our way!"

For the last two hours we had been exploring the shoreline, looking for signs of human activity, taking wildlife observations and mapping areas suitable for wilderness camping. A careful record was made of any natural hazards which might endanger future visitors to the area. Now we hastily stowed our gear and bucketed out of the inlet, to see the *Darby* already steaming south at a rapid rate of knots. Fortunately the sea was fairly calm that morning or I'm not sure we would have ever caught up to it. Even when we were alongside the captain did not stop as he usually did, but slung us on board with only a brief slowdown. Then he turned on full power and the old ship settled into her rock and roll rhythm, heading for Cape St. James at the southern tip of the Islands.

As it turned out, we were the unwitting intruders in a drama which had been covertly building for over eight months. When I went to the bridge to see the captain, he was noncommittal. He said that he had received orders from RCC Headquarters in Victoria, instructing him to sail to the east side of the Queen Charlottes, north of Scudder Point, and remain there until further notice. Apparently the last time he had orders like that, it had to do with drugs. When we listened to the news on the ship's television later on that evening, we realized that we had actually been happily poking around in the bushes only a few hundred yards from where 20 tons of Thai marijuana lay hidden on a hillside.

We would have been amazed to know that for the last 24 hours the telephones had been humming between RCMP and various U.S. law enforcement agencies, while perplexed officials asked what in hell the Canadian Parks Service was doing in an area where a major drug bust was about to take place. As for the smugglers, who might even then have been crouched with sweaty fingers on the triggers of automatic weapons behind their haystack of dope, they too must have been wondering "Who the ... are these guys?"

The arrests were made that afternoon, in Flamingo Inlet. Because the *Darby* became involved in logistical support for the drug bust operation, she was lost to us for the remainder of our survey and we were compelled to finish the work by helicopter. One thing that still puzzles me is why Captain Hall was kept in the dark about the operation until it was almost too late.

The following are excerpts from the 1990 spring issue of the *Canadian Coast Guard Fleet News*:

> (1988)   On August 18 at 21:00, Canadian Coast Guard Ship (CCGS) George E. Darby, under orders from the Rescue Coordination Centre (RCC), stood down from search and rescue (SAR) duties to assist the RCMP and an American agency remove 20 tons of marijuana and to provide logistical support to the surveillance team at Flamingo Bay, on the west coast of the Queen Charlotte Islands. The George E. Darby, working with Parks Canada, almost foiled the operation, because the crew did not know of the drug surveillance. The Darby was engaged in a hazard assessment of the South Moresby Park, and Flamingo Bay was one of the areas to be assessed. This task involved the ship for seven days, requiring two people from Parks Canada and special project officer, Dave Keige, to traverse every bay and inlet in the park and assess the various hazards that could be encountered by a visitor. Cool heads prevailed and quick-thinking surveillance team members contacted RCC Victoria to have the George E. Darby removed from the area. RCC dispatched a Secret Squirrel message to the ship to proceed to the east coast of the Queen Charlotte Islands,

north of Scudder Point, and to wait until further notice. That afternoon, the "bad guys" showed, and the arrests were made.

Note: Three small discrepancies occur between this account and mine. The first has to do with timing. The article has Darby "standing down" at 9:00 pm; my recollection is more like 11:00 am. Secondly, the map of South Moresby has it as Flamingo Inlet, not Flamingo Bay. Thirdly, the spelling of Dave Kaegi's name is not "Keige."

Horse Tales

One of the most unique and beautiful holdings of the Canadian Parks Service, and certainly one of the most controversial, is the "Little Prairie in the Mountains," the Ya-Ha-Tinda Ranch. Twice a part of Banff National Park, coveted by the Province of Alberta, and by wildlife and conservation groups along the entire eastern slope of the Rocky Mountains, the Ya-Ha-Tinda Ranch has been home to warden horses from the mountain national parks for nearly 80 years. It is the only federally operated horse ranch in Canada.

The Ya-Ha-Tinda Ranch, comprised of 9750 acres, is located along the upper Red Deer River Valley in Alberta. A narrow corridor of land now separates it from the east boundary of Banff National Park. The ranch is used for raising horses and as a staging area for warden patrol trips in and out of Banff National Park. It also serves as winter habitat for Rocky Mountain elk which migrate there from many of the surrounding areas.

Managing the Ya-Ha-Tinda became one of my responsibilities in 1980 when I returned to the West as Warden Operations Manager. I had to budget for horse feed and maintenance of the buildings and corrals, as well as the salaries for the foreman and two ranch hands. Together with the foreman, I was responsible for overseeing the horse-breeding program, for the ranch had its own stallion, and ensuring that Elk Island National Park and the six mountain national parks were supplied each spring with an adequate number of well-trained mounts for warden patrols into the backcountry. In fact, my last official task before retiring from Parks in 1991 would be to acquire a fine Quarter Horse stud and ten good, brood mares for the Ya-Ha-Tinda.

As with any ranch, there were certain management problems at the Ya-Ha-Tinda, but at least they were real problems involving horses and people and I relished the opportunity to be involved and effective in a tangible operation. It was so satisfying and rewarding to see the wobbly-legged little foals growing up to be fine horses and to hear the park wardens' words of praise—not readily given when it came to horseflesh. What joy it was to get away from the desk and spend a day greeting all the mares and their little ones, and sit in the sun by the barn door and talk about sensible stuff like hay, oats and the price of horseshoes. I grew to look forward to those days from which I invariably returned refreshed and with renewed faith. My first visit was on a cheerful morning, when the spring sun was drawing the first tint of green to the "Little Prairie in the Mountains."

On the drive, which took me first to the town of Sundre and from there west along the Red Deer River, I pondered over what I knew and had read about the history of the Ya-Ha-Tinda. The land was first used as a ranch by brothers, Jim and Bill Brewster, of Banff. Between 1904 and 1917, they leased the area at various times from Banff National Park and later from the Dominion Forest Service. Although some cattle were grazed then, the primary purpose of the ranch in the Brewster period was to raise and train horses for their outfitting and guiding business in Banff.

Meanwhile, the Chief Fire and Game Guardian of Banff was keeping a speculative eye on the Ya-Ha-Tinda. Due to its being situated just off the east boundary, the ranch was ideally positioned as a place from which to protect the park. On the other hand, given the assortment of colourful, if not to say, notorious characters who frequented the place, it would equally serve as a base for would-be poachers. Nor was Howard Sibbald blind to the fact that these free-wheeling types often used the Cascade Trail to go back and forth to Banff, a route which took them through some of the finest big game ranges in the park. He made up his mind that, if the opportunity ever arose, he would put a warden station at the Ya-Ha-Tinda. When the Brewster's lease ran out in 1917 and was not renewed, Howard quickly put his plan into action. Subsequently the ranch also became a home for warden horses.

Various park wardens and their wives came and went over the years. Some of the wives, like Mrs. Cliff Murphy, who arrived at the ranch in

1933 and stayed for 20 years, loved the place. Others, perhaps not properly prepared for the isolation and pioneer conditions there, fared poorly and have mixed emotions towards the ranch.

There were other illnesses and accidents over the years, including one in which a ranch hand suffered a badly broken leg; another in more recent times when a rider was dislodged by a bronc and landed on his privates on the saddle horn. His boss made the ribald comment to the effect that he was lucky the horn didn't catch him a couple inches further to the rear, or he might still be bobbing around out there. Generally speaking, however, the people enjoyed good health, and formed happy memories.

Meanwhile, the horse herd was expanded to serve all the mountain national parks and, as time went on, became an integral part of the Park Warden Service in the region. The source of endless arguments between chief wardens, all of whom were very opinionated on the subject of their beloved and not-so-loved horses, the Ya-Ha-Tinda Ranch became inextricably entwined with the history of the national parks.

As I drew near, I looked forward with considerable excitement to my first view of the legendary ranch. Since leaving Sundre, I had been driving for nearly an hour and was actually entering the first range of mountains to the west. The rough, one-way 4x4 road was leading me through a narrow cleft between two mountains, under a stand of big, over-mature spruce. Then suddenly, in a manner which surprised and delighted, the country opened up. I drove out into sunshine and entered a broad valley. On my left flowed the Red Deer River and, on my right, to the north were wide, grass-covered hillsides. Before long, a short piece of fence and a sign indicated the commencement of the Ya-Ha-Tinda Ranch property and soon after that the road crossed Bighorn Creek, just below the falls. Still travelling west, I passed a herd of about 40 horses grazing along the river flats; another band could be seen on an open hillside.

Then, for the first time, I saw the ranch buildings, clustered just below treeline where another stream flowed out of the mountains. The red and white maple leaf flag swayed in the morning breeze. As I drew nearer, I observed mares and their spring foals in a neatly fenced paddock At the same time I noticed the weather-beaten remains of an old corral at the top of the creek bank, a remnant of the Brewster era. Then, commencing a ritual which would be repeated on many subsequent visits, I drove slowly up to the corral gate in front of the log barn and turned off the motor.

Inside, two men with black hats could be seen easing a saddle onto a green-broke horse and, as I approached the gate, a tall, stoop-shouldered old cowboy emerged from the shadows of the barn and came to meet me. All three shook hands with me in a grave and courteous fashion, in the meanwhile taking my measure. I had a sense that my predecessor must have been well-respected here; I wondered how I would stack up in comparison.

After coffee at the foreman's house, we returned to the corrals and the tour began. It started with a walk-through of the main barn. There was a good reason for this. Each man was assigned a number of young horses to break and train over the winter months and in every stall was a well-groomed horse whose virtues were proudly extolled to me as we passed along. Here was a young gelding who tended to be a little lumpy in the morning, but would go all day once the kinks were out. And there was a little sorrel mare who never even offered to buck from the very first day. Next was a big black with a rather sulky eye. "Watch his feet! He's all right, but nervous with strangers."

Next was a good brown horse who showed up yesterday with a scrape just above the left front fetlock. "Must have got to runnin' and maybe hit a snag. May have got a whiff of that old grizzly up the creek, 'cause normally you couldn't faze him." And so it went, until each horse had been duly rubbed and petted, and his good points noted to me—the new man.

Having hopefully made a good beginning, the foreman now reluctantly led the way to the stallion's paddock. The reason for his dragging steps was soon obvious. The number one stud, a tall, nice-looking Thoroughbred, was a very sick horse. He stood head down, legs braced apart, sweating and shivering. The animal's nostrils were fouled with mucous and every few minutes a wracking cough travelled up the long thin neck. It was a sad sight and I looked in dismay at what appeared to be an advanced case of pneumonia. The vet had been out and the old foreman himself had taken charge of ministering to the horse, but so far there had been no improvement. Fortunately, they had a second stallion, a bouncy little Morgan with good bearing and a kind eye. Although he had been around for some time, his performance was still relatively untested.

The ranch hands were visibly relieved to move on from this disturbing part of the walk-about, and it was with lighter steps that they next took me down to a large Quonset barn, located at the entrance to the mares' paddock. Although the building was empty that morning, I saw that the stalls were quite small and each one was marked with a nameplate like Trudy, Sally or Socks. These were the names of that spring's little ones. As a start to their training, the foals were brought in at night, coaxed into halters and housed in their personal stalls until morning. The stalls were provisioned with plenty of hay and oats.

The highlight of the tour, a visit with the colts and their mothers, was always reserved for last. The foreman himself led the way into the mares' paddock and as he moved quietly among the horses in his gentle way, the young ones grouped behind him, much as though he were the Pied Piper. I had been unobtrusively observing the old man even as I looked at the horses and I was impressed. There was no mistaking the old horseman's love for his animals and that this feeling was reciprocated was obvious. My pleasure on this occasion increased when we went on to see the two-year-olds, many of whom were undoubtedly going to be fine horses, and found the same gentle curiosity and friendliness amongst that group. I was also delighted to find that I soon had my own following.

As I strolled around, having my collar nibbled at and my hat brim tugged at, I relaxed and my thoughts went back to the spring when I first arrived in Jasper. It had been in April, far too early to think of going out to my new posting—the Brazeau River District—so I was put to work around town for awhile. At first, the snow being still quite good, I was assigned to the ski patrol at Whistler Mountain and Marmot Basin. It was here, on an April evening, that I took part in my first search for an avalanche victim, Charlie Dupre, who died in the basin which now bears his name.

Later, in early May, I was put in charge of a small crew that was building a hiking path on the outskirts of town. In the meantime I had been introduced to the wardens' stable boss, a tall, slow-moving and even slower-talking horseman with incredibly bowed legs. I knew that the horses which I would eventually take to the district were going to be a big part of my life that first year, and I also realized that the nature and calibre of those horses assigned to me would be determined by this man. With that in mind, I cast about for some way to get in the stable boss' good books, and I came up with the idea of going to the barn early in the morning, before my own work day started, and helping to dung out the stalls. While doing this, naturally, I was also showing my own style with horses as I moved around them in my work, all under the watchful eye of the barn boss.

The first indication that this strategy was paying off came on the day when two new young horses arrived at the Jasper Warden Stable. One was a peppy, little bay mare—well-broke, and a slender grey gelding—green-broke. The mare was allocated to a young man who, that spring, was packing for the Park Warden Service, and the grey went to me. I couldn't have been more pleased. The gelding, named Silver, was a fine, intelligent horse who seemed to want to learn, and learned quickly. I spent my evenings and weekends getting to know the colt, and furthering its training. Only once did I sense that we were on the verge of a runaway. It was on a sunny, windy Sunday afternoon, when I had taken Silver for a ride on Pyramid Bench.

At one point the trail passed through a dense stand of young trembling aspens and a gust of wind happened to strike the trees just as we were in the centre of the grove. When a great rustling broke out among the leaves, the colt froze and began to tremble like the very aspens themselves. I felt the gelding's muscles tense, and knew that he was about to bolt. With one hand on the reins and the other on Silver's neck, I spoke to the horse quietly and guided him with a gentle pressure of the knees and a moment later the crisis was past. As we emerged from the trees back into friendly sunshine, I breathed a shaky sigh of relief. I was far more afraid of a runaway horse than a bucker.

Between barn cleaning, training my saddle horse and working my job, I was kept very busy, but again my efforts were not going unnoticed. I began hearing little things in the bar of an evening, like "Maybe that kid from Banff was OK," and the chief park warden commented on the fact that the grey colt seemed to be coming along nicely. Meanwhile, the stable boss remained his taciturn self, but I fancied that there was a friendly gleam in his eye of late. With the snows melting rapidly in the high country, I felt it was time to find out about the rest of my string. I decided to broach the subject one morning when we were taking a smoke break in between cleaning stalls and giving the horses their daily brushing. I considered the barn boss, carefully, where he squatted in the front doorway building a cigarette—hat down over his eyes.

Communication with the tall cowboy was something of an art, made so by the fact that he hated being crowded and also hated loud talk, so I squatted at the opposite end of the stable and took my time rolling a smoke. After a couple of thoughtful puffs, in a voice calculated to carry the distance but not offend, I said casually, "I suppose I'll be needing a few more ponies one of these days?"

There was silence for a minute or so, and then the battered old hat nodded imperceptibly. "I s'pose."

"Do you reckon there's something around that I might have?"

"I reckon."

I phrased my next question carefully; I didn't want to appear pushy. "When might be a good time to look at them?"

This time there was an even longer pause than before, while the import of the question and the correct response were duly considered. One of the horses shifted in its stall, groaned and something fell with a wet plot. Finally the hat moved again. "Could do it today, I reckon. Maybe after noon."

Following this remarkable outburst, nothing more could be gotten out of him until we were on our saddle horses, going out to the range. Most of Jasper's warden horses wintered in the park at that time, south of the townsite on a piece of range called Buffalo Prairie. Here we came, after awhile, to a drift fence which led to a squeeze made of pine rails and brush. Nearby grazed a fine, hefty bay mare and two other nondescript animals.

The stable boss waved a negligent hand at the bay. "What do you think of that one?"

"Looks okay to me."

"Well, you can have her, if you can put a halter on her."

I wondered a little at the comment, but said nothing while we hazed the three into the squeeze, where the tall horseman placed himself in the opening. Then I dismounted and with halter in hand approached the mare. I had suspected from the remark that she was halter shy, but just how shy I found out in the next few minutes. She began to tremble as I approached and at the merest proffering of the halter, she threw her head back and began to shake uncontrollably.

"Aha," I thought, "One of those." I studied the mare carefully. In spite of her nerves, she had large, kind eyes and the ears remained forward. So far there had been no attempt to strike at me. I decided this one needed kindness and assurance. Accordingly, I moved up against her neck, making firm but gentle contact through my hands, arms and shoulder, meanwhile keeping up a quiet line of chatter. Soon the trembling stopped and a moment later I charmed her into the halter, being careful not to cover her eyes or touch the ears in the process. Taking a surreptitious peek at the stable boss, I was quick enough to catch the surprised look before the hard-bitten old horseman adjusted his gaze to the far horizon and nonchalantly drowned an early dandelion in tobacco juice.

"May as well bring her on in," he said, "She'll both ride and pack. There's a couple of blacks over on the Malign River that'll pack as well."

And so I acquired Judy and the two black geldings, Billy and Frank. I learned from the blacksmith, who had already made their unwelcome acquaintance, that they were both as crazy as shithouse rats, and were calculated to demoralize any self-respecting outfit unfortunate enough to be blessed with them. The reader will already be familiar with our riotous arrival in the Brazeau District later that spring.

Meanwhile, back on the Ya-Ha-Tinda Ranch the tour was coming to a close. The two ranch hands retired to their respective houses for the noon break and the foreman and I went to the main house and discussed ranch matters over tea and bully beef sandwiches. By 2 o'clock everything seemed to have been pretty well hashed over and I had several items written in my notebook for follow-up. They waved good-bye as my car started down the long slope below the barns.

Turning the corner below the paddocks and heading east, my eyes roved to the top of a high hill; there in the sun stood an old horse, nearly white, the clouds behind him and the west wind riffling his mane. Something about that proud, patient way of standing tugged at my heart. It couldn't be! Or could it? Was Old Slippery still alive, after all these years?

A few years later, it was obvious that the breeding program at the Ya-Ha-Tinda was in serious trouble. After the Thoroughbred stud died of pneumonia, the Morgan became the number one stud, the only stallion at the Ya-Ha-Tinda. Put with the big mares which made up the majority of the breeding stock, he produced good, nicely-dispositioned colts, but with a very low impregnation rate. All efforts were made to assist him with his domestic duties, but to no avail. In any given year, we realized no more than 50 to 60 per cent of the potential colt crop. Then it was thought that the mares weren't getting enough nutrition during the winter and supplement was added to their feed. Still, there was no improvement. Finally, the number of young horses available to the parks dropped to an unacceptable level, so it was decided to purchase a new, certified stallion and 10 or so papered mares. We were also to look for some decent young stock to keep the parks allocations up to par until the new breeding program began to produce. While waiting the approval of funds, I pondered about what breed of horse to look for.

I knew from experience that the park wardens needed strong, sensible horses to carry them over the mountain trails. Together, the warden and his horses face long, gruelling trips over high mountain passes and spend days slogging through mud and snow with the cold rain running down the neck of the horse and rider. Together, they face the treacherous mountain river, swollen in flood, the shores lined with deadly sweepers that can ensnare and drown both horse and man. And together, they circumnavigate the unpredictable grizzly bear, where he feeds upon an elk carcass by the side of the trail.

The horses rely on the man to tie the packs on evenly and fairly, to give a rest break during an arduous climb, to remedy a loose shoe or a chafing sore. But most of all they rely on the boss to know the way and to know what he is about. Once this confidence is established, the horses will cheerfully exert every effort to do his bidding. When the confidence is lost, their gung-ho spirit is lost and a truly terrible confusion and lack of direction sets in.

For his part, the warden looks to his saddle horse, in particular, for good sense and a stout heart and, above all, instant response to the touch of the spur, the guiding rein and the quiet word at those times when hesitation can mean disaster. Through trial and error, it has been the aim of the ranch program to provide the Park Warden Service with horses bearing the attributes of strength and sure-footedness and, above all, courage and common sense.

While I was on the subject, I was reminded of two wardens, Gordon and Jim, who had tried to cross the Snake Indian River during high water. Gordon's horse was swept out from under him and he lost his hat. Finally reaching the far side, the horse tried to climb out of the water but couldn't get up the riverbank. It then tried to climb out by standing on Gordon and still couldn't get out. Gordon came up just in time to catch his hat as it went by. Jim, who possessed a scientific turn of mind, estimated the depth of the river to be approximately 18 feet at that point. This was deduced from the fact that the horse, a tall one, probably stood about 12 feet on its hind legs and by standing on Gordon gained another five-feet ten inches and even then only the tip of its nose showed above water.

On the other hand, I was very conscious of the fact that having too tall a horse could also be a problem. We had for some time, since returning to the west, been proud owners of a large, very handsome chestnut mare, which we boarded at the home of an old friend. Through some mysterious circumstances, which were never fully explained, the mare became pregnant by a long-legged Thoroughbred stud that also spent a winter on the same farm. The sorrel filly resulting from this clandestine affair, having inherited height from both parents, was now reaching truly awesome proportions. Not yet fully grown, she had already passed the 16-hand mark and was still zooming upwards, a situation which caused me no little concern when I contemplated having to break her.

While speaking with the Chief Warden at Pacific Rim National Park one day, I confided my trepidation at the thought of being tossed aloft by a horse standing 17 hands or better. The chief, who had come from horse country himself before trading his saddle for a bucket seat on the bridge of a warden patrol boat, came back at once with a typical cowboy rejoinder. "Hell," he said cheerfully, "not to worry. If that horse ever throws you off, you'll be so high up in the sky, the birds'll have time to build a nest under your ass before you hit the ground!"

All of which still left me in a quandary as to the best breed for warden mounts. A canvass of the chief wardens in the West and stable bosses actually produced a generic horse, just over 15 hands, with a deep girth, strong legs, reasonably large feet, pronounced withers—this so the pack saddles don't roll— and a sensible disposition. The colours ranged through sorrel, bay and chestnut, with the occasional grey. Out of all of the breeds available in southern Alberta, the Quarter Horse came closest to fulfilling the requirements, except for one problem. Purebred Quarter Horses, in the form favoured at the time, tended to be boxy-headed animals, with bunchy, overdeveloped muscles and small hooves. They were great in the cutting-horse arena, but not of much use for mountain travel.

I finally decided to look for Running Quarter Horses with enough crossbreeding to produce the height, girth and feet that we were seeking. Horses that were very much like the good range horse of the type used by cowboys years ago.

It was customary when buying horses for the parks for the Warden Operations Manager and ranch foreman to work together. This time, I decided to call in, as well, the two stable bosses from Banff and Jasper, for those two fellows were extraordinarily opinionated on the subject of horse-flesh. I also enlisted, as an advisor and consultant, the help of John Miller, a well-known horseman and Quarter Horse breeder from Longview, Alberta. John, or Jack, as he was sometimes called, proved invaluable as a source of contacts, as well as being a congenial guide in the travels that followed. Not only did he seem to know the location of every farm from the city of Red Deer south to the American border, he also seemed able to walk into the corral of every one of those farms and quote the pedigree of every horse on the place. The man was amazing!

And travel we did, for two weeks, back and forth across the vast spaces of southern and central Alberta; from the prosperous, well kept farms of the Olds-Red Deer regions, with their well-bred, well-fed animals, to the brush country of Caroline and the James River, where the cowboys wear their black hats pulled down tight, where the moustaches are scragglier, where the chaps are scarred and the cowboy boots a little downer at the heel than in the other parts. There, the horses, like their owners, are a bit thinner and wilder. Then south to Pincher Creek country, where the stones tend to be close beneath the grass and half the population would fall flat on their faces if the wind ever quit blowing. There, the tough old bronco busters try to sell tough old broncos for ridiculous prices. Finally, we went east towards Medicine Hat, where the sky gets bigger, the prairie drier, the winds flap the shutters on old, deserted farm houses, and many of the pastures seem little more than holding areas for poor, sad beasts.

There are numerous vicissitudes peculiar to the business of purchasing government mounts. First, there is the well-known fact that if you place 10 horsemen in a room, you may get 10 different opinions as to what constitutes a good horse. If one fellow likes the looks of a the prospect, someone else will point out that it's too long in the tooth, or too short in the back, or too flat in the withers, or too short in the pastern, or it tends to throw the left front foot. I was astonished to discover, as we went about our business, not only the predictable differences of opinion between buyers and sellers, but also a somewhat baffling divergence of viewpoints between the people on my own committee, whom I would have expected to be somewhat like-minded on the subject.

I started off, the first day, with reasonable confidence in my own ability to size up a horse; by the end of the second day, I conceded privately that I had a lot to learn. By the third day, having seen what I believed were several good horses dismissed out-of-hand by my companions, I began to wonder if I knew anything at all. At the close of the first week, however, having watched the other fellows treating each other's choices with the same feigned disparagement, I began to suspect that there was more than a little gamesmanship involved in the horse-buying business and my confidence slowly returned.

I also found out that you can't always believe what you hear over the telephone. It is very disappointing and frustrating to travel 200 or so miles, only to find out that the 16-hand-high mare, free of all blemishes, was actually a runty little roan with a wire cut leg. "You know, the darn horse got in the fence the day after you called!"

A typical example of that occurred on a day in March when we arose at a very early hour to travel to a farm north of Ponoka. My partner for the trip was to be Cal Hayes, the Ya-Ha-Tinda foreman, who incidentally, was not the quiet old man of former years, but a shorter, younger, more loquacious individual. He was the latest keeper of the "Cowboy Manual," a legendary document rumoured to be kept hidden beneath a slab of cement in the basement of the main ranch house, and to which the foreman refers late at night when seeking guidance in dealing with fractious horses and recalcitrant ranch hands. Cal kept a home in the town of Sundre and it was there that I picked him up on the morning in question.

We hoped the journey would prove productive. The person I had spoken to at the farm had seemed to be listening closely as I carefully listed our requirements and had then assured me that they had at least two, possibly three, nice mares that would fill the bill. The driving was miserable as we headed northeast towards Ponoka. There had been a wet spring snowstorm overnight so, that with each passing vehicle, my little station wagon from the office car pool was drenched in a hail of slush and crushed rock.

We eventually found the place we were seeking, having spent about two hours on dismal back roads and bumpy byways. Finally we arrived at an extremely messy farmyard where we had obviously been expected for some time. No sooner did we step from the car into a blustery north wind than the back door of the house burst open and what appeared to be the entire family spilled out into the yard. There were a young couple and several small children, a grandfather, two middle aged ladies, and a vacant-looking type of undetermined years with a patchy beard and a beer belly, all accompanied by an uncontrollable black-and-white mongrel dog. Appearances indicated that they must have been sitting around the kitchen table for most of the morning, speculating excitedly about the impending visit from the "Government Horse Buyers." My heart sank within me. I noticed that Cal had hardly moved from the car.

The first thing that struck us as odd was that the man asked one of the women, "Which is the best way to go?" This conjured up most un-welcome visions of an endless tramp through snowy fields, in that biting wind. But the woman merely gestured toward a corral about 50 feet away, and the whole group migrated in that direction. Once there we waited for at least five minutes while various people struggled to undo the rope that held the gate fast. In the end, it turned out the gate was frozen to the ground anyway so everyone climbed over the fence. Now we were ankle deep in half-frozen manure, amid a group of five or six of the meanest, crankiest-looking horses that we had encountered so far.

I was reminded of the expressions used by our advisor and consultant from Longview. Jack categorized horses as either "trash, common horses, na-ice horses," with the nice drawn out or, in exceptional cases such as his own animals, "real na-ice horses." There was no doubt we had hit trash that morning.

After some moments during which everyone stood around in the wind, the family glancing alternately from the horses to the visitors, as if to say "Aren't they wonderful?" and the visitors not sure whether to laugh or cry, the young woman approached the nearest of the sorry critters and cooed, "Here Baby. Whoa! Come to Mummy, do." At which Baby aimed a vicious kick at the lady's kneecap and dashed bug-eyed into the midst of the other ponies, causing a general melee during the course of which the assembled humans were generously pelted with clods of muck and manure. I wiped a piece off my cheek and caught Cal trying to hide a grin.

Already convinced that the visit was a waste of time, I began to plan our get-away but felt, that for the sake of the family, human decency called for at least a show of interest, no matter how brief. Therefore, with what courtesy I could muster, I turned to the husband and asked him what they wanted for a little mare, that although still poor, seemed a cut above the rest. The question apparently posed a dilemma. The family looked at each other foolishly and finally the head of the house gestured toward the fat, grey-bearded character who so far had remained wordless, and said, "It's Jake's horse."

I turned to Jake, who shuffled his feet shyly, and mumbled, "Wh— wh— would you give me for her?"

Afraid that even a ridiculously low bid might be accepted, thus landing us with an animal we really had no use for, I mumbled something about, "Think it over, I'll get back to you," and climbed back over the fence. Cal was already halfway to the car. I suspected that the shaking and twitching of the foreman's shoulders were a bad case of the giggles.

Following up on another lead on the way home, we stopped at Hobbema to see a man who purported to have a good Quarter Horse stallion for sale. While our feelings in the forenoon had been of pity for a family who were obviously naïve, what I and my companion saw at this place made us positively angry. Here we were asked to look at one of the saddest, most poorly conceived animals to be found outside of a glue factory. As if it weren't enough the poor beast had been wire cut and obviously uncared for, as it now carried about four pounds of proud flesh, under a layer of mud and manure, on the injured leg. As we turned wordlessly away from this sorry spectacle, the only sound to be heard was the contemptuous splat of Cal's tobacco juice hitting the floor. It pretty well summed up our feelings for the day.

The next trip took us into the bush country west of the James River, where the main criterion for picking a saddle horse is that it must have a leg under each corner. This time we were looking for a few young horses, broke or at least started, to augment Parks' riding stock until such time as the new breeding program would begin to produce results. As usual, we had a list of references. Arriving at our first destination, we found a motley collection of animals penned up for our inspection. A man who was obviously the owner came forward and introduced himself and then gestured at two young cowboys, who stood watching nearby, indicating that they should come and meet the visitors as well.

The two shuffled ahead a few steps, as if under duress, and paused. They were both of average height, and very thin and wiry, clad in tight jeans fronted with enormous belt buckles. They wore identical, dusty black hats set squarely on their heads and pulled low, over small, suspicious eyes. One was clean shaven, but the other had a drooping, scraggly black moustache, giving him the look of a Mexican bandit. The clean-shaven one, introduced as Ab, carried a lasso and a halter. The dark one, whose name was Frank, sported a scarred-up pair of chaps and well-worn spurs, and he carried a saddle. Both men looked as if they had been coaxed out into the open against their better judgment and stood poised to bolt back behind the Jack pine curtain at the first loud noise. They acknowledged the visitors with barely perceptible nods and a muffled "Howdy."

As our group approached the first corral, which appeared to contain four and five-year-olds, it was explained that all were halter-broke and many had been ridden. However, if the government buyers were particularly interested in any particular one, Ab would capture it and Frank would ride it for them.

Ab shook out a loop in his lariat and Frank tightened his grip on the saddle as the visitors hunkered up to the corral fence and peered through the rails. We soon decided that we were looking at a distinctly unsociable bunch of rang-a-tangs. When hazed back and forth in order to give me a better look, the broncs would stampede by, then go into a tight formation in the farthest corner. From there they eyed the government men with the same barely disguised mistrust as evinced by the two wranglers. No doubt, given half a chance, all would have liked nothing better than to vanish into the green timber.

Finally, a rather promising brown gelding was singled out for a closer look and Ab was instructed to put a rope on 'im. This he forthwith attempted to do but with a singular lack of success. The gelding dodged the first loop, ran by the second and ran over Ab on the next trip down the corral, trampling his black hat and leaving hoof prints on various parts of that cowboy's anatomy. Then, obviously according to a prearranged plan, the bronc ducked into a corner and hid its head, while all its buddies took up defensive positions around him.

Giving up for the moment on the brown gelding, we next tried to capture a big grey, but this animal flew at the side of the corral and, with eyes as big as saucers broke the top rail, scrambled over and promptly disappeared into the timber. The owner of the ranch, possibly sensing that his guests might need a little reassurance at this point, observed that, "The grey will make an awful good horse someday, tho' a bit shy, it'd already been ridden. In fact," turning to Frank, "you was up on 'im just last week, wasn't you, Frank?"

The wrangler's hat brim moved a quarter of an inch. "Yup."

The procedure was repeated for the next half-hour. Although Ab struggled valiantly to lasso several more horses, for all of the results he got, he might as well have gone hunting ducks with a rake. Frank, who had been looking more relaxed with every one that got away, finally put the saddle down altogether and built a cigarette. What had promised to be a scary morning, for him, was looking much better; with a bit of luck, he might even live until lunchtime. In the end we picked out a half-dozen colts and made arrangements to have them trucked to the Ya-Ha-Tinda Ranch.

As we drove away, Cal declared, with some heat, "I don't give a shit if Frank had been up on any of them or not. My boys would be up on 'em soon enough!"

Besides the seemingly endless miles, the hazards of weather, the disappointment of finding poor horses and the challenge of picking sound ones, not to mention the possibilities of being bitten, kicked, squeezed or trampled by unruly broncs, the dubious delights of eating in small town restaurants are also a part of horse hunting. Unlike my companions, I am a very small eater. My capacity for lunch is about half that of the average person and to be served with enormous platters of food when all I feel hungry for is a modest sandwich, tends to gross me out. Unfortunately for me, the tendency in restaurants, at least in this part of the country, seems to be to overwhelm the guest with food. This is usually done by adding a huge stack of greasy French fries to every order, whether the customer wants them or not.

Another one of my pet peeves is the quality of bread served in most restaurants. As a boy I was raised on good, honest homemade bread, baked in a wood stove. Bread with body to it, and a real crust that you could sink your teeth into. Occasionally one discovers a good bakery hidden away in an obscure corner, where they still make good, sturdy German loaves and crusty French rolls, but most days on the road meant doughy buns, greasy French fries and indigestion resulting as much from disappointment, as from the unpalatable nature of the food itself.

On another day, braving big west winds and drifting snow, we visited the Pincher Creek area. Fred Dixon, a retired park warden who had taken up a place in the hills west of there had been doing some scouting and met us at one of the coffee shops with a list of farms to check out. The first one belonged to a hard-drinking old bronco buster, who had given up the rough string some years ago and now raised and traded horses for a living. Fred advised my helper and I to try and visit this farm before noon as, due to the cowboy's habit, afternoons evidently were pretty much a waste of time.

As we approached the place, shortly before noon, we stopped to look over some horses in a pasture just east of the house. It was a poor-looking field; where the wind had scoured away the snow, the ground was bare and very stony. A couple of dozen horses, all rather thin, roamed restlessly back and forth in the wind, searching for food and shelter. There was very little of either. The buildings also seemed a bit poor when we reached them; the house was very plain, the yard unadorned, except for the usual abandoned vehicles. There were a number of corrals made of light rails, one of which held some young horses, standing huddled against a shelter.

The most outstanding feature on the place was the enormous snowdrift on the lee side of the corral, allowing a person to walk nearly up to the top rail. When we walked up to the back door of the house, a black-and-white dog rose stiffly from the doorstep where it appeared to be guarding a half-empty bottle of whiskey and came uncertainly toward us. A knock at the door was answered by a tall, lean man of about forty, who turned out to be the bronc rider's son. Once outside the house, this individual automatically leaned far forward from the waist, a posture peculiar to people raised in the windy, Pincher Creek-Crowsnest Pass area. He explained that his old man had gone to town but was expected back shortly. Meanwhile, there was some young stock in the corrals for us to look at.

Once into the corral, I was pleasantly surprised. The youngsters were friendly and inquisitive, nibbling at my collar and taking a great interest in my notebook. We saw some good black hooves, strong, straight legs and other indications that a number of these fellows would grow up to be decent horses. While we were thus engaged, we heard a truck drive into the yard, and a few minutes later a tall, stooped old fellow came slowly up to the outside of the corral. I climbed over to shake hands and pay my respects to this bronc rider, who was still remembered around Pincher for his feats in his younger days.

Although the creased old face was becoming mottled and the lower jaw had a tremble, the big splayed hand still felt like rope and leather, and the bow-legs told of tough days in the saddle. After we had dickered over prices for some time, during which I found myself up against a hard bargainer, I noticed the old man looking me up and down. The old rider seemed to be trying to make up his mind about something, as a man will when he is about to make a disclosure about himself. Finally, apparently having made up his mind, he took a step toward me and said, "You know, one summer when I was young, I got on the outside of better'n hunnerd head." Then he paused and was silent for some time, evidently reflecting on those days. Some time later, we concluded our business and departed in search of the next farm on the list.

The sun was casting long shadows on the snow when we started off for home, but partway up the Waldron Valley, we happened to pass a considerable bunch of horses corralled on a hillside by the road. I pulled over and stopped at the entrance to the property. To the right of the corral was a hillbilly sort of house, very rustic and kitty-whampus, with a porch facing the road. I was about to suggest they we stop and have a look at the ponies, when an arresting figure appeared from within and stood on this porch watching us. He was a large, fierce-looking man, wearing a black hat with a flat brim. He had long hair and a dark, bushy beard; he was dressed in a heavy army greatcoat, ragged jeans and tall boots.

My companion regarded this person uneasily and did not appear